As American
as Shoofly Pie

AMISH❤DUTCH Cookbook

50¢

Gensler

As American as Shoofly Pie

The Foodlore and Fakelore of Pennsylvania Dutch Cuisine

WILLIAM WOYS WEAVER

PENN

University of Pennsylvania Press
Philadelphia

Published by
University of Pennsylvania Press
Philadelphia, Pennsylvania 19104-4112
www.upenn.edu/pennpress

Printed in the United States of America on acid-free paper

10 9 8 7 6 5 4 3 2 1

Library of Congress Cataloging-in-Publication Data
Weaver, William Woys, 1947–
As American as shoofly pie : the foodlore and fakelore of Pennsylvania Dutch cuisine / William Woys Weaver. — 1st ed.
        p. cm.
    Includes bibliographical references and index.
    ISBN 978-0-8122-4479-3 (hardcover : alk. paper)
    1. Cooking—Pennsylvania—Pennsylvania Dutch Country. 2. Cooking, German. 3. Pennsylvania Dutch—Social life and customs. I. Title.
TX721.W365 2013
641.5943—dc23

2012027831

Frontispiece: The Amish-equals-Pennsylvania-Dutch equation comes together on the cover of the now-scarce 1961 cookbook shown in the frontispiece, written by Ruth Redcay and published by Ben Herman of Kutztown, Pa. Herman was long associated with the inner workings of the Kutztown Folk Festival. Roughwood Collection, Devon, Pa

Contents

Deep Fried Meets Dutchified: Food Mirrors the Culture

IN the Pennsylvania Dutch language "Dutchified" (*uffgedeitscht*) is slang for anything that is gussied up to look, taste, or in some way made to appear Pennsylvania Dutch whether or not it really is. A lot of locals use it specifically in reference to an overdose of decorative statement—such as a diner covered with neon hex signs—yet it can apply equally to people who accept or "convert" to the culture, to a peculiar way of talking, and even to a style of cooking or to a genre of folk art. Dutchification, if I may create that noun, is purely subjective and implies a heavily nuanced value judgment expressed within the Pennsylvania Dutch community; the general tenor is that the end result may border on gaudy and perhaps even tastelessly comic, since there is a hint of dry humor whenever the expression is used.

For aficionados of popular culture, things Dutchified probably represent a subcategory of kitsch (in Pennsylfaanisch *Edelkitsch*, something so tasteless it creates a new definition of "good"). Likewise deep-fried food, which is not a feature of traditional Pennsylvania Dutch cuisine except for festive fare such as *Fastnachts* (Shrove Tuesday fat cakes) has been served up in bountiful platters of grease as though it represents a taste of our authenticity. French fries, fried chicken, fried scrapple, fried everything: easy fast-food fare has been conjoined with Dutchification in the manner of culinary Siamese twins to create a tourist cuisine that has come to exemplify the worst of gluey tourist-trap shoofly pies, or more generally the ambiguous and overly saccharine food of family-style restaurants proclaiming the "Amish Experience." This is a tale of kitsch begetting kitsch. There is perhaps no better example than the stultifying aroma-therapy scent sold in Lancaster County gift shops under the name of "Amish Friendship Bread"—as though all the day-to-day realities of an Amish farmhouse kitchen can be released from a bottle. And yet behind this shopping cart filled with strange culinary mutants stand fascinating agendas that have pushed them to the fore. External issues from the larger world stage such as Hitler's accession to power in Germany, American isolationism, and the need of many urbanized Americans to take comfort or to seek reaffirmation in the old-time values of a lost agricultural age all bore down on the Pennsylvania Dutch in ways not well understood by the outside world.

The story that unfolds is a complicated one, not the least because the foods and foodways of the Pennsylvania Dutch represent the largest regional land-based cookery in the United States in terms of square miles covered, much of it outside Pennsylvania. Contrary to popular misconceptions, this is not the colorless, homogenized, deep-fried food peddled as the "Amish table" in the centers of Amish tourism in Pennsylvania, Ohio, and elsewhere. This is a food culture with authentic roots, a highly developed culinary tradition of classical preparation, and an extraordinary degree of internal diversity.

Within the original area of Dutch settlement in southeastern and central Pennsylvania—the cultural heartland about the same size as Switzerland—over sixteen hundred distinctive dishes have been documented, most of which are not available in restaurants or even in local cookbooks. When we consider that there are at least thirty variant forms of milk tarts (*Schlappkuche, Millichflitsch,* and so on), more than sixty variations of pocket dumplings or "mouth slappers" (*Mauldasche*), and several hundred sauerkraut dishes, the number sixteen hundred may even seem conservative; a great many more recipes lie waiting to be discovered through fieldwork. The complexity or diversity of this amazing regional cookery is one of the reasons that it has been difficult to encapsulate it in cookbooks and why there are so many mixed messages about its core characteristics in tourist literature today. Food, like culture, does not stand still; thus this is a book about food in motion, food moving from old forms toward new identities, new authenticities, and above all else toward a new culinary voice.

It is my hope that the common theme of food will draw together the disparate topics I have chosen as vantage points for viewing Pennsylvania Dutch culture from unusual angles: what it was, what it is today, how it is affected by class boundaries, how it is depicted in literary fiction, and of course how the Old Order Amish have been exploited as a lucrative culinary symbol. One of the recurring motifs in all that follows is an exploration of tourism and how in recent times this has imposed certain demands on culinary tradition. Over time these demands have shaped the way people within the culture, as well as those on the outside, have come to view the cuisine and to equate it with a stereotypical menu that evolved during the 1930s to fulfill the expectations of Lancaster County tourism. This was the beginning of the Amish motif in mass media culinary literature, which found its unintended endorsement at the Kutztown Folk Festival during the 1950s.

As we shall see, this tourist menu is a fictional cuisine. Rather than deriving its distinctive identity from actual home cooking, a subject taken up in Chapter 1, it was informed by local-color novels and by travel journalism and then grafted onto 1930s urban rathskeller cookery under the guise of Amish—the culinary epicenter being the 1935 menus of the German Village Restaurant in Lancaster, Pennsylvania. The Old Order Amish, who took no part in this evolutionary process other than to serve as objects of intense curiosity, were soon promoted as the only true representatives of the term "Pennsylvania Dutch," a misleading equation championed by the journalist and author Ann Hark, whose book *Hex Marks the Spot* and many magazine articles during the 1940s gave national currency to this idea. For Ann Hark, the plain sects and the other hoi polloi were Pennsylvania Dutch, while the true keepers of the culture were the Pennsylvania *Germans*, a nuanced distinction that was shaped by her personal construct of class and cultural divisions within the Pennsylvania Dutch world: a presumption of the fundamental superiority of the Moravian social circles in which she grew up.

Hark visited the Amish community much like a grand lady, moving from place to place in a touring car, arriving with a personal chauffeur (who was also her clandestine lover) in search of the quaint relics from the Middle Ages that she was convinced lay hidden in this closed religious sect. Like Ann Hark, I too have gone into the countryside and have spoken with the Amish and hundreds of other Pennsylvania Dutch of all religious persuasions, although I hope not in the same condescending frame of mind that distinguished Hark's Moravian worldview regarding the "other Dutch." In addition, rather than cast the Old Order Amish as players on a stage of my own making, I have let my subjects speak for themselves. They share many of the same concerns you and I have about the way tourism has distorted the truth about them and about Pennsylvania Dutch culture in general. The only qualification with my material is that several people I interviewed declined to have their names published, but I was comfortable with that, given that their answers were honest and uninhibited, and from their standpoint safe from unintended exploitation.

Another misunderstood voice heard from is that of the gentleman scholar and fellow Dutchman Cornelius Weygandt (1871–1957). I do not believe he was the nemesis of Ann Hark; they knew one another well enough, although his approach to the culture was entirely different, somewhat nostalgic but much more sensitive, much more in tune with the real roots of the Pennsylvania Dutch people, and he was deeply alarmed by the manner in which the Amish and other plain sects were being subsumed as the only symbol of who we are. Many writers on Pennsylvania Dutch culture have cast him as a maudlin witness to the decline of plain culture; that was not his foremost concern. He was disturbed by the wholesale loss of cultural identity then taking place in all parts of the United States and how this would play out for better or for worse.

For a long time it never dawned on me that Weygandt's firsthand observations and special clear-sightedness were among the key influences affecting my thinking about the culture of the Pennsylvania Dutch, but they were, and I have learned to read and reread his books carefully because they are written in the linguistic code of someone raised according to the mores of the old Philadelphia social elite. That side of his persona is probably best expressed in his elegantly written collection of essays called *Philadelphia Folks*, which says as much between the lines as it does within the text.

My loss is that I never knew Dr. Weygandt personally, but his early books such as *The Red Hills* and especially the later one called *The Dutch Country* captured the spirit of a Pennsylvania Dutch landscape very different from that of today, and his firsthand insights into people, events, and ideas of the times have created a framework for my own thoughts on these subjects. Unlike Ann Hark, Weygandt was conversant in Pennsylfaanisch, the language of the people: he could go to the heart of the problem with words only locals understood. He was also a wordsmith, an English professor at the University of Pennsylvania, and—perhaps surprising given his other interests—an expert on the Irish theater.

Ireland is where he and I first crossed paths intellectually, because while finishing my doctoral work in Dublin, I discovered that I needed Cornelius Weygandt to help me untangle the meaning of the term "Pennsylvania Dutch." I knew or at least thought I knew what this moniker meant, and yet the outside world is still confused, and even the Pennsylvania Dutch community is sometimes divided over the use of the name.

One thing I learned very quickly from Dr. Weygandt's writings is that the other name for our people, Pennsylvania German, was given new meaning in 1891 by the founders of the Pennsylvania German Society for elitist and not altogether spotless reasons, even though the term is tossed about today as a more "scholarly" label. Weygandt was adamant in his objection to the Germanophiles who embraced the Bismarckian racial concepts that lay behind this—he knew all of the major players. It disturbed him greatly that the society's founders attempted to define who was Pennsylvania Dutch and who was not based on the purity of their blood. One of the other subjects I deal with in this book is how the terms "Pennsylvania German" and "Pennsylvania Dutch" have been manipulated by certain segments of the Pennsylvania Dutch community with competing agendas. The dynamics of tourism often worked hand in hand with the goals of the Pennsylvania German Society, which in turn inspired museum curators to create a mythological lifestyle designed to fit decorative arts displays and by implication a cuisine to go with it. A number of living dioramas dot the Lancaster County landscape even today, and with stage sets of vastly more opulent and costly objects, they also furnish many leading museums with similar Dutched-up inventions.

The word "Dutchified" as I use it in the title of this introduction probably needs some explanation for people outside the regions where the Pennsylvania Dutch live. I did not invent the term; it first emerged in 1829 in the writings of Ernst Ludwig Brauns, who came to Pennsylvania to serve as a Lutheran minister, who was soundly defeated by the intransigence of the congregations assigned to his care (they disliked his petty personality), and who then returned to Germany as a self-appointed expert on the culture that had rejected him. He refused to learn Pennsylfaanisch and in all of his books maintained a sense of cultural superiority that many German Americans slip into when confronted with the farmish yet thoroughly American rubes of rural Pennsylvania.

This tension between the perceived superiority of Old World German culture over the raw creations of the New has shaped the way various Dutch communities view themselves. In turn this has influenced attitudes about the food and its traditional identity. A few years ago I interviewed an elderly lady in Berks County well known for her cookery and asked, "Are you Pennsylvania Dutch or are you Pennsylvania German?" She thought for a moment and responded, "No, I am American." Of course she had for the moment outwitted me: my question was intentionally loaded, but her telling answer was even more so. With uncanny predictability it echoed a similar answer to a similar question posed by the German travel journalist

Johann Georg Kohl, who toured among the Dutch in the 1850s: a denial of a cultural or emotional connection with Old Germany.

What the Berks County cook meant was that Pennsylvania Dutch culture is an American culture, a New World creation born on these shores, not a Little Germany captured like a butterfly in amber, a relic of eighteenth-century Europe frozen in time. The Pennsylvania Dutch are as American as the Cajuns, and the Old Order Amish are only one of several images used to represent this complex and ever-evolving culture. In terms of the larger culinary story, the Amish are mostly marginal anyway because the real centers of creative Pennsylvania Dutch cookery were in the towns and not to be found among the outlying Amish or Mennonite communities, even though today the Mennonites have attempted to preempt the Amish as their cultural public-relation handlers and in their Amish and Mennonite cookbooks to press for "Christian" culinary values—whatever that may mean.

Throughout this book I prefer to use the term "Pennsylvania Dutch," not only because I have a right to choose who I am—thirteenth-generation Dutch with Swiss rather than German ancestors—but also because this is the historical label used to describe my old highly diversified culture. William Shakespeare referred to all Germans as Dutchmen, and my own Swiss ancestors were called High Dutch by colonial Pennsylvania authorities because they came from the upper end of the Rhine Valley, while the Low Dutch lived in Holland. "Dutch" is the colloquial name used by the English for German-speaking peoples since the Middle Ages, and there is nothing wrong with it. It is good, basic Anglo-Saxon.

That said, the Pennsylvania Dutch are not German Americans who entertain a lingering nostalgia for the *Vaterland*; there is no interest among the Pennsylvania Dutch in German literature or art or the faux *Oktoberfests* that bring German Americans together in other parts of the United States. As that old Berks County cook stated in no uncertain terms, the Pennsylvania Dutch are Americans with a singular focus on their own landscape. That may sound hopelessly provincial, and yet the Pennsylvania Dutch are a special kind of American; they just happen to think and speak in a different language and to cook a different style of food. The centuries-old right to be who they are, to be different and yet one with mainstream American society, is another one of the complicated threads that make the culinary narrative in this book so unique and yet so much a part of the larger and ever-unfolding American story.

Now something about the recipes: from the very inception of this book, I always entertained the idea of including fieldwork recipes—they represent a sampling from many thousands of examples I have gathered during fieldwork devoted to this rich and diversified cuisine. Real local-harvest, home-cooked, belly-warming food is my métier, and its recipes provide excellent hands-on instruction to illustrate culinary concepts and terminologies unfamiliar to readers who are not Pennsylvania Dutch. After all, dishes such as *Gumbis* or *Schnitz-un-Gnepp* remain vague mental abstractions until you make them. Thus the recipes in this book are instructional: they are intended to give concrete shape and meaning, as well as firsthand enjoyment, to many of the core dishes of classic Pennsylvania Dutch cuisine discussed in the text.

There is also an ulterior purpose embodied in my recipe selection: a reality check against the highly artificial portrait of Pennsylvania Dutch foods and foodways painted by mainstream literature catering to tourism or to things Amish. Common poverty foods almost always are left out of that conversation; I have included a few of those dishes for ethnographic reasons as well as for their teaching value about the internal workings of the culture and the frugal mindset that shapes it—not to mention that these recipes represent the kind of warm comfort food almost anyone can relate to. Likewise the high-end cookery is never mentioned in tourist literature, and that too is represented here. Most important I have taken this opportunity to peel away the anonymity of the women who have contributed so many of the classic dishes.

Their names sometimes appear in early twentieth-century charitable cookbooks, but who were they? These women lived real lives and made valuable contributions. So instead of passing off the recipe for funnel cakes as the handiwork of an anonymous and long-forgotten "Mrs. John Weinhold" (to provide but one example), I tramped around the graveyard at Bowmansville, Pennsylvania, and found her: Lizzie Brendle Weinhold (1884–1958), a real flesh-and-bones Pennsylvania Dutch cook; a little further help from Ernest Weinhold, the family genealogist who interviewed her children, filled in a few more details about her life story. Wherever possible I have provided the names and dates of these remarkable home cooks. They deserve a special niche in the culinary history of the Pennsylvania Dutch; their descendants welcome the recognition, and their recipe contributions will hopefully find a new place in the continuously evolving cuisine of the Pennsylvania Dutch.

In several of the recipes I have called for a *Schales* pan (pronounced shah-less). A large, round, shallow dish that went by a wide variety of colloquial names, it was absolutely critical to any traditional Pennsylvania Dutch kitchen, and no Pennsylvania Dutch cook should be without one. Like the Spanish paella pan, which they resemble, *Schales* pans were handed down as valued heirlooms. On the other hand, few truly old specimens have survived because they were put to use for so many different cooking tasks that they were literally "cooked to shards." A good number of the very old iron ones were patriotically melted down during the Civil War to help with the shortage of metal for the war effort. I speak as a connoisseur of old iron when I say that the surviving cast-iron specimens from pre-1860 are still the best because the quality of the iron gives them special heat-transfer characteristics, and vigilant picking at Pennsylvania flea markets often yields rewards in this respect, especially when you know what to look for. Otherwise the more recent versions in heavy redware are just as good for baking. Dorothy Long's Eagle Studio reproductions of the 1980s are especially noteworthy.

Last I should mention that all the recipes have been revised to conform to a standard recipe format, and wherever possible the proportions have been adjusted so that each recipe is more easily doubled or reduced to half. I began testing many of these dishes in the early 1980s, so over time I was able to iron out some of the knots and kinks that surface in old sources. Most of the proportions will serve four to six persons, but in the case of preparations such as Amish *Roascht*, bread soup, *Gumbis,* or *Schnitz-un-Gnepp,* they are not practical unless made in larger quantities.

Another point worth considering: contrary to popular belief, real Pennsylvania Dutch cooking does not have to be starchy or heavy—unless you want to make it that way. In every single recipe using lard or butter, you can just as easily substitute olive oil or vegetable oil; true purists could use chicken fat, since this not only was preferred in many households but also was used in home remedies, whereas butter could be sold for ready money. Michelin three-star chefs in Alsace know the value of chicken fat (and goose fat) and are quite adept at transforming their basic traditional fare into delightfully creative *light* dishes. There is no reason the same cannot be done with Pennsylvania Dutch cuisine since we share the same basic culinary repertoire.

A new cuisine is already in the making because the younger generation of Pennsylvania Dutch cooks has converted enthusiastically to locally produced artisanal cheeses, not to mention wine, olive oil, hot peppers, and an abundance of fresh herbs—ingredients their grandmothers may have passed over. Perhaps also surprising to outsiders, there are many dishes, for example bread soup and the saffron-flavored potato potpie, that are meatless. *Neideitsche Kiche* (nouvelle Dutch cuisine) is actively reviving this traditional meatless peasant fare because it meshes very well with contemporary ideas about lifestyle and diet. On that note, I will finish here with the old Pennsylvania Dutch dinner expression that greets anyone coming to the table: *Hockt eich hie mit uns, un esst eich satt!* (Sit down with us and eat until you have had enough!).

CHAPTER 1

It Began in Bethlehem

IT was not my idea to drive to Bethlehem, Pennsylvania, in blowing snow. On the other hand the date was close to Christmas, the *Christkindlmarkt* (Christmas fair) was in full swing, and the town was alive with flickering candles in nearly every window and glowing Moravian stars on every other porch. Since 1937 Bethlehem has been the self-declared Christmas City, and I had been invited by the Moravian Bookstore to appear for a book signing for *Pennsylvania Dutch Country Cooking*. Since this is said to be the oldest bookstore in the country (it opened in 1742), the invitation was intriguing; and since the store was always thronged with people during the fair, it seemed the place to be while the toasty spirit of the holidays was in the air. That is where the seeds for *As American as Shoofly Pie* were first planted, because when I left Bethlehem later that evening, I left a changed person.

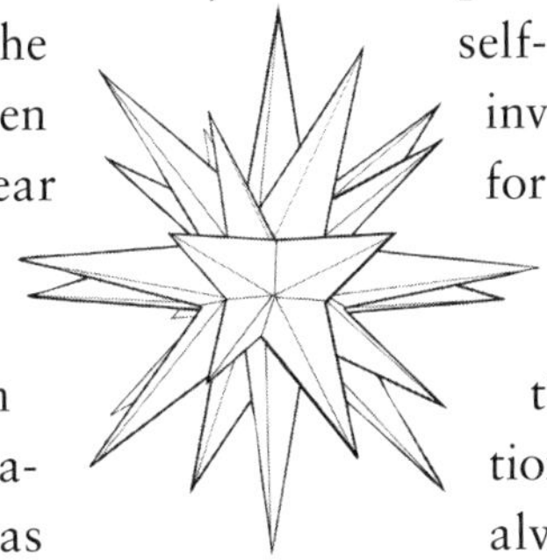

FIGURE 1.
Moravian star.

I imagine it all came down to the buzz I had created in the store because everyone there was soon caught up in the discussion of food, specifically Pennsylvania Dutch food, and opinions pro and con abounded. A well-dressed elderly woman came up to my table and glanced at my new book and its cover with a certain degree of studied disengagement. I encouraged her to leaf through the color-ful photography with the observation that the text contained recipes from all over the region and from all the major cultural groups that make up the Pennsylvania Dutch community—I had worked hard to be even-handed in that regard. She turned to me with a dark look of obvious disapproval and muttered, "I am *not* Pennsylvania Dutch. I am a Moravian. We are Germans." With that she walked away.

This lightning bolt illuminated a problem I had not foreseen: that the Moravian part of my Pennsylvania Dutch research would be shaped by their deep-rooted ideas about the Moravian place in the Pennsylvania Dutch universe. Yet to be totally fair, deep-rooted ideas abound in all the key groups that are part of Pennsylvania Dutch culture, ideas that cut across the verdant landscape and sub-divide it into small parts like crackled glass. The core issues go far beyond food; they deal with complex perceptions of identity that have tormented the Pennsylvania Dutch ever since they transplanted to these shores in the seventeenth century. Those issues can be re-duced to one question: Who *are* the Pennsylvania Dutch? Or more to the point: How do they know they are Dutch? What are the signs and symbols? What are the mutual understandings that draw them together to create a common mindset separate from the rest of their fellow Americans? On the other hand, another valid question could be asked: Is there a common mindset? If not, what holds the culture together?

Certainly if there is a mutual understanding, it is not expressed in Pennsylfaanisch because a good portion of the Pennsylvania Dutch community no longer speaks the dialect. The dividing line between who is Dutch and who is not is drawn in food even as food differentiates Dutch from Dutch: rich from poor, rural from urban, one religious sect from the other, even to the extent that there are localized cultural identities based entirely on neighborhood food-ways: for instance, Goschenhoppen (Montgomery County), the Tulpehocken Valley in Lebanon County, the Mahantongo region in Schuylkill and Northumberland Counties, Weaverland and the Eck in Lancaster County, Buffalo Valley in Union County, Kishacoquillas Valley in Mifflin County, the Bald Eagle and Buffalo Run Valleys in Centre County, the Glades in Somerset County, Morrison's Cove in Blair and Bedford Counties, and Snake Spring Valley in Bedford County. The list of these unique culinary pockets is long and continues to grow as new foodways are documented through fieldwork in Pennsylvania Dutch communities locally and far beyond the boundaries of Pennsylvania. There really is no one Pennsylvania Dutch culture; it is a composite of many parts.

This subregionalization is perhaps the defining theme of Pennsylvania Dutch cookery in that many dishes vary from county to county and even within a limited area, such as the fish pie of the Mahantongo Valley (a pie, incidentally, that contains no fish); the LuLu paste (*Lulu Bapp*), a cheese spread in the Millersburg-Sunbury area; the peach *Schnitz* dumplings of northern Chester County (recipe page 236); or the peach and new-potato stews of the Bald Eagle Valley (recipe page 234). Likewise every locality seems to have its own type of spice cookie or soft sugar cookie; in some areas potato filling (*Fillsel*) is common, while in others, such as York County, it is rare or not made at all. On the other hand, peach and tomato pies (recipe page 235) and pig stomach stuffed with potatoes as opposed to meat (recipe page 266) are less geographic variations than preferences very much dictated by family backgrounds. Some households within the same neighborhood may choose yellow tomatoes instead of red when making the pies or follow certain stuffing traditions over others and view their particular choices as the most authentic. That said, there are certainly many localisms tied to nonregionalized dishes, such as the York County preference of serving horseradish with stuffed pig stomach (which York Countians call "hogmaw"), the Lancaster County potpies flavored heavily with saffron, and the Lehigh County practice of eating scrapple with molasses.

Venison cookery is an excellent example of regionalization because it creates its own map in terms of consumption patterns. In the lower counties, which are primarily agricultural or suburban, venison is more of a specialty dish. Beef and pork are the basic ingredients of winter mincemeat (eaten throughout the winter, not just

FIGURE 2. Deer hunters at the Hegins Hotel, Hegins, Pa., 1909. Real Photo postcard by Charles Schrope. Roughwood Collection, Devon, Pa.

at Christmas). However, in the northern-tier counties of the Dutch Country, where hunting is still an important cold weather activity, venison is widely consumed in many different forms. Since the tallow in venison is unpleasant tasting and of a dry, waxy texture, especially from deer that have grazed on mountain laurel and other evergreens, the meat is not commonly converted into scrapple or pot pudding unless combined with generous portions of pork or beef. However, venison mincemeat is popular, and some traditional butchers even pickle the hearts in the same manner as they do beef. This is considered a great delicacy. So are venison hams, which are brined and smoked and which resemble Italian prosciutto di Parma in appearance and flavor.

The French food historian Philippe Meyzie explored the evolution of regional cuisine in southwest France for roughly the same time period (1700–1850) during which Pennsylvania Dutch cookery was assuming its own distinctive character. While the particulars of these two cuisines are worlds apart—yet also with many surprising similarities—his study about the one has much to teach us about the other. Meyzie argued that all regional cuisines are evolutionary, part of a dynamic process that is constantly open to the flow of new ideas and new foods. Most important, regional cuisines are not single entities. They are amalgamations defined by many overlapping social groups in spite of the winnowing modifications of cookbooks and food literature—especially travel journalism, which tends to cherry-pick and decontextualize unusual dishes or customs.

On that one point, the study of Pennsylvania Dutch cuisine, or what has been written about it over the years, has fallen grievously short of representing the food culture in all of its many diverse components: the urban elite now largely gone due to shifts in demographics, the sectarian now overmagnified through the lens of the Amish, and the rural poor now remembered through a few stylized one-pot dishes. Following are some thoughts on the cuisine and its component parts.

The Classic Cuisine and Its General Structure

While it is true that the early waves of settlers from German-speaking Europe who arrived here in the eighteenth century brought tangible reminders of Germany with them in their massive travel chests, the cultural baggage was not as homogeneous as that of Anglo-Americans. It is a mistake to imagine that beyond sauerkraut there was an easily recognizable "German" cuisine as practiced by the early Pennsylvania Dutch any more than there is a "Chinese" cuisine or an "Italian" cuisine today. These are cuisines composed of distinctive regional cookeries, and a similar mix of regional identities (Swiss, Alsatian, Palatine, Hessian, Swabian, Saxon, Westphalian) was brought to American shores by people who in any case never thought of themselves as Germans. Their cultural loyalties were defined by religion and by petty dukedoms and principalities, and these were expressed in regional dialects much older than standard German. However, once in America they quickly underwent a melding process that was further shaped by the English-speaking colonials who lived around them.

For one thing, colonial Pennsylvania was home to many iron foundries, so the Pennsylvania Dutch were forced to adopt an array of iron utensils not available at the time in Germany and designed for the most part for use on English-style floor-level hearths. This culinary shock was perhaps the first step in their Americanizing experience. Buckwheat cakes (recipe on page 199) and other griddle breads, not to mention johnnycakes and cornmeal, were immediately absorbed into the diet. The frugal recipe for peas and bacon on page 237 is an example of this adaptation of the Old World to the New—remarkable because as a poverty dish it survived well into the late nineteenth century and even found its way into an almanac.

One key characteristic of the immigrant diet was the low amount of fresh meat consumed during much of the year, a pattern echoing the situation in the Old World. This demanded an alternate cuisine based on many kinds of meat substitutes. Flour and dough dishes served this purpose, with browned flour (roux) forming the base for all sorts of soups and gravies; *Gereeschte Mehlsupp* (browned flour soup, recipe on page 199) can be considered one of the cornerstones of this type of cookery. The Pennsylvania Dutch were famous for their flavorful soups, which were an expedient way to deal with odds and ends in the kitchen and to extract the last bit of nutritional value from old bones and scraps. Of course dumplings could be added to soup since they stood in for meat, although among the well-off, meat *and* dumplings or dumplings made of meat defined their special economic status (as I explain further under the discussion of *Hooriche Gnepp* ["hairy" dumplings] on page 219). If we dissect the soup customs of the Pennsylvania Dutch, many truths about the culture in general emerge.

Soups were a core feature of classic Pennsylvania Dutch cuisine, so their preparation and method of serving received considerable attention in culinary literature. Soup was not soup without bread in it, and yet there were complex social codes embedded in both the quality of soup bread and its appearance. In his 1778 encyclopedic guidebook on household management, *Die Hausmutter in allen ihren Geschäfften* (The Housewife in All Her Duties), Christian Friedrich Germershausen brought up this point. His book is pertinent to this discussion because a copy belonged to Catharine Schaeffer (1750–1835), the wife of Frederick Augustus Muhlenberg, who lived at Trappe in Montgomery County, Pennsylvania. Catharine was the daughter of the wealthy Philadelphia sugar refiner David Schaeffer, and she and her husband were among the cultural elite of Pennsylvania Dutch society and served as conduits for information regarding diet, medicine, and moral advice among the Lutheran congregations of the state. This is what Germershausen had to say about serving bread in soup: "For everyday soups, bread is broken up and served in large pieces; for company, the bread should be neatly diced. It is inelegant to serve guests soups that contain large, irregular chunks of bread. Dinner rolls cut into thin slices for soup should be served on a wooden platter or pastry board; they are then cut into neat strips and diced."[1]

While the thrust of this passage deals with food presentation, there is also a differentiation in quality when it comes to entertaining visitors: only the best sort of white bread should be brought to the table. In the Pennsylvania Dutch context, this would be *Millichbrod* (milk bread, white bread or rolls made with milk instead of water). Furthermore, while it is not stated here, elsewhere in his book Germershausen made it clear that the crusts should be removed. These trimmings could be dried, ground up, and used as thickeners in soups or gravies, as liners in well-buttered cake pans, or for giving body to *Grimmele Schaumkuche*, a type of bread-crumb omelet. Otherwise they could be transformed into *Gruscht Pannkuche* (bread crust pancakes), a poverty food for which a recipe is provided on page 195.

We think nothing today of buying a bag of ready-made croutons at the market, and yet the idea of serving beautifully diced bread in soup was a nuanced refinement that can be traced to the aristocratic cookery of the Middle Ages. It cannot be said that it was particularly novel by the eighteenth century when Germershausen mentioned it, but just the same, it did serve as a visual code for defining the importance of the situation. Thus we could expect to find bread croutons either freshly sliced or browned in butter on the tables of the urban and rural elites. This was not the case in most working-class Pennsylvania Dutch farmhouses.

The late Isaac Clarence Kulp (1938–2007), who was a passionate cultural historian of the Pennsylvania Dutch in Montgomery County, once recalled for me the poverty soups that he had known as a child growing up in the Dunkard sect.[2] In the Kulp household, which entertained many Brethren and Mennonite farmers from the area around Vernfield, coarse country bread was served with meals, and when bread was wanted for soup, it was simply torn up into pieces and dropped in. Pieces of bread were also used as sops to wipe up the bowls. In fact soup was generally eaten with bread in it because the bread became an extender and the soup assumed a porridgelike consistency. In a number of cases, foods acquired the designation of "soup" simply because of the presence of bread, as for example the common breakfast meal known euphemistically as *Kaffeesupp* (coffee soup), hot coffee with bread broken into it, or the baked *neideitsch* casserole known as *Brodsupp* (recipe on page 197), which consists of layers of stale sourdough bread, sautéed onions, mushrooms, and shredded cheese flavored with ample quantities of sage. The latter soup has a thick soufflélike texture when hot from the oven.

Once supermarkets and the fast-food revolution penetrated rural Pennsylvania during the 1970s, the old social connotations of soup and croutons quickly disappeared. Croutons could be purchased by the bag or box in any convenience store, and mainstream restaurants began featuring French onion soup with its buttery mass of croutons submerged in an abundance of melted cheese. For better or for worse, the crouton shifted in popular culture to something viewed as French, especially since it was not encountered in standard Pennsylvania Dutch restaurant cookery served to the world at large. Nor was it standard practice in traditional Pennsylvania Dutch cookery to add croutons to salads; that was introduced at salad bars in the 1970s.

Were soups consumed by all Pennsylvania Dutch economic levels? Of course; for the most part soups shared by all classes of Pennsylvania Dutch were basic convenience foods, such as *Riwwelsupp* (rivvel soup), which could be made quickly with milk and rivvels (tiny crumb dumplings) as a dish for children or the elderly, with chicken stock for the convalescent, or with hearty ham or beef stock as a first-course starter. Another soup in this category was *Gereeschte Mehlsupp* (browned flour soup or roux soup), which also served as the basis for seemingly infinite variations, one of the most popular being browned flour soup with potatoes. Potatoes took the place of bread; potato dumplings carried this evolution one step further with the creation of different classes or qualities of soup extenders, from the poor man's *Hooriche Gnepp* ("hairy" dumplings) to the more refined *Buweschpitzle* ("boys bits," recipe on page 193), known more modestly in French Alsatian cookbooks as *quenelles de pommes de terre*.

The *Vollständiges Kochbuch für die deutsch-amerikanische Küche* (Complete Cookbook for the German-American Kitchen), published at Philadelphia about 1856, was a major source of recipes for republication in nineteenth-century Pennsylvania Dutch newspapers, especially those in Lancaster, Reading, York, Pottsville, Gettysburg, Chambersburg, and Allentown, where there were large concentrations of urban Dutch—not to mention large Dutch readerships across the border in Maryland and in and around Cincinnati, Canton, and Lancaster, Ohio. Browned flour soup was called *Gebrannte Suppe* ("parched" soup) in this cookbook, and the middle-class character is clear at the end of the recipe: "Heat four Loth (60g) of lard in an iron stew pan until quite hot, and then brown three to four not-too-large spoonfuls of flour; dissolve this with cold water [and cook until thick], adding salt and nutmeg. Serve over diced white bread; the bread should cook in it only a short time."[3] Needless to say, soup recipes calling for croutons were themselves evidence of bourgeois cookery, and for this reason we find this kind of fare in cookbook literature: a world very much set apart from everyday oral-based cooking in the countryside.

Meats and Seasonal Consumption

Pork and pork products—especially an amazing array of sausages—constituted the meat of choice, and annual pork butchering was as much a ritual for processing food for the winter as it was a time-honored celebration of harvest and plenty. Stuffed pig stomach, an ancient (pre-Christian) festive dish common in southwest Germany and Alsace, became a status and icon food among all the Dutch regardless of their province of origin. While it may stand out as unusual to non-Dutchmen, this dish is little more than a species of sausage; its British Isles counterpart is haggis, a form of mincemeat wrapped in sheep's caul (stomach lining) rather than in the stomach itself.

Aside from small game, which was free, or the Sunday roast chicken, consumption of fresh meat was low among most rural households, especially during hot weather. Thus dried fruit was often cooked in combination with dumplings to form one-pot dishes that were served in a wooden or earthenware bowl in the center of the table. The family and even guests ate from this communal dish, a custom that has survived even today under the comic generic name *Schlappichdunkes* ("slop pot" gravy). Beans, lentils, and peas baked in earthenware pots were served in a similar fashion, sometimes cooked with smoked meat, such as bacon, or with squirrel, groundhog, or pigeons. Families that sold produce at local markets tended to have much more diversified diets because they could interact with other vendors and purchase a wide range of "town goods" such as pretzels, cheese, smoked fish, fancy baked goods, wine, and even imported food products.

German farmers in Europe lived on gruels and porridges, and in this respect they differed little from their English counterparts, and both groups were united by their shift to corn-based dishes once they settled in America. Cornmeal mush was a universal poverty dish or dish of convenience, especially when served with milk for children or the elderly. What set the Pennsylvania Dutch apart from their English neighbors were extensive vegetable gardens and a much broader range of food plants (both domesticated and wild) that found their way to the Pennsylvania Dutch table. For example, it was the Pennsylvania Dutch who first began to harvest native American ramps (a species of wild onion) because they closely resembled in taste and appearance the wild bear garlic of German forests. The eighteenth-century herbal of the Germantown apothecary and book printer Christopher Sauer enumerated the culinary uses for many plants not found in colonial English kitchen gardens, but the lack of specifically native plants in this herbal also reminds us that for the urban Pennsylvania Dutch or for those literate farmers who read books for their source of information prior to the Revolution, a heavy dependence on a continuing influx of ideas and even food imports from the European homeland prevailed. This changed after 1780 with a period of rapid Americanization and by 1830 the evolution of a distinct regional identity, selectively dropping out Old World foods and customs that did not adapt to the American landscape.

In addition to a willingness to consume a broader range of food plants than their English counterparts, the most traditionalist portion of the Pennsylvania Dutch community was noteworthy for cooking on raised hearths. This imposed different cooking technologies and cooking techniques, including the use of a broad range of earthenware utensils of specific design, especially squat, one-handled cook pots and various types of braising pans that were set on trivets when in use. Rural Pennsylvania Dutch potters continued to produce these wares well into the latter part of the nineteenth century because they could be adapted to cook-stove technology and, perhaps most important, because locally made utensils were cheaper than the iron and tin factory goods available in stores—and they could be paid for through barter.

For this reason many vegetables, especially turnips and cabbage, were either boiled in earthenware cook pots or braised under hot coals in enclosed earthenware pans. A dish that consisted of layers of shredded cabbage, perhaps some fresh or dried fruit (apples or pears, for example), and leftover meat was a common one-pot meal. Called

Gumbis in Pennsylfaanisch, a corruption of the Latin term *compositum*, this type of dish survived in many forms and with many subregional variations into the 1930s. A skeletal recipe is even included in Berenice Steinfeldt's 1937 pamphlet mentioned later in my discussion of Amish tourism. One type of *Gumbis* called *Schnitz-un-Gnepp* (dumplings cooked with dried apples) is still made today, and in spite of its original role as a meatless poverty dish, it has become one of the food symbols of Pennsylvania Dutch cookery.

FIGURE 3. *Gumbis* pot.

Gumbis and *Schnitz-un-Gnepp* were dishes of convenience that could be made in a bread oven on baking day and reheated during the course of the week on top of the ten-plate stoves that used to heat the stove rooms of Pennsylvania Dutch farmhouses. Plate-stove cookery, now a lost art, could produce such a rich range of recipes outside normal dish categories that it may be an oversimplification to delegate Pennsylvania Dutch plate-stove preparations under the general heading of poverty foods. On the one hand, they were indeed simple, and many became poverty foods after the shift from hearth to iron cook stove in the 1840s. On the other hand, they were originally intended as convenience dishes made away from the kitchen hearth after the hearth had been put to rest for the day.

This meant that they were cooked in the *Schtupp* (stove room) where the family normally ate. This was also the common living area of the traditional Pennsylvania Dutch farmhouse. Thus these dishes generally served as snacks or supper foods, reheated and eaten in the early evening using up leftovers from the primary meal consumed several hours earlier. The ease with which these recipes could be executed guaranteed their continued popularity with busy Pennsylvania Dutch housewives regardless of economic consideration, although the benefits of frugality should not be overlooked.

Included in this group of foods are mock fish (*Blinde Fische*), slow-simmered potatoes (*G'schwelde or G'schwelde Grumbiere*), and *Backet* or *Baecket,* for which there is no satisfactory English translation beyond "a little morsel baked or fried." Two recipes for *Blinde Fische* are supplied on page 226; this was essentially a preparation composed of minidumplings that were then shaped into "fish" fillets and fried on the top of a hot ten-plate stove with a little pot of gravy simmering at the back. This procedure was then transferred to cook stoves in the nineteenth century with a heavy skillet or iron *Schales* pan taking the place of the baking surface of the plate stove.

Likewise *G'schwelde* moved from plate stove to iron cook stove. These are potatoes that have been simmered slowly at a very low temperature in one of four basic broths that were then thickened and used as gravy over the potatoes to make a one-pot meal. The broths of historical record are as follows: *Brieh* (any type of stock on hand); *Grosse Brieh* (strongly flavored meat broth usually so rich that it will jell when cold); *Weisse Brieh* (the rich, white, meaty stock left over from butchering, and thus a special-occasion dish); and *Zwiwwelbrieh* (onion stock), made by cooking sliced onions until clear in butter or lard along with a little chopped slab bacon. The broth is then thickened with flour or browned flour and thinned to soup consistency with water and seasoned with salt and pepper. The potatoes are then simmered in this mixture until tender. All of these several forms of *G'schwelde* were served hot over a slice of bread, toast, or rewarmed *Mauldasche* (pocket dumplings).

Pennsylvania Dutch *Backet*, sometimes pronounced *Baecket,* is called *Bäckes* in the Palatinate. Potatoes are simmered in a cook pot on top of the stove until tender, the skins are removed, and then the potatoes are cut in half lengthwise. The top of the plate stove (or griddle) must be very hot; it is then greased with butter or lard. The potatoes are placed on the stove top flat side down and cooked until crispy golden brown on the bottom. They are then served brown side up smeared with apple butter or with a layer of old-style cottage cheese (smooth curds) covered with apple butter. This dish was eaten as a bread substitute in poor households and was often given to work hands as a snack or as supper. Hard cider was the standard beverage. This old traditional method of cooking potatoes as

Backet is still practiced in the Lykens Valley of Dauphin County, in the region around Shamokin, and in several counties west of the Susquehanna River. It also surfaces as a popular sandwich filling in many parts of the Dutch Country. A recipe for fried potato and sauerkraut sandwich from the old potato belt around New Tripoli (Lehigh County) is supplied on page 214.

Aside from the preparation of *Gumbis* and the snack foods made on the plate stove, baking day also meant that a variety of shallow-dish casseroles could be assembled from the overflow of vegetables and fruit from the garden. They were generally meatless or else flavored with bits of bacon, ham, or smoked sausage. Called *Schales* for the shallow pans in which they were baked (see Figures 52–53, page 249), they represented yet one more category of dish that could be warmed over on the ten-plate stove or served at room temperature. Recipes range in texture from dense puddings (when made with shredded potatoes, for example) to the equivalent of hot, slightly tenderized salads and are probably old-style dishes well worth reintroduction since they are light and can appeal to a variety of dietary demands. For this reason *Schales* was more generally a hot weather dish, while hearty *Gumbis* supplied the table during winter.

Baking day (usually Friday in preparation for the weekend) was probably one of the most important in the culinary cycle of the old Pennsylvania Dutch household. Bread was the key element of every meal since food was eaten on it or with it. By the middle of the nineteenth century most Pennsylvania Dutch farmhouses were equipped with outdoor bake houses situated at a safe distance from the dwellings due to the danger of fire. The Pennsylvania Dutch were at one time famous for their variety of hearty country-style breads, some of which I re-created, photographed, and included in my book *Pennsylvania Dutch Country Cooking*.

Aside from breads there was also a large subset of dishes made with extra bread dough, mostly flat breads or tarts similar to Italian focaccia or pizza. *Zwiwwelkuche* (onion tart) is perhaps one of the most commonly mentioned in Pennsylvania Dutch poetry since it served as a universal snack food even during harvest. *Schlappkuche* (milk tart with sugar and spices; see page 273 for a recipe), usually given to children, is still one of the nostalgia foods mentioned most by Pennsylvania Dutch during interviews. But there were also many others, including for example *Schmierkeeskuche* (cottage cheese tart with apple butter topping) and *Nesselkuche* (nettle tart with eggs, cottage cheese, and nettle leaves); any ingredients then in season were easily transformed into delightful meals.

The advent of the cast-iron cook stove during the 1840s altered the cuisine by introducing a standardized cooking technology, and with it a plethora of mainstream American dishes designed for the cook stove: chemically leavened breads and pastries for example. This marked the gradual displacement of the true *Kuche* made with yeast-raised dough in favor of the common pie shell of Anglo-American cookery. This shift occurred over the course of about two generations and accelerated during the period of intense industrial-ization following the Civil War. The Dutch borrowed the pie shell made with lard or butter (or both) from mainstream culture and adapted it in unusual hybrid ways, such as in the well-known shoofly pie, which is an old-style molasses crumb cake (*Streisselkuche*) baked in an Anglo-American pie shell. This hybridizing process is still at play, for example with "Whoopee Pies," which were not in-vented in Pennsylvania by the Amish, contrary to popular myth, but which have acquired in the hands of Pennsylvania Dutch cooks a new range of types and flavors—even giant ones easily the size of wedding cakes.

If classic Pennsylvania Dutch cookery can be reduced to a few words, it is a cuisine with Continental European roots with an em-phasis on a great range of soups, pasta dishes (in the form of dump-lings and noodles), flat breads (*Kuche*) that served as bases for sweet or savory toppings, and a striking variety of casseroles, deep dish in the case of *Gumbis* or shallow in the case of *Schales*. The one unify-ing element and the key dish that made the Dutch different from all the other American groups was their preference for sauerkraut. This is the cornerstone that holds up the entire cuisine, and I have more to say about that in Chapter 7, "The Cabbage Curtain."

FIGURE 4. Wealthy *Hasenpfeffer* Dutch from Lancaster, Pa., posing for a photo prior to their departure for a grand tour of Europe, ca. 1880. Original photograph by Otto E. Weber, North Queen Street, Lancaster, Pa. Roughwood Collection, Devon, Pa.

CHAPTER 2

The *Hasenpfeffer* Dutch:
The Urban and Rural Elites

"*H*ASENPFEFFER Dutch" is an old euphemism for the Pennsylvania Dutch well-to-do, the merchants and professionals who lived in towns as well as the *Grossbauer*, the large landholders whose fine stone or brick farmhouses still dot the Pennsylvania landscape. Their money allowed them to mingle and intermarry with other social elites and to live a lifestyle much like that of other upper-class Americans. The term was once common parlance among certain Lancaster County circles, and I distinctly recall my grandfather mentioning it in connection with the J. H. Beers 1903 *Biographical Annals*. People paid a fee to get into the *Annals*, so there was a certain disdain for the ne'er-do-wells who for a fee managed to pass themselves off as *Hasenpfeffer* Dutch in spite of vague origins and inflated family accomplishments.

It is relatively easy to pick out names of the better-known individuals who belonged to this social category: the writer and antiquarian Cornelius Weygandt; the Pennsylvania Dutch historian Julius Friedrich Sachse; the art collector Albert Barnes of the Barnes Foundation—his mother was Pennsylvania Dutch, and he preferred that term; the Lehigh County "potato baron" and politician Mark W. Hoffman; and perhaps the greatest Pennsylvania Dutch booster of them all, Pennsylvania's governor Samuel Pennypacker (governor 1903–1907). Any of the earlier Dutch governors such as Simon Snyder would also qualify, not to mention the Reading, Pennsylvania,

Hiesters, the Muhlenbergs, the Wistars, the Rittenhouses, the cookbook author J. George Frederick, and the novelist Elsie Singmaster.

Also included in this group were the politically connected hotel keepers such as Colonel Tilghman Good, whose venison cutlet recipe is published on page 209 for the first time, and not least, the beer barons: the Yuenglings of Pottsville, the Lauers of Reading, and the Wackers of Lancaster. The expression "*Hasenpfeffer* Dutch" may have originated from a linkage between the dish sour braised rabbit and the socialite Mary Wacker, wife of the brewer Charles V. Wacker, who was prominent among the culinary elites and whose recipe for *Hasenpfeffer* was considered one of the best (see her recipe on page 257). The essential point is not the "who" but rather their influence, since many of these individuals shaped Pennsylvania Dutch haute cuisine and how it was perceived by the other Dutch.

For one thing, these people ate differently and often drank wine with their meals. Many of them read and spoke fluent German; they used the German-language almanacs and newspapers common in Pennsylvania until World War I. Parlor dishes such as potato balls, sweet-and-sour marinated shad, and mock hare were part of their culinary culture. Cabbage dumplings and onion sauce were just a few of the many rich dishes that one was more likely to find on the tables of these Dutch families than in a middle-class farmhouse. Julius Friedrich Sachse reminisced in 1899 about goose liver pies for Christmas—a recipe was actually published in *Der alte Germantown Calender* for 1863—because these families ate goose stuffed with sauerkraut (and chestnuts) instead of roast chicken on Christmas Day, hence goose in all its culinary expressions became a code for status.[1] These Dutch also consumed a wide variety of American-style layer cakes; thus it was these "cake families" to whom the local church committees looked for material when compiling fund-raising cookbooks.

If you go into the countryside and ask farm cooks about *Hasenpfeffer*, more likely than not the question will draw a blank. In Pennsylvania Dutch *Hasenpfeffer* is both a rabbit dish and a popular card game. There are probably two hundred people who know how to play the game for every one who may know how to cook the dish. Like its "daughter dish" rabbit souse, a rich aspic made from the leftovers, this is one of those braised raised-hearth preparations from classical Pennsylvania Dutch cuisine that has begun to fade from the scene because it was part of a culinary tradition associated with the old, educated elite; hence it was never embraced by our local tourist industry, which has always fixated on noble peasant roots. This dish took its place beside *Gansepeffer* (made with goose), *Endepeffer* (made with duck), *Harzepeffer* (made with beef hearts and often served with pretzel dumplings), and *Fleeschpeffer,* perhaps the lordliest of them all: beef and pork eye of the round stewed together in red wine. The latter dish was a Berks County specialty given pride of place many years ago on the menus of the Water Gate Inn in Washington, D.C., and before that, during the 1930s, on the menus of Mary Elizabeth, a well-known Fifth Avenue restaurant in New York that belonged to Pennsylvania Dutch–born Martha Evans Stringer. Both of these popular restaurants also served *Hasenpfeffer.*

Like those other *Peffer* dishes, *Hasenpfeffer* was considered the centerpiece of the meal. It was prepared in marinades of wine or vinegar or both, to which were added spices and even gingerbread crumbs in some cases. The dish can be traced directly to the Middle Ages and calls to mind jugged hare, its old English equivalent. Indeed during the era of open-hearth cookery in colonial Pennsylvania, the Pennsylvania Dutch dish was traditionally baked in a *Rutscher,* an earthenware pan that resembles a jug cut in half lengthwise (Figure 44). Many of these pans sported matching lids, and the fancier sorts were ornamented with rabbits or some other animal alluding to the contents (Figure 5). The pans were in every case status symbols for their owners and like the food inside, clear statements about the families' place in local society. These were the prized possessions of the *Hasenpfeffer* Dutch.

Since they lived mostly in towns, the *Hasenpfeffer* Dutch also enjoyed a distinct café culture, and a unique menu to go with it surfaces from time to time in pre-Prohibition literature. It was often called "Bohemian" in reference to this café lifestyle, even though that now-dated term is misleading. In the 1907 book *Suppers,* author Paul Peirce, publisher of the national magazine *What to Eat,* described a Bohemian supper for single men. "Bohemian" was a loose word in those days; in this case it applied to culturally adventuresome aristocratic gentlemen with refined interests in the arts and food, and perhaps each other. This ambiguous term (which was sometimes equated with today's term "gay") was popular in the early 1900s with society writers such as Clarence Edwords—for example, in his 1914 *Bohemian San Francisco*—and was often applied with unflattering overtones by rural Pennsylvania hotel keepers to rich townies in search of rustic culinary epiphanies.

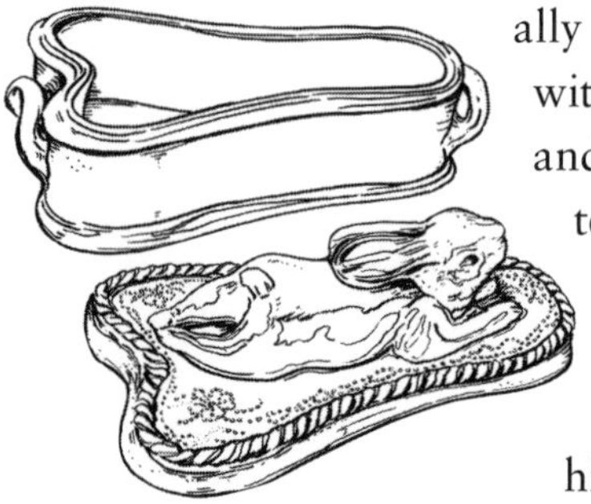

FIGURE 5. *Hasenpfeffer* pan. Poterie artisanale Gérard Wehrling, Soufflenheim, Alsace.

This is how Peirce described his Bohemian supper: "The menu includes one hot dish, a rabbit fricassee or stew. Any chef (especially German) can prepare what is called 'Hasenpfeffer stew.' This is rabbit soaked in vinegar and cooked with certain herbs and is liked by Bohemians. With this serve potato salad and cold dishes, Swiss cheese on rye bread, Westphalian ham, Frankfurters, Bologna, cottage cheese with chopped chives, dill pickles, Spanish onions sliced in vinegar, French mustard, radishes, spring onions, pickled beets and pickled eggs, pickled herring."[2]

This menu with its highly cosmopolitan range of components could easily have been inspired by the famous meals served at Kuechler's Roost, one of the best-known of the Pennsylvania Dutch haute cuisine eateries of the late nineteenth and early twentieth centuries. Named for Jacob Louis Kuechler (1830–1902), a mountain hermit who made his own high-quality wines, the Roost was the first (1882) of several wine houses that later sprouted up along the Gravity Railroad on Mount Penn overlooking Reading, Pennsylvania. Like Fred Kiedeisch's Wine Resort at Lauterbach

FIGURE 6. Pennsylvania Dutchmen enjoying Mt. Penn wines at their *Schtammtisch* in a Reading, Pa., wine saloon. *Carte de visite* by Reading photographer F. M. Yeager, ca. 1868. Roughwood Collection, Devon, Pa.

Springs, Reininger's Vineyard and Wine House, and Steigerwald's Winery—all on Mount Penn—Kuechler's Roost was a Pennsylvania Dutch–style *Weinstube* (*Woischtupp* in Pennsylfaanisch) where fine cooking and locally made wines went hand in hand with a style of cuisine that was European in tone and yet thoroughly Pennsylvania Dutch in character.

Anywhere else in the United States, the style of cookery at the

Roost would have been called German American, but in Pennsylvania, under the interpretive direction of the so-called Swabian culinary aristocracy or "dumpling gentry" (*Gnepp Adel*), it was redefined in local terms and hybridized into something uniquely Pennsylvania Dutch. This was no marginal rarity in the Dutch Country; even the consumption of local wine made from American grapes was an integral part of this food scene. It is said that during any given season Spuhler's Mountain Resort (another eatery along Reading's Gravity Railroad) sold as much as fifteen thousand gallons of local Mount Penn wines, so in the sense that these restaurants were serving food to accompany their own local vintages, they resembled the type of classical *Heurigen* that sprang up around Vienna, Austria.

Kuechler's in particular was legendary for its pig roasts, *Hasenpfeffer* lunches, and domestic red as well as foreign (mostly German) wines, not to mention weekly offerings of chicken and waffles in either of two ways, with fowl roasted or stewed. Paul Peirce referred to this type of cookery as the "genuine Dutch supper, in all its glory of Limburger and sour-krout."[3] And so it was. Yet it was an authenticity that did not survive Prohibition. The rich style of cookery that evolved around the old Pennsylvania Dutch upper-class habit of drinking wine as an integral part of the meal declined to the point that by the time J. George Frederick published *The Pennsylvania Dutch and Their Cookery* in 1935, the culinary traditions of Kuechler's Roost (which Frederick had visited during its heyday) were little more than a nostalgic memory.

This brings to the table the heretofore sotto voce reality that there were noteworthy class and economic divisions in Pennsylvania Dutch cuisine, that this was not the food we know from tourism but a cuisine highly evolved and with its own distinct social boundaries. In practice this culinary code in all its complex divisions as it evolved from the land is what we still have, and it will be with us as long as American society uses food to express social divisions between differing economic groups. Quite surprising, in spite of the members' Germanophile leanings and emphasis on colonial tradition, the pre–World War I menus of the Pennsylvania German Society banquets reflected nothing of their culinary heritage but rather high-class Philadelphia-style hotel cookery (mock turtle soup, lobster cutlets, Roman punch, Neapolitan ice cream, and similar old clubby standbys). The society was not at that time comfortable with anything that smacked of lowbrow Dutchness.

The actual cultural gatekeepers of high-end Pennsylvania Dutch cookery as practiced in urban and rural hotels, in wine cafés on the edges of large towns, and in the homes of rich landowners and economic elites were the Swabians who dominated the culinary business class of the culture. This "dumpling gentry," as the group was euphemistically labeled, formed a social "culinocracy" (a term of my creation) by virtue of overlapping business ties and marriages. We refer to them and their larger community in Pennsylfaanisch as 'S *Schwowe Drittel*, the "Swabian Third," since they represented about one third of the total Pennsylvania Dutch population. Also not to be overlooked, a large number of Swabian-born ministers filled the pulpits of Lutheran churches throughout the state. The "Swiss Third" gave us the food producers and the plain sects (Amish and Mennonites); and the "Palatine Third" gave us the "rural majority," the middle-class Lutheran and German Reformed farming backbone of the state. Proof of the lasting influence of the *Schwowe Drittel* is Pottsville's Yuengling beer (the Yuenglings were Swabians) and the iconic Philadelphia soft pretzel, but the Swabian contribution to Pennsylvania Dutch culture was far more extensive than simply beer and pretzels. The Swabians brought to Pennsylvania a highly developed cuisine based on dumplings and noodles and a culinary world ruled from hotel kitchens.

The Famous Kuechlers Roost and Wine Vault on Mt. Penn, Reading, Pa.

FIGURE 7. View of Kuechler's Roost, ca. 1912. Tinted postcard. Roughwood Collection, Devon, Pa.

CHAPTER 3

Our Dumpling Culture and the "Swabian Third"

THE Swabians of Baden-Württemberg were attracted to Pennsylvania because they were for the most part Lutheran Protestants, unlike Catholic Bavarians who headed for New York or the Midwest, and they shared many cultural customs with other German-speaking groups who emigrated with them from the Rhineland. The American pretzel story was largely built on networks of Pennsylvania Dutch Swabians, such as the brothers Frederick and John Schwab, who set up bakeries in Pottstown, Pennsylvania, in 1860 and Shelby, Ohio, in 1866 and used the railroads to ship pretzels and bakery products back and forth. Indeed it was the Swabian-born bread baker Andreas Beyerle of Lancaster, whose 1745 case clock was carved with dinner rolls and a pretzel, who has provided posterity with the earliest documented image of a pretzel in Pennsylvania. All Pennsylvania Dutch bread bakers also baked pretzels; that was part of their training, and the pretzel was a symbol of their trade.

The Swabian culinary hegemony is probably best illustrated by the family connections of Swabian-born Karl August Schaich, who purchased Kuechler's Roost in 1905, demolished the original hermit's lodge, and erected in its place the rustic stone restaurant preserved in popular postcard views (that reincarnation of the Roost was accidentally burned down by fireworks on July 4, 1919). Schaich was born in Württemberg in 1863 and came to the United States in 1889, eventually settling in Reading, Pennsylvania, in 1891.

His sister Louisa was the wife of Frederick Glasser, a well-known
Philadelphia butcher and sausage maker. Schaich's brother Frederick
was a brewer in Baltimore. This microcosm of relations in the food
business could be replicated over and over in every major Pennsylvania Dutch town, and it was this segment of the Pennsylvania Dutch
community for which much of the German-language culinary literature was published and from which many of the core dough dishes
emanated into larger Pennsylvania Dutch culture.

William Vollmer's *United States Cook Book* (1859), which originally appeared in German for Pennsylvania Dutch readers, was one
such source of recipes. Born in Swabia and trained as a hotel cook,
Vollmer worked for a time in a Philadelphia dining club. Not
only were his recipes—both German and English—
reprinted in local newspapers and almanacs, but also the nomenclature of
many of the dishes was adjusted to account for Pennsylvania Dutch sensibilities.
Thus *Mauldasche* (pocket dumplings), one of
the popular foods in urban Dutch cookery,
are called by Vollmer "Swabian Filled Noo-

FIGURE 8. *Mauldasche.*

dles" in reference to this popular specialty that is still considered a
"national dish" in Württemberg.[1]

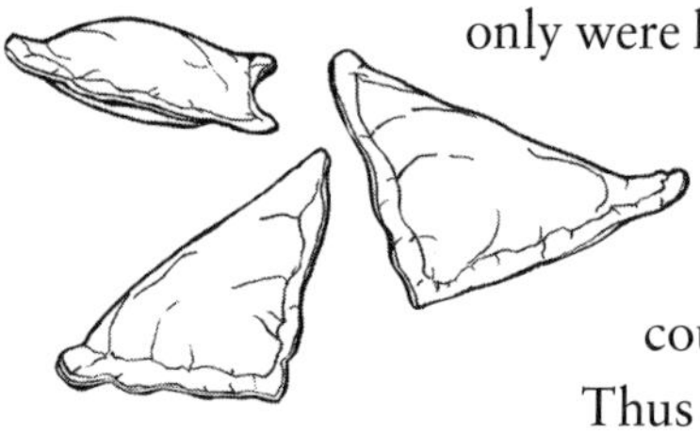

The oldest Pennsylvania reference discovered thus far for the
term *Mauldasche* appears in Johann Georg Hohman's 1819 *Das
Evangelium Nicodemus* (The Gospel of Nicodemus) in material
Hohman added to this apocryphal work. In it Hohman has Jesus
addressing Saint Matilda, Saint Bridget, and Saint Elizabeth: *Weis-
set, liebe Töchterlein, ich habe hundert und zwei Maultauschen
von den Juden empfangen,* which someone recently mistranslated
as "Know ye, dear daughters, that I have received one hundred and
two raviolis from the Jews."[2] This hilarious error arises from the
fact that *Maultaschen* is folk slang for *Maulschelle* (slaps across the
mouth); thus the most accurate way to translate *Mauldasche* (the
food) is "mouth slappers"—just as Americans use the euphemism
"pot sticker" for nearly the same thing in Korean cookery.

Most of the thirty-two recipes for classic *Mauldasche* listed in Herbert Rösch's *Schwäbisches Maultaschenbüchle* (Handbook of Swabian Pocket Dumplings) were also known to the Pennsylvania Dutch. Just the same, Dutch cooks took the pocket dumpling much further and adapted it in creative ways to American ingredients, ingredients not used in the Old World, such as squirrel and groundhog, snapping turtle, smoked buffalo tongue, corn, squash, beans, ramps, and even catfish, chinquapins, and pawpaws. The fillings for *Mauldasche* were as varied as the Pennsylvania landscape, although the most ubiquitous recipe, commonly called "parsley pie," was stuffed with parsley and served with parsley gravy—which to me is parsley overkill. Yet who would not be enchanted by the *neideitsch*-style *Mauldasche* stuffed with fresh spring morels and served with a green sauce of wild asparagus, or stuffed with toasted hickory nuts and smoked pheasant and served with a creamy chestnut sauce? These too are Pennsylvania Dutch, but these 1930s experimental recipes were never destined to turn up in Lancaster County tourist brochures.

The Swabian segment of the population was not limited to towns exclusively, for we find strong evidence from settlement patterns that groups of immigrant families often settled together, thus creating cultural pockets with distinctive food patterns. This was true, for example, in the Mahantongo Valley, where the Swabian Hepplers, Massers, and Reinerts settled together, thus giving rise to local names such as Swabian Creek (*Schwowegrick*) at Rebuck in nearby Northumberland County and the Mahantongo expression "Swabian Dumplings" (*Schwowegnepp*) for steamed dumplings. Otherwise these dumplings are more commonly called *Dampfgnepp*, and at one time they were geographically pervasive in Pennsylvania Dutch cookery, although never considered a poverty dish. Yet not everything in Pennsylvania Dutch is that simple.

"Swabian dumplings" could be several things. Carrie Haas Troutman's Mahantongo recipe for *Schwowegnepp* consisted of boiled rather than steam-baked egg-size dumplings served in bowls of hot milk topped with a mixture of sugar and breadcrumbs browned in butter—a dessert dish reserved for Sunday dinner. The distinction between something familiar and everyday as opposed to food with an outside connection (Swabian hotel cookery) suggests that not only were most types of dessert dumplings considered food of the affluent, but also they probably found their way into rural cuisine in conjunction with the adoption of the cast iron stove, that is, during and after the 1840s. The cook stove and its heavy iron utensils made *Dampfgnepp* easier to prepare from a technological standpoint, and the concurrent introduction of baking powders gave dumpling cooks a convenient and fail-safe replacement for yeast.

The urban high-culture origin of *Dampfgnepp* (often served with sweet wine sauce or molasses) and its close culinary relatives is confirmed by the presence of prototype recipes in old German cookbooks intended for the literate elite. The 1691 edition of the *Vollständiges Nürnbergisches Koch-Buch* (Complete Nuremberg Cookbook) outlined a recipe for *Heffen oder Ofen Knötlein* (yeast or oven dumplings) in which the dumplings were placed in a pan with a flat, tight lid. Hot coals were scattered on top of the lid and underneath the pan, which was set on a trivet. The dumplings were steam-baked in milk, which was also common in Pennsylvania, although the process is tricky because it is easy to scorch the milk, especially when sugar or honey is added to give the dumplings sweet, sticky bottoms.[3]

The French in Alsace call these steam-baked dumplings *petits pains gouflés à la vapeur,* while the Old World Palatines call them *Dampfnudle,* and one might even see these same terms appearing simultaneously on old menus. Added to this culinary Tower of Babel is the *Dampfgnopp*, a Pennsylvania Dutch variation known among the Beachy Amish, who made it mostly on baking day because they fashioned it from an extra lump of raised bread dough. This consisted of one large dumpling (hence the singular *Gnopp*) steamed over simmering water rather than steam-baked in a skillet like the others. This latter type of steamed dumpling can be treated as the poor man's version of the recipe, although when properly made, it will acquire the texture of a "cumulus cloud," to quote Annie Glick, one of the Amish cooks who used to make the dish on a regular basis.[4]

The Old Order Amish are also beholden to the *Schwowe Drittel* for the wedding dish they call *Roascht* (roast). In spite of its name, it is not a roast but rather a species of baked filling that is in fact a chicken-and-bread variation of common Pennsylvania Dutch *Fillsel* (potato filling, recipe on page 213), now ubiquitous in most parts of the Dutch Country. Like potato filling, *Roascht* is served either by itself or as part of a suite of dishes for special occasions. The Amish version is served primarily at weddings or for Christmas and consists of chopped or shredded roast chicken (hence the reference to roast in the name), diced or chopped bread, chicken stock, and perhaps some herbs and chopped celery. This wet mixture is baked with ample quantities of butter (one recipe calls for over one pound) so that it develops a golden crust on the sides and bottom. The Amish like it because it feeds a large number of people. Contrary to popular myth, the Amish did not invent this dish as many writers on the Amish claim. The Amish have adjusted it to meet their needs and in that way have changed it, but the origin of *Roascht* lies outside the community.

The prototype recipe for *Roascht* can be found in William Vollmer's *United States Cook Book* under the name "Chicken Stuffing."[5] This is just one of several similar dishes that were served by the hotel and restaurant keepers in nineteenth-century Pennsylvania Dutch towns. In short, the Amish borrowed it because it was something other religious groups around them found expedient when entertaining large numbers of people. Technically speaking, all of these old-style stuffings doubled as the bases for boiled dumplings, a point made by Vollmer, so in this respect baked Pennsylvania Dutch fillings replaced dumpling cookery as more and more commercial kitchens shifted to baking the preparations in large pans. Instead of serving it as a dumpling, the filling could be served with an ice-cream scoop in perfectly round imitations of the real thing. Who would have thought that the invention of the ice cream scoop would replace an icon of traditional cuisine?

Yet this transformation began in earnest during the early 1930s under the lead of restaurants catering to the tourist industry. It eliminated the need to make large numbers of dumplings by hand, the need for a kitchen station where they would be boiled right before serving (an additional staff salary), and the need for soup bowls and people to serve them (a further reduction of salary overhead). *Roascht* can be served family style without any of this fuss, and it does not require specialized culinary training to assemble, although it does require an experienced palette to create the right balance of flavors.

This simplification process originating in the commercial food sector is typical of the way the Amish assimilate ideas via contact with the world around them. Indeed if their cookery is examined carefully, at least as it was practiced before the 1960s and the onslaught of junk food that has greatly affected everyday Amish diets, there is a fascinating range of recipes belonging to this transfer cuisine.

Since bread-based puddings and dumplings are essentially meat substitutes, one of the stark differences between the cookery of the Pennsylvania Dutch economic elites and that of the average farmer was the prevalence of fresh meat on the table, and not just any sort of meat but pork, beef, game, or poultry prepared in richly flavored dishes, such as *Hasenpfeffer*. This is coupled with a general preference for boiled dumplings as a side dish rather than transforming the dumpling mixture into baked puddings. This type of cookery, with two "meats" (the real one and the dumpling as a meat substitute), would have persisted much longer and in a much more vibrant fashion had it not been misconstrued as German during the anti-German frenzy of World War I. Furthermore its total integration with the custom of wine drinking signaled further decline during Prohibition.

Friedrike Löffler's popular Swabian cookbook *Oekonomisches Handbuch für Frauenzimmer* (The Gentlewoman's Handbook of Domestic Economy), first issued in 1793 and reprinted into the 1930s, also contained material that appealed to the urban Pennsylvania Dutch community, especially cooks of Swabian ancestry; she included a recipe using *Bubenschenkel* ("boys thighs"), a type of large stuffed roll of dough still popular in the Allentown area. The urban/rural dichotomy surfaces in even the plainest of Löffler's recipes; let her *weisse Wasser-Suppe* (white water soup) serve as a final example. It is closely akin to Pennsylvania Dutch *Oiersupp* (egg drop soup), although country cooks would have dispensed with the ginger. This soup is to Pennsylvania Dutch cookery what *stracciatella* is to Italian cooking and is sometimes called *Gehacktesupp* ("chopped" soup, recipe on page 206) in Pennsylfaanisch, in reference to the shreds of cooked egg. Löffler's recipe reads: "For four people, take three *Schoppen* (1.5 liters) of boiling water, add the necessary salt, and a little parsley, pepper and ginger; add only a pinch of the last three ingredients. In a work bowl, beat five eggs until frothy. As soon as the water boils up, remove from the fire. Slowly swirl in the beaten eggs and serve over the fried crumbs of white bread or the crumbs of dinner rolls."[6]

The rustic home-cooking version of this soup would have called for gribble or bread crumbs made from crust trimmings instead of the best part of the white bread and crumbs fried in lard or more likely bacon drippings rather than butter. In households where milk was plentiful or overly abundant, milk might take the place of water, and depending on local taste, saffron might be introduced instead of ginger. Soups served with bread or bread crumbs in them eventually thicken the longer they stand; these thick soups were then used the next day as gravy over other foods: over bread as a breakfast or supper dish or over meat such as fried ham or sausages for dinner. They were also added to dishes baked in earthenware pots, such as beans, or even to one-pot meals such as *Gumbis*, in which the day-old soup acted as both a thickener and a flavor enhancer. These soups could also be combined with the stuffing in *Seimawe*, a sausage about the size of a football that is considered, along with sauerkraut, the "national dish" of the Pennsylvania Dutch.

CHAPTER 4

Seimawe: Tourism Reshapes a Food Icon

In plain English the Pennsylvania Dutch word *Seimawe* means "sow's stomach," although this is commonly translated as "pig stomach." This is one of the iconic dishes of Pennsylvania Dutch cuisine, and recipes vary greatly. In the Dutch Country west of the Susquehanna River the same thing is called "hogmaw." Regionalisms aside, the distinction about the sex of the pig is important because boars (male pigs) were not traditionally eaten by the Pennsylvania Dutch; they were breeding animals, and once sexually mature their meat acquired a rank-tasting gaminess resulting from the production of androsterone and skatole. Male piglets were sent to tables as roast suckling pigs because from an economic standpoint they could not have babies and certainly did not make good pot roasts or sausages once fully grown. All you needed was one boar to keep the sows in litters; the rest were redundant. Male pigs sometimes went into army rations in the nineteenth century or were castrated and raised for lard.

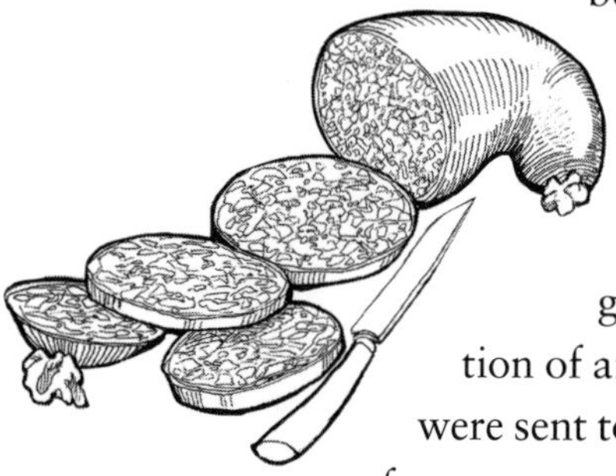

FIGURE 9. *Seimawe.*

This critical footnote on the connoisseurship of pork is important from the standpoint that Pennsylvania Dutch meat cookery is largely pork-based, although beef is now probably running neck and neck. When a country butcher describes with obvious pleasure the "sweetness" of good-quality pork, what he is telling you is that it is not boar's meat; it is a superior cut from a sow or a barrow (castrated boar). In the nineteenth century when it came time to butcher the family-raised pigs—usually sometime before Christmas or right before the new year—the event was cause for celebration because the intestines were recycled into sausages and the stomach was saved to make a once-a-year specialty called stuffed pig stomach. This name does not ring well in English, although stuffed pork tripe would do just as well. All economic levels of Pennsylvania Dutch culture celebrated this food as a symbol of plenty and the consummation of the harvest in the same manner that the rest of America ascribed this imagery to the Thanksgiving turkey.

This custom came to Pennsylvania with the *Pelzer Drittel* (the Palatine Third), and yet stuffed pig stomach quickly evolved into one of those unifying foods with which all segments of Pennsylvania Dutch culture—rich or poor—could identify. Today the announcement of a pig stomach dinner will draw people for miles around. This has become one of the surefire ways to raise money for charitable organizations, and it is possible to spend each weekend of the winter tracking down these dinners in various parts of the state. In fact there are people who do this as a form of weekend entertainment, and they are the ones with whom to network to learn about the places where pig stomach is cooked in the tastiest manner.

The mention of pig stomach to non-Dutchmen more often than not invites scowls and comments of disgust, when in fact *Seimawe* is nothing more than a large sausage filled with ingredients similar to those found in any common turkey stuffing, but of course with a number of Pennsylvania Dutch twists such as diced potatoes, chopped smoked sausage, small sections of pork ribs, or even some dried fruit. There are well over thirty recorded variations of stuffing recipes, which means that there are doubtless many more waiting for discovery. Two recipes in the last chapter, one with a potato filling and one with a meat filling, provide examples of two very different cooking traditions (see pages 266 and 267).

Properly made, pig stomach is stuffed and sewn up and then boiled, similar to the method used for an English bag pudding, until the filling expands and sets into something soft yet perfectly slice-able. The stuffed stomach is then roasted in the oven, basted with butter or bacon drippings to develop a golden brown skin, and then brought to the table whole with considerable fanfare. It is sliced and served like sausage, and there are as many people who do not eat the crispy outer skin as there are those who prefer it over the filling. In some households where several pigs were butchered at once in earlier times, one or two of the pig stomachs were cooked until tender and then chopped and added to the stuffing; otherwise they would be pickled like tripe, since there was no other way to preserve them in the days before refrigeration.

Aside from mentioning *Seimawe* as a Pennsylvania Dutch icon food, the tourism industry more or less stayed away from it because it was not a dish outsiders could easily embrace. Furthermore this is not the kind of food safe to serve at outdoor events such as the Kutztown Folk Festival because pork tripe would spoil much too easily during the oppressive heat that normally accompanies the festival in early July. Nonetheless commercial restaurant cooking has slowly influenced the way in which pig stomach is now served at church suppers and fire hall dinners.

The stomach is cooked and chopped up, mixed with the stuffing, and then baked in large pans, similar to the way potato filling is cooked. The texture is loose and sometimes very moist if a generous amount of pork stock has been added. The appearance is not that of a large sausage nicely sliced, but rather a pork tripe version of Amish *Roascht* in which pig stomach takes the place of chicken. For the uninitiated tourist, this ambiguous form of presentation is less off-putting. This is how pig stomach is now served at Shady Maple in Lancaster County and at many other places that on occasion feature the dish on their menus. This simplification of procedure was borrowed directly from tourist fare along the lines of the similar transformation of dumplings into pan puddings. It eliminated the need for someone in the kitchen expert enough to know how to sew up the stomachs; it eliminated a station in the kitchen where they were boiled; and it eliminated the need to roast and baste them once cooked. Everything could now be poured into large pans and baked like chicken potpie and then served by the scoop. Many people have never seen it served any other way.

This simplification process has also been adopted in the German Palatinate, where the Pennsylvania dish originated and is still considered a regional food icon. In an interview with chef Volker Gilcher, owner of the Restaurant-Weinkeller von Busch-Hof in Freinsheim, a popular spot for Palatine specialties and game dishes, I was provided with a rather full discourse on the present state of pig stomach cookery. I was also introduced to a book by the local food journalist Judith Kauffmann, who touched lightly on the history of the dish and provided a pictorial overview (with recipes) of how the preparation is being handled by various Palatine chefs.

Like many other foods that have become tourist food icons, stuffed pig stomach was popularized by one person and then widely copied. One recurring theme in food tourism is the spontaneously evolving shadow industry of knockoffs, look-alikes, and copy-cat marketing. In this case stuffed pig stomach was first made famous as a regional Palatine food at the Weinhaus Henninger in Kallstadt under the watchful oversight of the owner and cook Luise Henninger (1871–1951). Thus the evolution of stuffed pig stomach into a Palatine culinary icon is fairly recent, even though the dish itself has been around since early medieval times, perhaps even dating to the pre-Roman Celts, as some historians have suggested. More important, the dish did not become an icon food in Pennsylvania until it became an icon food in the Palatinate. While the Palatine tradition was preempted by hotel cookery, the Pennsylvania Dutch tradition evolved directly out of home cooking.

Kauffmann's book is a classic example of food tourism since it is both a well-illustrated cookbook and a culinary guide outlining where to go and what to expect. Against that background I sampled a number of variations that Gilcher has listed from time to time on his menus paired with the local wines of his recommendation—

from which I concluded that he has been influenced by Kauffmann's survey, especially by the recipes of other well-known chefs that he has adapted to his own taste preferences. Clearly the literature of food tourism has an effect on the product it is packaging; indeed in this case it has created a new reality.

Aside from butcher shops and a few traditionalist country inns, such as Henninger's, that still make and sell old-style stuffed pig stomach, most of the restaurants in the Palatinate no longer serve the dish in its stomach casing for economic reasons similar to those in the Dutch Country. In Germany commercial artificial casings have entered the scene in the form of oblong, tube-shaped "Bohemian" dumplings—"Bohemian" in this case refers to the region of that name in the Czech Republic. These casings are now the defining standardized shape of all nonartisanal dumplings across German-speaking Europe and are also used for pig stomach.

FIGURE 10. Butchering a sow, New Cumberland, Pa., November 1908. Roughwood Collection, Devon, Pa.

Gilcher's pig stomach dishes are not quite that industrialized. He forms the mixture (with some of the cooked skin included) into sausages about 2¼ inches (5.6cm) in diameter. These are poached and then cut into ¼-inch (6mm) thick slices that are lightly browned on both sides right before serving. In one of my favorite recipes, the flavor is lush and full of depth because it is created via a concentrated mixture of chopped cooked pork, ground pork sausage, pureed dried tomatoes softened in wine, marjoram, and a pinch of hot pepper. Goat cheese runs through the middle of the sausage so that each slice has a small spot in the center, a dab of creamy texture that adds to the richness of the mouth feel.

This intense-tasting morsel was intended to be eaten with a local wine and other complementing foods; the important point is that the pig stomach was not stuffed with bread or diced potatoes as is the norm in Pennsylvania. The experience of sampling Gilcher's various renditions of the classical dish brought home the realization that our own talented chefs could do likewise with ingredients more indigenous to us, such as corn or hickory nuts or even whole grains such as spelt and buckwheat. I have long heard rumors about the Pennsylvania Dutch poor and how they put buckwheat into just about everything they ate. It would seem an odd inversion of class values that this kind of poverty food may be destined to become the artisanal health food of the well-to-do.

FIGURE 11. A typical Buckwheat Dutch two-room log house, now demolished. Built by the Vanasdall family, Hampden Township, Cumberland County, Pa. Original photograph ca. 1896. Roughwood Collection, Devon, Pa.

CHAPTER 5

The Buckwheat Dutch:
"We Ain't Towner"

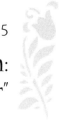

THE rural poor among the Pennsylvania Dutch have never been given much notice in regional literature, even though most of the practitioners of folk medicine (or powwow doctors, as they are called) came from this marginal stratum of society. The diet of this group, which was by no means homogeneous aside from the shared factor of poverty, is certainly the most interesting from an ethnographic standpoint because it was in every respect closest to the land, based on subsistence farming and a large dependence on foraged foods. These were the people who not long ago traveled door to door selling blue mountain tea (*Solidago odora*), hickory nuts, wild asparagus, ramps, and poke. In this respect, embedded as they were in the natural environment around them, they were thoroughly American in spite of certain foodways that clearly traced to Europe. Mima Faust (now deceased) of Hegins, Pennsylvania, expressed it well in this popular Dutch saying: "*Sie wore so orum ass sie ken Brod im Haus iwwer Nacht hatte*" (They were so poor they did not even have bread in the house overnight).

Local-color novelists such as Helen Reimensnyder Martin stereotyped these people in her character portraits of the Pennsylvania Dutch. Access into their world was perhaps one issue; class prejudice was certainly another. Just the same, the Buckwheat Dutch were used (or misused) metaphorically by writers such as Martin to represent all Pennsylvania Dutch under a more general characterization of country rube. In her 1910 novel *The Crossways*, Martin set the stage for the social tensions between the Kunz sisters in rural Lebanon County and the outside world brought into their household by their brother, who had just married a southern woman. The prospect of her arrival and the disruptions she would cause were voiced by Martin through the mouth of Lizzie Kunz:

> "I've been considerin', Sallie, mebby Matthew's wife will think that us we're too common."
> "To be sure we ain't towner," responded Sallie, as she and her sister busied themselves with kitchen chores and contemplated their new role as spinster in-laws to a woman with no ties to Pennsylvania Dutch culture.[1]

"We ain't towner" was the key phrase. It defined Helen R. Martin's own worldview of the Pennsylvania Dutch, and it fortified the negative image of the "dumb Dutch" that was promulgated by writers such as Martin and a public school system originally established with the one key goal of stamping out the culture. Thus Dutchness was equated with inferiority and shame. Even the term "Pennsylvania Dutch" was abjured by those who felt that "Pennsylvania German" was a more dignified descriptor. As uncomfortable as it may have been to rub elbows with the rural poor, who most certainly crowded the states' many farm markets to beg, barter, and sell, they existed in large numbers, and their foodways left a mark on Pennsylvania Dutch culture. For certain their eating habits were not glamorous, and yet their food had its own story worth telling.

The starkest dietary difference between the well-to-do Dutch and the Buckwheat Dutch lay in the consumption of meat. Among the rural poor, fresh meat was not eaten on a regular basis, aside from small game that was readily available in neighborhood woodlots. Rabbits, squirrels, groundhogs, and even raccoons were considered pests in any event, so they were hunted regardless of the season and generally cooked in a very simple manner: first boiled until tender (often described as being boiled until "brown") and then fried in lard or butter. Otherwise the meat was simmered together with fresh or dried corn or with steamed dumplings, such as in the squirrel recipe on page 263. The inevitable side dish consisted of cornmeal mush, potatoes or turnips, or a mixture of these two vegetables. Sauerkraut was a staple cold-weather dish. Salt pork, bacon, or ham represented the general sort of meat eaten once the supply of fresh pork had been used up; and fresh meat was not consumed during warm weather unless served at a wedding or a funeral. Funeral dinners were once extremely popular as social events because they offered an opportunity not only for the exchange of local news but also to sample foods not commonly eaten at home.

Fresh meat, whether pork from mid-winter butchering or game or even a mix of the two, was normally converted into mincemeat, which could be conserved in crocks as a food supply throughout the winter. While mincemeat pie is now associated in general American culture with Christmas, it was in fact a common country dish throughout nineteenth-century America and provided the Buckwheat Dutch in particular with a staple for breakfast, dinner, and supper. Eating pie three times a day and even in between defined these people as pie families as opposed to cake families, and everything imaginable was encased in pie crust. Pies could be eaten at breakfast in a bowl of milk or they could be eaten handheld, with no need for silverware.

There were many families in the Dutch Country who lived according to these general patterns, and their small log, frame, or stone houses can still be seen today in the hills where the hardscrabble land was cheap and only borderline productive. Figure 11 shows the Vanasdall two-room cabin in Cumberland County with its old central chimney replaced by the 1890s with a stove pipe to accommodate a more modern cast iron stove. Note the young man shooting squirrels from the porch and the corncobs hanging overhead, the swept yard, the corn rick (corn stalks thrown over a four-post frame) to give protection to chickens, and the picket fence surrounding the entire yard and kitchen garden (off camera to the right). Small farms like this were once common and belonged to a large class of marginal people who preserved old ways longer than many others by virtue of their poverty. They earned the collective name *Buchweetze Deitsch* (Buckwheat Dutch) because this was one crop that would grow well on poor or worn-out land. As several eighteenth- and nineteenth-century travelers observed, buckwheat was popular with small-scale farmers because they could get more bushels per acre than with wheat. Thus for many households buckwheat was the dietary mainstay and provided the family with a source of grits and flour. In addition the plant was good fodder for milk cows, and if the farmers were industrious, a few beehives could supply their tables with dark buckwheat honey.

Buckwheat also had market value because it could be sold to local mills, where it was ground and reprocessed for an array of food products that called for buckwheat flour. Perhaps the best-known Pennsylvania dish made with buckwheat flour today is scrapple; buckwheat is what gives it its distinctive dark color and nutty flavor. The history of Pennsylvania's scrapple tradition is outlined in my book *Country Scrapple*.[2]

Dutch farmers who could not afford the rich bottomlands that demanded high prices turned to squatting or clearing rocky land in the hills. These people lived off foods of opportunity rather than a well-supplied pantry: squirrel potpie, roast groundhog, and processed dishes such as rabbit pot pudding or sap porridge (tree sap boiled down with cornmeal). The farming practices of the Buckwheat Dutch were based on grubbing hoes rather than plows, so patches of turnips, cabbage, onions, and parsnips assumed center place in their kitchen gardens. Buckwheat cakes and apple butter or apple butter cooked together with fox grapes provided staple food throughout the winter. The bare-bones peas and bacon recipe on page 237 is typical of the winter fare that characterized this back-hill form of cookery.

Many of the Buckwheat Dutch foodways are preserved in county histories, and some specific dishes have been recorded in early state grange cookbooks, mostly for their nostalgia value or appeal to hunters. But few, if any, of these dishes have been romanticized in local-color novels or have achieved the status of identity foods the way, for example, goulash—also a poverty dish—has come to symbolize Hungarian cookery.[3] No similar fate has blessed the likes of sweet buckwheat bread, a richly flavored flat bread from the hill country of Perry County (page 270), or for that matter gribble (*Grippel*), one of the most common poverty foods among the Buckwheat Dutch, although this is a dish remarkable for its versatility and long genealogy.

Gribble is made by mixing hot water with buckwheat flour to produce stiff dough and then toasting this on a griddle while the dough is chopped and stirred until it is reduced to small, crispy crumbs resembling Grape-Nuts. The crumbs are then reserved in an airtight container for later use as an addition to soup, as topping on casseroles or dumplings, or to be mixed into baked dishes and stuffings to give them a crunchy texture. I published the basic recipe, which came from the Goschenhoppen area of Montgomery County, in *Pennsylvania Dutch Country Cooking*.[4] Buckwheat gribble is actually the poor man's version of a related dish known as *Siesser Grippel* (sweet gribble). It was made in many parts of the Dutch Country prior to the Civil War, and the little bits of pasta were known in Philadelphia as "pop-robins"; several manuscript cookbooks preserve recipes for pop-robin pudding. Instead of buckwheat flour, sweet gribble consisted of egg pasta chopped very small. It was then boiled in milk and served with sugar, honey, or molasses, or it was boiled and then baked in the form of a pudding. A *neideitsch* recipe is provided in the last chapter (page 271) for the pudding known as *Grippelboi* (is baked in a pie shell) as served at the Black Horse Hotel at Reinholds, Pennsylvania, while it belonged to the Bowman family.

The technique for making sweet gribble is probably ancient, although its premedieval origins are murky. Regardless it was a class of food far removed from poverty cookery. The 1691 *Vollständiges Nürnbergisches Koch-Buch* included a recipe for pasta gribble under the heading *Ein gehacktes Kooch* (A Minced Porridge).[5] The gribble was created by mincing freshly made egg pasta into tiny oatmeal-like crumbs, drying them in a slack oven, and then cooking the crumbs in milk "gilded" with saffron to create porridge with a texture somewhat like soggy couscous. This bright yellow side dish could be served either as a savory or as a sweet—that is, with salt and herbs or with spices and sugar. Made with milk it was appropriate during periods of religious fasting, although meat stock could serve as a cooking medium. While it also appears to have served as a light one-course supper dish, it was a direct holdover from the Middle Ages when gruels of this type appeared instead of soup at the beginnings of lengthy meals. All things considered, the 1691 minced porridge is not much different in texture and appearance from Pennsylvania Dutch saffron-flavored *Riwwelsupp,* for which crumbs are created by rubbing pasta dough into little balls rather than chopping it.

More common even than buckwheat gribble was "black mush" (*schwartzer Brei*), which was cornmeal mush mixed with buckwheat flour. The precise proportion of cornmeal to buckwheat varied from household to household and depended to some extent on the type of cornmeal used, since some old varieties were starchy, while others could be surprisingly sweet. While black mush was long considered poor man's fare, it was nonetheless nourishing—it is rich in thiamine—and even the Victorian-era cookbook author Eliza Leslie tried to imbue it with middle-class dignity in her *New Receipts for Cooking* under the name buckwheat porridge.[6] Her version consisted of buckwheat flour or meal (no cornmeal in this case) boiled in milk and eaten with molasses and butter and promoted as a healthy breakfast dish for children. The true poverty version would have been boiled with water or perhaps small-game stock instead of milk.

In this same cookbook, Leslie also included a recipe for buckwheat batter pudding, which was boiled in a bag like an old-style English pudding. Her promotion of buckwheat was less motivated by an interest in regional cookery than by the fact that she was searching for suitable substitutes for potatoes, which at the time had become expensive due to shortages arising from the devastating blight then attacking the American potato crop. In the Middle Atlantic region buckwheat had always served as a fallback even when corn failed, and its widespread popularity as a breakfast pancake provided a degree of familiarity to readers willing to experiment with some of Leslie's more unusual suggestions. However, Pennsylvania Dutch buckwheat noodles (*schwartze Nudle*) never earned the imprimatur of Miss Leslie, perhaps because they were just too odd for Anglo-American palates; yet today *soba*, their Japanese counterpart, is readily available in health food stores, Asian markets, and Japanese-style noodle shops. No one would ever guess that buckwheat noodles were once viewed as a stigma of poverty in rural Pennsylvania.

"Hairy" Dumplings: The Essence of Frugal Housekeeping

When the Pennsylvania Dutch first came to North America, potato cookery was not as highly developed as it is today. The turnip still reigned as the king of root vegetables and was used in multitudes of ways: cooked and mashed, boiled with duck or small game, shredded and fermented like sauerkraut, and prepared to yield a variety of dumplings. By 1800 potatoes had begun to replace turnips in rural Pennsylvania Dutch cuisine, and by the middle of the nineteenth century potatoes had graduated into the one vegetable that was almost certainly consumed three times a day, as many old-time songs and folk sayings relate. *Hooriche Gnepp* ("hairy" dumplings) originated as a turnip-based recipe dating to the Middle Ages, but after the general conversion to potatoes during the late eighteenth century, these dumplings quickly found their place as a fulsome meat substitute in the diets of the rural poor.

The reason was simple: these dumplings were best when made with year-old potatoes; hence they were a perfect solution for using up long-stored tubers before the new potatoes were harvested. Thus they provided poor families with a source of food during that period in the early to late spring when many vegetables had been planted but were not ready for harvesting, a period known as the *Sechs-*

woche Noth (six-week privation). This was a worrisome period when many of the poor relied on foraged greens such as dandelion, sorrel, patience dock, bladder campion, chickweed, charlock, and white mustard, foods that helped correct winter diets deficient in important vitamins and minerals. Just as diced milk bread marked clear class and economic distinctions between urban and rural Pennsylvania Dutch soup cultures, so too did *Hooriche Gnepp* (leaving aside those individuals who ate them simply because they liked the dumplings regardless of economic circumstances).

"Hairy" dumplings never entered the modern food lore of the Pennsylvania Dutch because they were not embraced by the early forces of tourism. For one thing, it would be risky to assume that outsiders would want to sample, let alone pay for, a menu featuring an authentic poverty dish. Furthermore the dumplings were not among foods found on the fictional groaning tables described in popular literature where the emphasis was on meat dishes. They were, therefore, less ripe for commercialization than some other regional specialties. From the standpoint of food tourism, other marks against the dumplings were based on practical considerations: they required two days of preparation and, of course, a ready supply of cellar-aged potatoes. This would be a hard sell for any mom-and-pop restaurant hoping for a fast turnover of Sunday excursionists. From a cultural standpoint, though, the dumplings were insiders' comfort food, and one would need to speak Pennsylfaanisch in order to fully appreciate the humor in the dialect name and the image of *Gemütlichkeit* that it evokes.

"Hairy" dumplings acquired their name from their appearance. They are made with shredded potatoes, so when boiled, little strands lift up from the surface of the dumplings to give them a fuzzy appearance even after they come out of the pot. In households where fresh meat was consumed at most once a year (during seasonal pork butchering, for example), "hairy" dumplings became a menu standby, a highly adaptable one-pot dish that could be adjusted to accommodate all sorts of wild greens and odds and ends from the pantry.

During my interviews with rural Pennsylvania Dutch cooks, a number of individuals had heard of the dumplings and knew that they were poverty food, but the general consensus was that the dish began to disappear in earnest during the 1930s as the older generation born before the Civil War died out and as more and more packaged food recipes, especially baking powder dumplings, which could be made in a matter of minutes, entered the scene. This raised the question, did anyone know of families who still made these dumplings, and specifically, was there someone who could relate to me the general techniques of preparation? I happened to mention this research problem to a friend of mine in Germany, and while there during a conference in 2009, I was introduced to Theo and Gertrude Adam, who lived in a tiny village in the Palatinate, in a farmhouse that had been in the family for several generations. In the nineteenth century their forebears had derived their livelihood from three cows and a pig; more recently the family had lived more or less under the same roof as the cattle stall. Gertrude Adam knew all about *Hooriche Gnepp.*

For certain, Frau Adam had risen above the norm because she had developed her considerable culinary talents into those of a well-known champion of traditional cookery—especially poverty cookery—and over the years had gathered recipes for unusual dishes from all over the Palatinate. "One never knows when we will need to fall back on these old dishes," she cautioned. "We must learn to live very well off of nothing, this is the lesson of working people everywhere since the Middle Ages, because the rich only look after themselves."

Over the years Frau Adam had acquired firsthand culinary knowledge that proved invaluable to my own quest for the true *Hooriche Gnepp,* a goal I finally reached during a meal in which this poor-man's dumpling in all its variant forms was served. While "hairy" dumplings were also recognized as poverty food in this part of Germany, here they carried none of the stigma that had shadowed them in Pennsylvania; they were instead a romantic and rather comic reminder of the past, indeed of a time when life was simple yet rich in ways not easily measured in terms of money. Furthermore "hairy" dumplings had evolved into one of those colorful nostalgia foods that had joined a roster of dishes associated with Palatine regional identity. Oddly enough the name was the same in both Palatine dialect and Pennsylfaanisch, linguistic evidence of its Old World roots.

The process for making the dumplings well, which means turning them into something remarkably palatable without the use of eggs and leaveners, hinges largely on technique. The basic proportion is as follows: to each 6 pounds (3kg) of raw, grated potatoes, add 3 pounds (1.5kg) of peeled, mashed potatoes that were cooked the day before. Year-old potatoes are preferable in this case because they shred better and the shreds do not disintegrate when cooked. If the potatoes are not old enough, Frau Adam adds potato starch; in former times some type of flour—spelt or barley flour, for example—would have been used. This mixture of mashed and shredded potatoes is then hand-formed into two types of perfectly round dumplings each weighing about 6½ ounces (200g) as well as a copious batch of smaller dumplings about one-fourth the size of the large ones.

Of the two types of large and perfectly round dumplings that Frau Adam made, one was left plain; the other was stuffed with about two tablespoons each of ground beef and ground pork mixed with liver sausage for moisture (this would otherwise be supplied by pork fat). This meat-filled dumpling was considered a festive dish that would have been eaten only on special occasions, such as butchering day, Christmas, or after a successful hunt; in the latter case ground game would supply the filling.

The large meat-filled dumplings were a meal by themselves and were intended to fill the belly quickly (which they do). The unstuffed dumplings were boiled and then set aside for other meals during the week; they were sliced and then lightly browned with sliced onions in lard or butter. Frau Adam made small dumplings too, each about one-fourth the size of the large ones. These were not cooked immediately but held over for later consumption for stewing with dried fruit (as in *Schnitz-un-Gnepp*) or with sauerkraut. Thus from one batch of old potatoes a menu for an entire week could be devised. The meat-filled dumplings and the sliced, browned dumplings were served in shallow bowls with hot sour cream or hot sour milk broth poured over them. This broth might also include vinegar and chopped herbs, such as marjoram or savory.

The cooking water in which the dumplings were boiled was not discarded. Thickened with grated potatoes and browned flour (*gereeschtes Mehl*), it made another poverty dish called *Rappsupp* in Palatine dialect or *Geriewwenesupp* ("grated" soup, recipe on page 218) in Pennsylfaanisch. This soup was served before the dumpling course with large pieces of toasted bread in it, the idea being that it would satisfy hunger and cut down on the consumption of the dumplings, which had to be rationed for other meals.

The broth of this soup was enhanced in several ways to make the meals less monotonous: with the addition of sauerkraut juice for those who liked sour soups; with milk or meat stock; or even with grated turnips and herbs. Carrots, which now appear regularly in Palatine restaurant versions of *Rappsupp*, were never included in the original poverty dish. According to Frau Adam they spoil its authenticity and probably disguise the fact that certain key flavors are missing. The use of carrots was generally unknown in rural Palatine and Pennsylvania Dutch poverty cuisine; only turnips, Hamburg parsley (root parsley), and parsnips were the basic root vegetables in the diet. Like diced croutons, carrots were a sign of "cake" families and the urban elite.

In this brief excursion into the finer points of "hairy" dumplings, I hope we can better understand the complex ways in which the rural poor among the Pennsylvania Dutch created a variety of frugal dishes from one food source. We see none of this replicated in restaurants catering to tourists or on the menus of fire halls, church suppers, or other similar events catering to the Pennsylvania Dutch themselves. All of this has been replaced by chicken potpie.

The critical feature of *Hooriche Gnepp* was the dumplings' largely meatless character, a recurring theme in most peasant cookeries whether Old World or New. As several Pennsylvania Dutch cooks pointed out to me during interviews about their food memories, in the more affluent families where fresh meat was eaten regularly, dumplings were more or less absent from the household menu because there was no need for a meat substitute. This means that among the Pennsylvania Dutch, alongside cake families and pie families there were also meat families and dumpling families, since dumplings stood in for meat and implied a different range of dietary choices. The idea of serving sauerbraten with potato dumplings, a ubiquitous combination in rathskeller cookery, was originally a break from traditional eating patterns: in essence offering the consumer two "meats" on one plate. Eating them proved that your economic status was several levels above fried potatoes or a platter of bacon: in short, one or two notches above working class.

Meatless dumplings also fulfilled religious dietary requirements during periods of fasting, which in Pennsylvania applied mostly to the Lutherans and a small Roman Catholic minority. Thus dumplings made richer with the addition of bread toasted in butter or with various kinds of dried fruit took the place of prominence on tables where abstinence was practiced. This added a further qualifier to the meat family/dumpling family dichotomy, since eating patterns sometimes shifted not out of economic necessity but rather from religious duty.

Nevertheless there are any number of Pennsylvania Dutch cookbooks featuring dumplings and especially potato dumplings. For the most part the more recent recipes are derived from a common body of dishes discussed in *Mary at the Farm* (1915), a book written in Quakertown, Pennsylvania, by Edith Bertels Thomas (1859–1941) and heavily influenced by period local-color fiction. In fact the essential parts of the *Hooriche Gnepp* recipe as made by Frau Adam in a village in Germany can be found in *Mary at the Farm* under the rubric of *Kartoffel Klöse*, a standard German term that is not used in Pennsylfaanisch.[7]

This linguistic ambiguity in *Mary at the Farm* may reflect the fact that Edith Thomas grew up in Wilkes-Barre well beyond any real contact with Pennsylvania Dutch culture. Her cookbook represented an enthusiastic rediscovery of her own Pennsylvania Dutch culinary roots on the Bertels side of the family—with all the pitfalls of a reconversion known as selective ethnicity (choosing only a small range of positive aspects of a given culture). If we consider *Hooriche Gnepp* the absolute basis upon which to compare all other similar forms of dumpling cookery, the addition of browned croutons to her dumplings and to the many later recipes that are based on hers points in the direction of urban cookery or even hotel or rathskeller cuisine.

The difficulty with "hairy" dumplings was in their translation from farmhouse dish to restaurant fare. There were no cooking-school shortcuts, no chemical additives to lighten the work, no requirement other than an innate sensitivity to the lifespan of the potato and to the culinary potential created not by retardant chemical sprays designed to keep it from budding or wrinkling (such Dorian Gray cosmetics are widely in use on storage potatoes today), but simply by long, careful storage in a root cellar and the unique starchy manner in which such a potato shreds when sliced on a very sharp grater. There is a special nutty aroma to potatoes aged in this way, and it penetrates the dumplings. Although a poverty dish, "hairy" dumplings taste of *terroir*. In contrast, in the case of chicken potpie one could argue that aside from the substitution of noodle dough for short crust, there is not much about it that is Pennsylvania Dutch, not even the name.

The Rise of Chicken Potpie

Chicken noodle stew would be a more accurate description for most of the chicken potpie now sold in the Pennsylvania Dutch region, and there is also a distinct difference between the homemade dish that uses freshly made noodles and the one that is sold in restaurants or at the Kutztown Folk Festival using commercially packaged noodles.

In its most widely available form, chicken potpie presents itself as a rather bland species of tourist fare that does little justice to the appetite or to the visitor's impression of Pennsylvania Dutch cookery. This downward evolution of a dish with two converging genealogies has gone one or two steps further down the evolutionary scale with the recent practice of using bowtie noodles to thicken the potpie. This is a positive development much favored among the Amish, since factory-made bowtie noodles can be purchased cheaply and in bulk in Lancaster County's many outlet stores.

"How can they spoil potpie?" one of my interviewees exclaimed, which is to say, how can something so plain be made any plainer? This goes to the heart of the subject: potpie was always working-class fare. Among the Pennsylvania Dutch it was never a special dish to commemorate a festive occasion or to be served to guests; it was food designed to use up leftovers from the weekend's big Sunday dinner. No one made it from scratch the way it is now presented in cookbooks; you started with the boiled carcass of Sunday's roast chicken or the remnants of a roast ham.

It is indeed odd that this leftover fare for wash-day Monday should become an icon of Pennsylvania Dutch cookery. Then again, it found a convenient place on the menus of the tourist industry because, as any Dutch restaurateur can attest, pasta is cheap, and the profit margin is "wonderful good." Remember too that like the filling dishes that once were dumplings, potpie can be made in vast stainless-steel casserole pans and kept simmering all day long—slow food in the saddest and most literal sense of the term. Perhaps most important of all, the dish resembles common American potpie, so it is not off-putting to the kind of picky customer who might be dubious about the rustic appearance or the sort of indeterminate meat inside real *Hooriche Gnepp*.

Noodle squares have a long history in German cookery, dating back at least to the Renaissance, either as extenders for dishes using cheaper cuts or qualities of meat or more commonly as a stand-alone dish cooked with milk and sweetened with sugar—the same manner in which noodle squares were prepared in Byzantine cuisine. Unlike dumplings, they were not treated specifically as a meat sub-

FIGURE 12. Originally created as a 1950s recipe note card promoting potpie for the tourist industry, this image of an Amish table was later recycled as cover art on recipe booklets and as coasters. Roughwood Collection, Devon, Pa.

stitute even though they originally played an important dietary role in medieval fasting. In Ann Hark and Preston Barba's *Pennsylvania German Cookery* (the title reads *Pennsylvania Dutch Cookery* on the cover: evidence of a war of minds between the authors and the publisher), there is a recipe for chicken potpie contributed by Marie Knorr Graeff (now deceased). It can be traced not to Berks County, where she lived, but rather to the 1751 Black Horse Hotel at Reinholds, an old Lancaster County institution once held in high esteem for its fine local cookery while it was under the management of the Bowman family (1898–1933). In Clara Bowman's recipe, which employed generous amounts of saffron (one of the features of cuisine in "the Eck," where Reinholds is located), the chicken, sliced potatoes, onions, and square noodles were arranged in layers. This is about as Dutchified as chicken potpie gets, unless we accept that Henrietta Beam's potato potpie with saffron on page 246 stands out as the last word.

There is also another culinary line of descent. Thus there are now two types of potpie circulating in the Dutch Country, for an ingredient of Continental origin, the egg noodle, has been inserted into a dish originally from the British Isles. Their distinctiveness became blurred during the transition from hearth to cook-stove technology in the 1840s, a process of hybridization and fusion that has affected many aspects of material culture in southeastern Pennsylvania (Amish quilts and bonnets, for example—both derived from outside the Amish community).

I turn again to the 1854 edition of Eliza Leslie's *New Receipts for Cooking* for what I would characterize as the classic Anglo-American type of chicken potpie; this was the sort of potpie made in Philadelphia's middle-class hotels and boardinghouses or in the hotels catering to the produce vendors who came into the city for weekly markets. It was also general farmhouse cookery commonly served for Sunday dinner and not a dish made with leftovers as among the Pennsylvania Dutch. After all, it was created from scratch, and chicken was not something people ate every day, at least not in the nineteenth century. It served the practical function of making good use of old hens that had stopped laying eggs or roosters whose time had come. Boiling them to shreds only made the potpie better.

Leslie instructed her readers to use an iron pot, meaning a vessel with a neck (as opposed to a kettle with straight sides); hence the name.[8] This pot was lined with pastry made with beef suet or butter (suet or lard was a far more common choice in rural households). The pastry was laid against the inside walls of the pot about two-thirds of the way to the top; the bottom was not covered. The pot was then filled with sliced potatoes, cooked chicken, onions, and pieces of the pastry cut in squares, and then the broth from the cooked chicken was poured over this. A pastry lid went over the filling and was attached to the dough along the sides.

Since the pastry was essentially a *pâté brisée,* like common pie crust, and rather dusty with flour, it served to thicken the contents of the pie while the squares cooked into lumps of soft dough. Other cookbooks sometimes explain how this was sent to the table: the contents of the pie were poured out into a tureen or large bowl, and the crusts from the sides and top were broken up and served on a hot platter. Individuals eating the potpie would transfer crust to their plates and then ladle the filling over this. Otherwise the whole thing was brought to the table and served communally from the pot. There was no elegant way of serving this dish unless it was miniaturized into individual pies, which is the method used by most restaurants featuring American cooking today.

It should be clear from Eliza Leslie's example that the most common sort of chicken potpie now served in the Dutch Country is little more than a localized variation of an old mainstream American dish, with German-style egg noodles taking the place of pie crust. In Pennsylfaanisch these noodle squares are called potpies (*Botboi*), a term also derived from English. The acquired name resulted from a common association with potpie cookery of the sort described by Miss Leslie but traceable, ultimately, to the kitchens of medieval England.

The year-around availability of commercially made potpie noodles since the 1920s altered the role that old-style potpie played in rural diets. It quickly evolved from a convenient way to recycle left-overs in large households of extended families and live-in help to a nostalgic symbol of early twentieth-century country life and commu-nal eating, a relic of the good old days that could be easily prepared for fund-raising purposes by fire halls, churches, and other local organizations. As a dish prepared by the Old Order Amish, noodle potpie was readily canonized by the tourist industry as an icon of Pennsylvania Dutch culture. Contrary to what has been written to date about the Amish, most of their food culture is derivative—for example, Whoopee Pies—borrowed in one form or another from the people living around them. They did not bring chicken potpie from their Swiss homeland; what we know today as Pennsylvania Dutch chicken potpie is an American invention.

CHAPTER 6

The Creation of the "Amish Table"

THE flowering of Amish food tourism during the 1930s and its gradual preemption of the *neideitsch* culinary movement was not a spontaneous development. Certain local and international events did indeed set the stage for what transpired during that tumultuous decade, and yet for a good sixty years prior to it, a gradual convergence of new cultural currents helped shape the outcome in profound ways. One was the grassroots dialect revival following the Civil War, and the other was the birth of local-color fiction written for a national audience. While these literary developments ran counter to one another both in essential material and in philosophical objectives, Pennsylvania Dutch foods played an inordinate role in the creation of a sense of place and an aura of authenticity.

FIGURE 13. The earliest known depiction of the Amish table. Ornament on a menu from the German Village, Lancaster, Pa., October 1937. Roughwood Collection, Devon Pa.

The dialect literature movement, which was launched in 1870 with the publication of Henry Harbaugh's *Harfe* (The Harp), was created by Dutch speakers for Dutch readers. It represented one further step in the evolution of Pennsylvania Dutch culture away from all things German. The dialect writings generally consisted of poetry or newspaper columns focusing on themes that were humorous satires of everyday life. Many topics were also patriotic and thus reaffirmed the culture's uniquely American roots. Yet one overwhelming subject was food or situations dealing with food, such as schnitzing parties, making sauerkraut, or a dinner of *Schnitz-un-Gnepp*. This preoccupation with food was an attempt to internalize the culture by focusing on the family table as opposed to tavern life, village events, the landscape, or higher philosophical questions.

The Civil War had acted as a formative experience for the Pennsylvania Dutch who served in the army, since the men came home with the realization of just how different they were from other Americans. Furthermore the burning of Chambersburg and the huge destruction and loss of life at Gettysburg served to remind all Americans that unlike anyone else in the North, the Dutch had paid a high price at the hands of an invading army. The state public school system had been established in the 1830s with the ulterior objective of eradicating all vestiges of Dutch culture and especially the language, so the dialect movement, fortified by the Civil War experience, served as a form of resistance to the school system's relentless pressure for cultural conformity. The success of this resistance can be seen in the 1876 *Gettysburg Centennial Cook Book,* a local fund-raiser that included the earliest known published recipe for *Schnitz-un-Gnepp.*[1] This recipe marks one of the first crossovers from oral Pennsylvania Dutch cookery into more mainstream regional culture under the protective and symbolic guise of red, white, and blue bunting. It also launched *Schnitz-un-Gnepp* as an icon food mentioned time and again in the local-color novels that followed.

For certain, *Schnitz-un-Gnepp* culinary fantasies represent one of the most nostalgic and iconic of all Pennsylvania Dutch farmhouse preparations, although there are many others, *Seimawe* for example. This is not to say that sliced dried apples cooked with ham and dumplings (or no meat at all) represent the cultural nectar of all Pennsylvania Dutch families; some Dutch do not like it, and some families never made it. Furthermore this was a food selected early on by people outside the Pennsylvania Dutch community as a symbol of Dutch cultural inferiority. The earliest known published reference to *Schnitz-un-Gnepp* appeared in the January 31, 1821, issue of *The Balance,* a Philadelphia newspaper that chose to mention the dish (in this case made with apple *Schnitz* stewed with bacon, parsnips, and dumplings) as an example of just how bad a Pennsylvania Dutch Christmas dinner could be. This was the meal of an Allentown Dutchman: no goose, no cranberry tarts, no plum pudding; just a mess of greasy apples and "dotschy" dough.

As already mentioned under the discussion of *Hooriche Gnepp,* the little dumplings made from old potatoes were part of a strategy to economize on pantry supplies; *Schnitz-un-Gnepp* was not something people made for Christmas dinner. It was one of those mid-week dishes assembled from leftovers, so the dried fruit might be apples, but much better were dried pears or peaches with meat or no meat at all. There is also ample evidence for using dried or canned sour cherries (alone or by mixing them with dried apples)— in the Schoeneck area of Lancaster County, for example. In fact some Dutch households treated the mixture as a sweet dish, adding a little brown sugar and perhaps some raisins or currants in the dumplings. The dumplings were supposed to stand in for meat in any case, so this was one of those cheap and easy-to-make creations that were intended to feed many mouths from one pot. In spite of this low-brow origin, *Schnitz-un-Gnepp* gradually assumed a role as an iconic food among the Dutch, mostly because it became a pet detail in local-color fiction; for certain it was much more exotic than sauerkraut. The trouble with most local-color fiction is that the process of selecting authenticities is highly subjective and quite often manipulated to make a point quite out of context with cultural reality. That is the discussion now before us.

Parallel to or in contradistinction to the local dialect movement and its outpouring of culinary nostalgia for indigenous consumption were the culture wars fought in early twentieth-century pulp fiction. By the late 1890s the effects of Phebe Earle Gibbons's protoethnographic 1860s carriage tours of Lancaster County and her intense interest in plain sects, especially the Dunkards, who at the time were more picturesque than anyone else, had found their counterparts in mainstream literature. Until then Gibbons's book *"Pennsylvania Dutch" and Other Essays* (which first appeared in 1872) was the only place to go for insights into Dutch culture and foods. Books soon appeared on the popular market using Pennsylvania Dutch settings depicting clashes between old ways, religious beliefs, and the progressive world outside Pennsylvania. Unfortunately the message usually meandered far afield from reality and at best planted curious if not fully egregious ideas about the Pennsylvania Dutch, among them seeds for the "Amish table" that eventually took shape in the 1930s.

At first this was encouraged by a surge of interest in the "medieval lifestyle" as practiced by the relics of cloister life at Ephrata. Indeed the whole package of odd lifestyle choices among the Church of the Brethren was far more interesting to the world at large during the 1880s and 1890s than the Amish were. The real turning point came when the Brethren, like the Quakers and many other religious groups, gave up plain dress in the 1920s after women won the right to vote. Female couture of the plain sects was suddenly transformed and the focus redirected toward the Amish mainly because they became the last holdouts against change. Thus by degrees the Amish mystique began to take shape.

However, the Amish were not the sole interest of the local-color novelists; food is woven into this literature so thoroughly that it offers a unique perspective into the mentality of the period. Elsie Singmaster (1879–1958) was one of the most credible of the writers because while she employed culinary imagery to provide touches of authenticity in her short stories and novels, she also considered herself Pennsylvania Dutch (and used that term in spite of her biographer Susan Hill's assertion that she was "German") and thus approached her cultural heritage through sympathetic eyes. Much of her material was based on firsthand experience, a far cry from the equally popular works of her contemporary Helen Reimensnyder Martin (1868–1939). This brings us to two very different worldviews regarding the way Pennsylvania Dutch food was portrayed in novels and how this eventually played out in the literature of food tourism and ultimately in the creation of the mythic Amish table.

Both Singmaster and Martin were daughters of Lutheran ministers and graduates of Radcliffe College, and yet their visions of the Pennsylvania Dutch were entirely different: where Singmaster gave the country Dutch a certain redeeming grace, Martin cast them in the role of rustics and did much to widen the divide that separated the urban Pennsylvania Dutch from their rural counterparts. Martin largely ignored the urban, upper-class culture of the pre–World War I Pennsylvania Dutch, a curious blind spot in all of her writings. To the Dutch, she was dismissed as an outsider, which did little to settle the many valid criticisms of her works.

Unlike Elsie Singmaster, who was descended on her father's side from an old Pennsylvania Dutch family, Helen R. Martin was the daughter of an immigrant Lutheran minister. She launched her successful career as the author of a

FIGURE 14. The Tillie the Mennonite Maid cookie cutter was sold in gift shops during the 1930s. Roughwood Collection, Devon, Pa.

long line of pulp novels with the publication in 1904 of *Tillie: A Mennonite Maid*. While this often-reprinted book has been styled a charming photographic portrait of Pennsylvania Dutch culture, the underlying framework of the plot is not flattering to the Pennsylvania Dutch, nor is the book honestly photographic in all its details.

In fact due to its negative treatment of the Mennonites, the book created a firestorm of controversy as soon as it was published.

The novel deals with a young girl who became a member of the New Mennonite (Reformed Mennonite) sect centered on Longenecker's Meeting near Strasburg in Lancaster County. This breakaway sect from the Old Mennonites was founded in 1812 on a nearby farm belonging to Jacob Weaver, where the first baptisms took place. While similar to other conservative Mennonite groups who advocate plainness, Reformed Mennonites are well known for their refusal to read spiritual writings other than those of their own ministers or to listen to preaching from anyone outside their own church. Both of those themes were touched upon by Martin in *Tillie* because the author was determined to demonstrate the narrow-mindedness of this sect and by extension the suffocating provincialism of the Pennsylvania Dutch.

Tillie's misery was the result of an obsessively strict and bullheaded father (who was also depicted by Martin as pitifully ignorant) and a colorless yet overbearing stepmother. She was also the victim of physical abuse since in order to break her of perceived transgressions, her father whipped her until she nearly fainted. Her parents were so selfish and so grotesquely drawn that they seemed like trolls in a fairy tale, but like a princess wakening from deep sleep, Tillie found salvation not in the heavy hand of the Reformed Mennonite Jesus but in a handsome Harvard graduate who became an English professor at what was then Millersville State Normal School (now Millersville University).

He appeared at the precise moment when all seemed lost for Tillie and (the intentional metaphor equated him with an angel) spirited her away from her fate: living in penurious servitude with her parents. In the time it took her to pack her valise, Tillie abandoned her family and joined the world, thus triumphing over her Pennsylvania Dutch roots. This thematic tension between two worlds became the framework for all of Martin's local-color novels. For Helen Martin, any fate was preferable to remaining Pennsylvania Dutch. The redemptive influence of the state normal-school system (for training public-school teachers) as a tool for assimilating the Dutch into mainstream culture was a recurring leitmotif in many of Martin's books, and all the heroes of her stories were men with a proficiency in good English.

Martin's novels were especially popular with impressionable female readers and did much to strengthen negative stereotypes in the minds of those outside the immediate Pennsylvania Dutch community. Martin was clearly a propagandist for English-only doctrines, and her effect was real. As retired college professor Charles Fegley pointed out to me during an interview about his Pennsylvania Dutch childhood, the atmosphere of fear was so stifling that he was mortified to speak the dialect in school during the 1920s lest he be ridiculed or even bullied both by teachers and by his fellow students. Fegley grew up over the family grocery store on South Franklin Street in Allentown and learned to speak Pennsylfaanisch not from his parents (who discouraged it out of concern that it might "hold him back") but from neighbors and farmers who patronized the shop. Against this setting of prejudice and fear that at one time permeated the Pennsylvania Dutch region, we come to the subject of food.

In Helen R. Martin's *Sabina: A Tale of the Amish* (1905) she acknowledged that she drew her "facts" from William H. Richardson's "Picturesque Quality of the Pennsylvania-German," an address presented at the twelfth annual (1902) meeting of the Pennsylvania German Society. In line with the society's founding philosophies of heredity and class distinctions, Richardson (an expatriate Pennsylvanian then living in Jersey City, New Jersey) coined a polite-sounding code phrase for ethnic or racial peculiarities with the expression "picturesque quality." These were the perceived qualities that defined the character of the common Dutch as opposed to the better sorts (Pennsylvania German Society members). Martin went straight to the peculiarities when describing the Amish table:

The table, as well as those who sat about it, had its peculiarities: there were two dishes of everything—potatoes, cabbage, stewed "snitz" (dried apples), stewed dried corn, platters of fried ham, and plates of bread cut in mammoth slices; there were at least four kinds of "spreadin's" or jellies on the table and three kinds of pie. The idea in this Amish table custom of duplicating every dish is that the food may be within reach of everyone, so that, the necessity of handing things to another being dispensed with, undivided attention may be given to the business in hand of staving off starvation. Each one cut his own piece of pie with his own knife.[2]

What takes shape here is the image of a table groaning with food. Ham is the only meat, and more likely than not (if this is an actual meal), the *Schnitz* were cooked with some of the ham (she does not mention *Gnepp*, although it could easily be assumed). This is not a special-occasion menu; it is a workingman's dinner, a meal for the men, work hands, and boys who generally ate first in Amish households of that period (hence the use of male pronouns in the passage quoted). There are other features notable for their absence: seven sweets and seven sours. When Martin published *Sabina* in 1905, this mythic array of pickles and preserves was not yet associated with the Amish table and not yet spread beyond Henry Croll's Valley House Hotel in Skippack, Pennsylvania, where it had been invented some years before.

Henry G. Croll (1858–1930) may claim—with tenuous justification—the laurels for founding the *neideitsch* culinary movement, if we allow that his hotel's seven sweets and seven sours represent an evolutionary step forward, or at the least something *new*. Croll was descended from a long line of Montgomery County tavern and hotel keepers (his father had operated the Keystone Hall Hotel in the same village) who were masters in the art of Pennsylvania Dutch hospitality, yet worlds away from the Amish country. If the Amish had embraced the custom of seven sweets and seven sours, Helen R. Martin would have mentioned sweets and sours because she was acutely interested in customs that reinforced the picturesque, the superstitious, or the slovenly character of the Pennsylvania Dutch; in the not-too-subtle remark about each man cutting his slice of pie with his own knife, clearly gross table hygiene was what she had in mind. She repeated this theme in her description of the Amish Sabbath, where everyone in the congregation drank from shared coffee cups without washing or rinsing between servings.

On the other hand, the meal Martin described was not limited to the Amish; it was a common, simple Pennsylvania Dutch sit-down midday dinner that one could find almost anywhere in the Dutch Country. She was careful to keep the menu plain and to mention a few dishes that were even then viewed as Pennsylvania Dutch identity foods, but she missed her opportunity with the bread and jellies, which leads me to conclude that she probably acquired even this bit of dinner information secondhand. Had she witnessed it (being female she would not have sat at the men's table), she would have noticed that the coarse-crusted farmhouse bread cut in large slices was the core component of the dinner, that everything else was eaten on it or with it, and that it also would have served as sop to clean up the plates.

Furthermore the jellies would have been eaten first, passed around and sampled by everyone present the way the outside world would savor an aperitif; some people would even dissolve spoonfuls in their glasses of water to create sweet beverages. This custom is still prevalent today among some Old Order Mennonite families belonging to the Groffdale Conference (most conservative), and the drink appears to serve as a substitute for sweet wine or more generally anything alcoholic, since the universal table beverage among these plain sects is water. If the family does drink wine (many among the plain sects do), it would follow the meal, after coffee and dessert as a type of remedy to help digestion. When I visited Salome Beiler (Old Order Amish), she uncorked a velvety homemade strawberry wine worthy of any dessert wine at a high-class restaurant; it was carefully portioned out and served in the equivalent of a shot glass.

Funeral Cookery as Cultural Marker

Very different from the everyday fare described by Helen R. Martin, funeral cookery was one social arena where Pennsylvania Dutch cooks lavished great attention on tradition or novelty, depending on their persuasion. Funeral dinners were a real mark of the family's place in the community, for it was here that many people could sample foods that were too costly to consume at home on a regular basis or explore foods considered new and fashionable. Funeral dinners were free, which gave rise to a whole class of Pennsylvania Dutch known as "funeral runners," who made it a point to seek out free meals for the small price of a few sanctimonious tears.

In *Tillie,* Helen R. Martin described a frugal Reformed Mennonite funeral meal: "cold meat, cheese, all sorts of stewed fruits, pickles, 'lemon rice' (a dish never omitted), and coffee." The "lemon rice" mentioned here is a lemon-flavored rice pudding baked in a pie crust (recipe on page 222); a prototype recipe can be found in *Die geschickte Hausfrau,* compiled by Harrisburg printer Gustav Peters,under the odd transliterated moniker *Reis-Pei* (rice pie).[3] The fact that "lemon rice" can be traced to that cookbook, and to other more mainstream American cookbooks of the 1840s, points to an origin outside the Pennsylvania Dutch community.

The vector of introduction for "lemon rice" was most likely through the Lancaster County Quakers, who must have served this dish on special occasions, such as Quarterly Meeting, when large numbers of Friends gathered together for business and socialization. "Lemon rice" took its place beside "lemon butter" and other rich fare served at these events. The Quaker cookbook author Elizabeth Ellicott Lea called it "Pudding of Whole Rice" (as opposed to ground rice pudding) in her *Domestic Cookery,* and like the recipe in *Die geschickte Hausfrau,* lemon was the primary flavoring. Perhaps the most important point about "lemon rice" was that it was meant to be served cold or at least cool, so from a practical standpoint it meshed well with the other items on the funeral menu, all of which were served at room temperature in order to avoid the onerous logistics of a hot-from-the-stove, sit-down dinner. Furthermore this is a "dry" pie without a runny filling (ground rice pudding is a thick custard), so it can be eaten out of hand and even dipped in hot coffee.

I asked the Reformed Mennonite Lydia M., a ninety-two-year-old member of Longenecker's Meeting, which served as the setting for the Tillie story, whether Helen Martin's description of the funeral meal was accurate. Lydia, who was born in Virginia and did not grow up among the Pennsylvania Dutch (even though her mother was a Landis from Lancaster County), observed that funeral meals had changed radically over the past fifty years and that the meal described by Martin was no longer so iron-clad in its format. In fact she was of the opinion that it probably passed out of fashion during the 1930s when German was dropped from Reformed Mennonite religious services.[4] In short, lemon rice has faded from living memory and has been replaced by lemon-flavored tapioca pudding.

When I asked the Old Order Mennonite Nora Martin Hoover whether or not she knew this pie, she was startled by the idea of putting rice in a pie; she had never heard of it and in fact thought it was an extravagant way to use rice. Nora grew up in Clay Township, Lancaster County, and began cooking for the family at age fourteen; since her father had operated a produce and meat stand at the Olney Market in Philadelphia, her world was much more open to outside culinary influences. This was an intriguing test of the kind of invisible culinary borders that exist between the various Pennsylvania Dutch religious groups. Nora also admitted—half joking—that she did not know how to make noodles without saffron in them and never considered them "right" unless they had that distinctive flavor and yellow color. Reformed Mennonites do not use saffron much—certainly not in noodles, which only further reinforces the complex fabric and subtle cultural borders that delineate Pennsylvania Dutch food customs and eating habits between religious groups living practically side by side.

Helen R. Martin may have been justified in singling out rice pie as peculiar to the Reformed Mennonites even though it was a passing thing and not a core custom such as stewed fruit. Nonetheless she mentioned the funeral meal not for ethnographic reasons but rather to take a jab at the parsimonious character of the smug, self-righteous Christians with whom Tillie was affiliated, especially parsimonious when set against the much more lavish funeral meals prepared elsewhere in the Dutch Country, as will be described shortly.

Ironically this scrimpy feast is one meal described by Martin that actually approaches reality, at least as the custom survives among the Old Order Mennonites (Groffdale Conference). Members of that group have assured me in interviews that cheese and cold meats are still standard and so are stewed fruits; one of the "old time" compotes consists of stewed prunes. It was only at funerals that many of them ever sampled stewed prunes, and yet no one I spoke with knew why this was such an invariable item on the menu.

Ada Burkholder, who lives near Fleetwood in Berks County, speculated that perhaps eating prunes would increase the sadness of the situation, or its gravity; every time she saw prunes at the market, she said she immediately thought of funerals and someone who had recently died. However, the original underlying reason—now long forgotten—was expense. Like the raisins in raisin pie (a standard funeral item), dried plums represented an extra financial outlay and thus defined the occasion as special, at least in the days when dried fruit was far more expensive than it is today and required hours of preparation to remove the stems and pits (even more so with old-style raisins, which were dried whole on the stems). Additionally, stewed prunes can be served at room temperature and eaten with cold pork or beef or with cheese, so they conform to the demands of convenience when serving large numbers of people. This brings us back to the Amish table in its embryonic phase.

We can dismiss Helen R. Martin's use of "ethnic peculiarities" as a reflection of the mind-set of her era when it came to dealing with minority cultures. Unfortunately these same ideas have played into the hands of later racial theoreticians such as the National Socialist Liesel Meixner, whose "theories" of *Stammeseigenheiten* (ethnic peculiarities or ethnic traits) formed the foundation of Nazi categorizations of cultural expression.[5] This moves us directly into the present-day questionable "ethnic peculiarities of the Amish," to quote David Weaver-Zercher in his book on Amish tourism,[6] as though there is an Amish cookery, an Amish taste to food, an Amish persona, an Amish decorative style, and on and on. Ethnic peculiarities as racial theory or mind-set has represented a dangerously tainted concept since the 1930s. Yet in an offhand way this unfortunate ethnic ideology has established formative ideas about the Amish table as they began to evolve in the late 1920s, and they are unfortunately continued in Amish scholarship today. The irony of this is that by singling out specific dishes (such as lemon rice pie or *Schnitz-un-Gnepp*) as symbols of cultural identity, we overlook the fact that it is the people who give food its cultural vitality, not the other way around.

This dichotomy between fiction and reality is further confirmed by an 1880s funeral dinner prepared by the cook Stella Siegfried at the Slate Exchange Hotel in Bath, Pennsylvania. The meal is a study in contrasts not simply because it was served in Northampton County far beyond the Amish sphere of influence and the attention of local-color novelists, but also because the original handwritten recipe book used by Mrs. Siegfried recorded a number of dishes of extremely local character (rivvel soda cake and Quaker cake, for example). They are not mentioned anywhere in printed cookbooks.

Under the entry "What I made for Mrs. Hoffman's funeral," Stella Siegfried listed her purchasing order for the dinner: eight pounds of beef, one small ham, two pounds of cheese, two pounds of coffee, fourteen pies, two layer cakes, five light cakes (sweetened yeast-raised potato bread), seven loaves of bread, and celery. This represented only the special purchases, not the items already on hand in the hotel pantry (such as jams, jellies, and pickles). The dinner was planned for sixty people, which was extremely small as funerals went in those days, not to mention that Mrs. Hoffman was a relatively poor widow, so the financial outlay was undoubtedly limited. While the actual menu does not survive, much can be interpolated from this list: the standard cold meats, cheese, a preponderance of pies (probably raisin and apple butter)—in short the range of items one would expect at a light buffet as opposed to a cooked sit-down dinner.

Siegfried's kitchen notebook includes many recipes for chow chow, apple butter, sour mixed pickles, and pickled tomatoes and cucumbers, so we may presume from this that she kept these items on hand at the hotel. Likewise the only clear layer cake in her recipe book was chocolate; the other cakes were shellbark cake (flavored with chopped hickory nuts), Quaker cake (a type of scone), several light cake recipes (made with mashed potatoes and eggs), wine cake (flavored with madeira), and Mrs. Hoffman's own recipe for tea cake.

This latter recipe would have been highly appropriate for the occasion not only in honor of the deceased, who was a friend of Mrs. Siegfried, but also because this cake was meant to be cut into small square portions—ideal finger food with hot coffee. In any case the picture is somewhat different from the Reformed Mennonite meal described by Helen R. Martin, mainly because it took place in a town where a more elaborate style of Pennsylvania Dutch cooking prevailed. Furthermore the cake culture represented in the Siegfried cookery book is very much like that found in *Die geschickte Hausfrau*: a medley of dishes from outside the Pennsylvania Dutch community, including tea cake, which appears to have been a ubiquitous symbol of urban hospitality set in motion via the early nineteenth-century cooking school lectures of Philadelphia's Elizabeth Goodfellow. In Philadelphia tea cakes were called "rusks" even though they were not twice baked as true rusks ought to be.

To put Mrs. Hoffman's funeral dinner in perspective and to add contrast to the Amish meal described by Helen R. Martin, an extensive account for the funeral dinner of Jacob B. Mensch (1835–1912), a Mennonite preacher who was buried at the Upper Skippack Mennonite Church in Montgomery County, Pennsylvania, is helpful.[7] No meat was ordered or cooked, although provisions from C. R. Hunsicker's store in Harleysville included 35 pounds of cheese, 3 pounds of coffee, 25 pounds of prunes, 15 pounds of dried peaches, about 11 pounds of honey, 15 pounds of apricots, and a small amount of tea. This outlay of food again reflects the preference for stewed fruit and other items easy to serve at room temperature. Perhaps more illuminating was the list of baked goods ordered from J. M. Moyer, a baker in Harleysville: 125 loaves of bread, 20 dozen doughnuts, 6 dozen cinnamon buns, 6 dozen Vienna buns, 3 dozen light cakes, 3 dozen knot cakes (a type of yeast-raised cake shaped like pretzels), 3 dozen butter buns (butter *Semmels*), 15 fancy cakes, and 34 mixed cakes. The latter two items were small loaf cakes of various compositions (pound cakes, sponge cakes, currant cakes, and the like).

This food was served by members of the congregation in the home of the deceased preacher's daughter. Judging from the purchase inventories, it represented a mix of popular Victorian-era cakes and a few items peculiar to the Pennsylvania Dutch region: cinnamon buns, light cakes, knot cakes, and butter buns, to name four. In any case the quantity of food was prodigious because the Mensch family was expected to provide not only for friends, neighbors, and members of the congregation but also for anyone else who showed up to pay respects. As it turned out, a blowing snowstorm prevented all but the hardiest of travelers from attending the funeral, so the family returned about one-third of the groceries sent them by Mr. Hunsicker.

What these long grocery lists tell us about the rural Pennsylvania Dutch table is quite simple: funeral food was highly varied from one region to the next, and it reflected both the religious values and the economic status of those serving the meal. In addition a great range of foods might appear together on the same table: some traditional; others quite novel and up-to-date. Nowhere in any surviving funeral records is there a mention of *Schnitz-un-Gnepp* on the menu. Considering its role as an everyday food, this should not come as a surprise, and yet it is good to find it confirmed over and over in primary sources. In spite of this, a winnowing process occurred in fiction that was then parroted in newspaper articles about the Dutch, thus creating expectations in the minds of tourists contemplating a trip to the Dutch Country. *Schnitz-un-Gnepp* became a core dish that gradually came together with other foods as part of the Amish table by the mid-1930s, as we shall see in Chapter 10.

If the culinary conversations initiated in local-color fiction are found guilty of launching *Schnitz-un-Gnepp* into commercial realms that might puzzle, amuse, or perhaps even shock Dutch cooks of the nineteenth century, at least it can be said that Elsie Singmaster had the last word. Her most famous novel, *The Magic Mirror* (1934), contains a passage that more or less redeems the sort of Dutch Christmas parodied in the 1821 reference to *Schnitz-un-Gnepp*.

The Magic Mirror

Allentown has always served as a cultural mirror of Philadelphia, just as York mirrors Baltimore. Allentown was the setting for Singmaster's *The Magic Mirror*, which in an uncanny way brought together all the conflicts and issues of identity that have surfaced thus far in this discussion of the forces shaping Pennsylvania Dutch foods and foodways. Singmaster was keenly aware of the English-only sentiments then prevalent and cast her character Llewellyn Reeder in the role of an English-only advocate. Reeder was the wealthy Allentown owner of an iron foundry who declined a high-placed invitation to join the Pennsylvania German Society because of its Germanist views—a silent vote for Cornelius Weygandt, whom Singmaster greatly admired. But her story did not focus on the Reeders; they were a foil, the wealthy family who lived next door to the Hummers. Jesse Hummer was the central character in the novel, even though his sister Mamie eventually married Llewellyn Reeder's son.

The Hummers were working-class Dutch who lived very much as did the real-life Allentown family of Charles Fegley, one of my interviewees, urban Dutch whose culture was somewhat different from that of their country brethren. This urban/rural dichotomy was sketched vividly by Singmaster during Jesse Hummer's bicycle peregrinations through the Pennsylvania Dutch countryside with the object of selling Bibles and copies of *The Royal Path to Life* in order to raise money to go to college. This provided Singmaster with ample material for vignettes about the rural Dutch, their eating habits, and cultural life in general. Yet it was her Christmas description of the Huber dining room (the Hubers were neighbors of the Hummers) with its *Putz* (crèche), festoons of ground pine, red candles, and numerous little pine trees in pots that seemed to capture the real spirit of the Pennsylvania Dutch, even in households where every penny counted: "Half the dining-room was taken up by the large tree and a *Putz*, the scene of the nativity. On a carpet of moss stood the stable; in the doorway sat Mary, the babe in her arms; from one side approached the shepherds, from the other the magi. Arnold Auerbach passed plates of little cakes, animals such as Mrs. Hummer made, sticky flapjacks, *Springerle, Lebkuchen,* and tiny spice cakes shaped like nuts."[8]

In this one passage Singmaster essentialized the traditional Pennsylvania Dutch Christmas with unerring accuracy: *Lebkuchen,* or in Dutch *Leppkuche* (recipe on page 223), are still very much a part of festive cookery; but the sticky flapjacks (sweet pancakes similar to blintzes) are now almost forgotten, although they were doubtless sticky with Christmas preserve (recipe on page 207). The *Peffernisse* (pepper nuts) really did look like nuts because they were shaped with wooden molds or, lacking that, with walnut shells saved expressly for this purpose. *The Magic Mirror* was published during the depths of the Great Depression, so for that painful experience it became a talisman for survival during hard times, a backward glance to the days when small things carried greater meaning.

Singmaster was hard at work on this book during the early years of the second revival in Pennsylvania Dutch culture following World War I, a new time frame in which the very term "Pennsylvania Dutch" was openly rehabilitated and the culture's decorative arts featured in museum exhibitions. Her book was so well received that it was republished in Germany, although the German motives behind that edition may have been political, given what was then transpiring under Hitler. If it was an attempt to win over Elsie Singmaster's political sympathies, it failed. She was as sensitive to the larger implications as anyone and represented a group of Pennsylvania Dutch writers who worked single-mindedly to distance the Dutch from all things Old World German.

This movement found many voices, but perhaps the most adamant and vociferous was that of J. George Frederick (1882–1964), whose *The Pennsylvania Dutch and Their Cookery* (1935) was not only the first nationally marketed Pennsylvania Dutch cookbook (and emphasized that term in its title) but also a carefully orchestrated apology for Pennsylvania Dutch culture packed with little homilies about the patriotic contributions of the Dutch to the American way of life. Not one dish in this book is attributed to the Amish. In fact they are quite peripheral to his discussion.

Frederick was a collaborator with the New York theater critic Bland Johaneson in establishing the Society of Pennsylvania German Gastronomes in 1928 and the publication of what may be considered a manifesto for the *Neideitsche Kiche,* which first appeared in the *American Mercury* in 1926.[9] H. L. Mencken was part of that circle, but it was Hitler who indirectly made Frederick's book an instant success. *The Pennsylvania Dutch and Their Cookery* was part of an isolationist reaction to events in Europe that ultimately led to the adoption of the Amish, the pacifist farmer, as a symbol of Pennsylvania Dutch culture. The German Village restaurant in Lancaster, Pennsylvania, picked up on these themes by featuring pictures of both the Amish and *Schnitz-un-Gnepp* on its menus, and thus the mythic Amish table was born. Yet the truth of the matter is that the dividing line between who retains Dutch identity and who does not is not drawn across a bowl of *Schnitz-un-Gnepp* or an imaginary Amish menu; it is defined by sauerkraut.

FIGURE 15. Trade card depicting a popular stage spoof of the stereotypical Dutchman with his Meerschaum pipe and drumhead cabbage. Jacob Kuechler cultivated this image as host of the Roost. Buffalo, N.Y., 1878. Roughwood Collection, Devon, Pa.

CHAPTER 7

The Cabbage Curtain

Unlike the Berlin Wall or the fortified borders that once divided Europe, the "cabbage curtain" is invisible and crisscrosses the Pennsylvania landscape like the willy-nilly flight of a distelfink. Yet it is the sturdiest of borders because it defines who is and who is not Pennsylvania Dutch by virtue of one odoriferous, iconic dish: sauerkraut. Nothing in the repertoire of Pennsylvania Dutch cookery is as much a key to preserving traditional foods and foodways as fermented cabbage; this one preparation serves as the pointed end of a phalanx of traditional dishes that depend on sauerkraut for their perpetuation in everyday diet. Thus the Pennsylvania Dutch who keep up their cultural identity may be readily identified as eaters of sauerkraut: they are the true "Sauerkraut Yankees." They eat sauerkraut, and they eat it often in a variety of ways.

The expression "Sauerkraut Yankees," which served as the title of a book I published in 1983, was coined by Confederate soldiers during the Civil War as an insult to the Dutch. At the time the Pennsylvania Dutch cultivated a deep dislike for New Englanders (the true Yankees); thus among the Pennsylvania Dutch the term was so laden with negative weight that calling any Dutchman a Yankee was tantamount to picking a fistfight. Yet in an odd and perhaps accidental way, the southern stereotype of the Dutchman as a sauerkraut eater fit the cultural reality: sauerkraut was indeed the invisible border that separated the Dutch from the rest of Pennsylvania and Americans in general.

I arrived at that conclusion while undertaking the research for *Sauerkraut Yankees*, but it was at best an intuitive inference because nowhere in the historical literature (published or manuscript) did anyone claim that sauerkraut was indeed the matrix dish that cemented together the many disparate parts of Pennsylvania Dutch culinary identity. Then again, that type of cultural/ethnographic question was not being asked—I may have been among the first to consider it, and sauerkraut was strangely absent from most nineteenth-century cookbooks, at least those used by the Pennsylvania Dutch.

In hindsight this made perfectly good sense when one took into consideration that the production of sauerkraut on the family farm was more often than not a male activity (no need for such information in kitchen manuals) and that the various methods for making sauerkraut or its variants, made with turnips or even string beans, were mostly oral information. Recipes were irrelevant in any event because much depended on the type of cabbage used, the time of year, and a host of other variables—even the choice of salt—that only a well-seasoned farmer would understand. Thus while sauerkraut was a key dish, its production belonged to the arena of folk knowledge. After all, if you were Pennsylvania Dutch and made your own sauerkraut every fall, as most rural Dutch families did in the nineteenth century, you would have known since childhood how it was done.

The absence of sauerkraut recipes of any kind was glaringly apparent in *Die geschickte Hausfrau*, the 1848 cookbook that served as the core text for *Sauerkraut Yankees*. How could this pamphlet cookbook, which was most certainly sold to a largely Pennsylvania Dutch audience, represent Pennsylvania Dutch cookery without including a recipe or even a reference to sauerkraut? It did not occur to me until quite recently that this was a book for Dutch townies, educated people who spoke decent German but whose basic lifestyle was more or less similar to that of other mainstream Americans.

For the farmhouse cook, this recipe collection represented a window into a larger world outside Pennsylvania, the flip side of the Pennsylvania Dutch personality that is American, as the old Berks County cook so aptly revealed to me during her interview.

I inserted a sauerkraut recipe into my translation of *Die geschickte Hausfrau* because in my mind it needed to be there in order for the book to be Dutch; yet in reality the contents were not Dutch except in the nuanced ways in which they may have been interpreted in Pennsylvania kitchens. As I explained in the book's introduction, most of the material was borrowed from cookbooks published outside Pennsylvania, and many of those cookbooks were already old-fashioned by the time the compiler, Gustav Peters, raided them for

FIGURE 16. Fifty-three hundred pounds of drumhead cabbage on its way to sauerkraut. Real Photo postcard taken near Roaring Spring in Morrison's Cove, Blair County, Pa., October 17, 1912. Farmer Jimmy Replogle is wearing a buffalo-hide coat. Roughwood Collection, Devon, Pa.

recipes. Such recipe borrowings are common in cookbook literature and say more about the popularity of certain dishes than about plagiarism (in traditional cultures, imitation—the replication of certain motifs—is one measure of authenticity).

In any event, over the course of interviewing many different sorts of Pennsylvania Dutch from many different economic and religious backgrounds, the common theme of sauerkraut emerged as the one element all of them shared, the one rare thing they all agreed on, and the one dish that served to keep Pennsylvania Dutch culture alive in the home. Where sauerkraut was served, so were the traditional pork dishes made with it, and so it formed a basis upon which families relied for perpetuating their cultural identity, even if most Pennsylvania Dutch are at best ambivalent about their cuisine. They do not think about it as special; it is just something they happen to eat. However, I can now write with a certain amount of relief that fieldwork has eventually vindicated the conclusions I made about sauerkraut almost thirty years ago. Since then I have taken to making my own sauerkraut, so I have decided to share my family's recipe on page 251. It is fairly easy, and no expatriate Dutchman should be without it.

Grubenkraut and Its Evolution in Pennsylvania Dutch Cuisine

In Pennsylfaanisch the term is *Gruwegraut,* and there is no easy way to translate this into English other than to call it "pit cabbage," even though this does not sound appetizing. Quite the contrary, it is much more delicate than cabbage fermented in crocks or barrels, and since this method was the only way to make large quantities of sauerkraut in colonial Pennsylvania, it deserves a few words of discussion, especially since the technology was eventually applied to other agricultural practices, namely the development of silage for livestock. In short, the iconic silo of the American barn started out as an underground structure for storing cabbage—an idea borrowed directly from the Pennsylvania Dutch.[1]

Perhaps this is the juncture for a little background information regarding the underlying reasons why pit cabbage was at one time so heavily relied on by the rural Dutch. The basic problem was that once it was made, how did people stabilize the sauerkraut so that it would not spoil? Modern canning methods and simple refrigeration have completely resolved these issues; indeed the former seasonality of sauerkraut has virtually disappeared. It is no longer a cold-weather dish.

Pit cabbage was essentially sealed in the ground and would keep that way for many months since there the temperature was even and exposure to air was inhibited. Normally the pits were lined with planks after the fashion of a barrel so that the wood would expand and thus form a perfectly tight seal. Because of its density and antimicrobial qualities, the wood of choice was black birch (*Betula lenta*), also called sweet birch. The twigs have a distinct wintergreen flavor, and either these or, lacking that, strips of fresh bark were also sometimes added to the pit cabbage.

A small article in the 1872 *Neuer gemeinnütziger Pennsylvanischer Calender*, an almanac printed in Lancaster, alluded to the widespread use of black birch: "Sauerkraut can be protected against spoiling if a birch wood stake is stuck into it; this keeps the sauerkraut good."[2] In this case the stake should be cut from sappy green wood; it was not necessary to remove the bark. This same practice was also applied to sauerkraut made in crocks or barrels because there was no way to stabilize the kraut aside from storing it in a cold, unheated room or pantry. This is one reason for the popularity of three- and five-gallon stoneware crocks. Once the local potteries began producing them en masse after the Civil War, families could make small batches every few weeks and thus have a series of crocks coming ripe over the course of the winter.

My great-great-grandfather Abraham Weaver made his sauerkraut in three twenty-gallon crocks: one in September, one in October, one in November. This large quantity of fermented cabbage made sense for his household, which operated on a boardinghouse scale, considering the number of live-in relatives and work hands on the farm. These crocks were kept in the summer kitchen, which also doubled as a bake house (thus it did not freeze inside during the winter), because once filled, the crocks could not be moved. Other people built actual sauerkraut sheds, special outbuildings in which the crocks or barrels of sauerkraut were stored during cold weather.

This alleviated the problem of odors wafting into the house from an enclosed porch or pantry.

Gumbis: Sauerkraut's Culinary Cousin

Earlier on I mentioned *Gumbis* as one of the basic cold-weather dishes that has come down to us from classic eighteenth-century Pennsylvania Dutch cookery. Its French cousin is easy to locate in Alsatian cookbooks under the dialect name *Baeckoeffe* or under its French moniker *potée boulangère* ("baker's pot"). The French name refers to the custom of taking the big casserole pot, already filled with the ingredients, to the local bread bakery, where it would be baked Saturday evening for retrieval after church the next day as the centerpiece of Sunday dinner. This same custom prevailed in large Pennsylvania Dutch towns where many specialized bakers resided; the side industry of renting space in commercial-size bake ovens was always profitable. People even took their meats to the bakers for roasting, especially since many urban kitchens were small and ill-equipped.

In farmhouses at a distance from towns and the convenience of bakeries, *Gumbis* had to be prepared downhearth, or in special baking compartments that were often built into the sides of raised hearths. They could be heated with coals from the hearth, thus alleviating the need to fire up the bread oven and waste valuable cordwood on one dish. All the same, *Gumbis* was probably more of an urban dish than something commonly served in the country, at least until the coming of the iron cook stove, which changed the dynamics of energy consumption and expanded the culinary repertoire of household cookery.

Aside from my discussion of *Gumbis* in *Pennsylvania Dutch Country Cooking* in 1993, readers curious about this dish would be hard-pressed to find any reference to it after the 1930s; by then it was one of those preparations beginning to fade from living memory. That is probably why Berenice Steinfeldt included a recipe for a dish she called *Knabrus* in her 1937 pamphlet *The Amish of Lancaster*

County, one of the first tourist brochures about the Amish.[3] The recipe she published without giving a source was a fairly straightforward preparation of *Gumbis*, albeit with the curiously botched dialect name. It also appeared under that same misspelling on the menus of the Water Gate Inn in Washington, D.C., during the 1940s and 1950s, evidence of just how pervasive Steinfeldt's influence was beyond the borders of Lancaster County. There is absolutely no documentary proof that this dish was peculiar to the Amish; if it were, they would still be making it. More to the point, it was mostly an urban dish, and the Amish did not live in towns. On the other hand, this was a dish Steinfeldt may have suspected of being appropriately old and Dutchy; thus including it in her booklet lent greater authenticity to the other contents, riddled as they were with all sorts of myths and strange notions—more on that in Chapter 10.

So how does *Gumbis* connect to sauerkraut? For one thing, *Gumbis* can be made with sauerkraut instead of shredded cabbage; in its oldest known medieval form, it was certainly a fermented preparation much like sauerkraut but with the addition of other ingredients; hence its old Latin name, which means "a composition." To date, the earliest printed American reference to *Gumbis* appeared in an 1841 German-language cookbook written by George Girardey, a Pennsylvanian who settled during the 1830s in Ohio, where he established a local reputation as a booster of Philadelphia ice creams. His last name is generally rendered in Pennsylvania Dutch as Sherardin or some variation thereof, and the main concentration of that large, extended clan is still in Berks County.

While Girardey's cookbook drew heavily on French, especially Alsatian, sources, it is peppered with all sorts of curious and highly colloquial add-ons, among them a recipe for *Gumbis*, a baked deep-dish casserole composed of layers of shredded cabbage, meat (generally ham), dried fruit, and onions. This is just one of the innumerable variants derived from a medieval *compositum*, which could be a pickle, a type of preserve, a one-pot meal, or all of the above. The word "compote" in English traces to this same Latin root, except that in the case of Pennsylvania Dutch *Gumbis*, the preparation was savory or sweet and salty rather than something put down in honey or sugar. Girardey's recipe was designed to imitate the main features of its meatless fermented counterpart (fermented layers of shredded vegetables), which could be eaten uncooked like a pickle or served hot like sauerkraut. Thus it is a dish that does not fall neatly into modern culinary categories.

The most ancient form of this preparation, which was made with turnips rather than cabbage or with shredded turnips and kohlrabi, probably traces to late antiquity—there were certainly many Byzantine counterparts. By the Middle Ages it was pervasive in the food cultures of southern Germany and Switzerland and southeastward into the Danube Basin, and there is still considerable debate among European food historians about whether it was a relic of indigenous Celto-Roman culture that passed into Alemannic (German) custom or came out of Byzantium via medieval trade contacts. Since it was a so-called folk dish, it does not appear in medieval culinary texts, at least not in any that are known to survive, although the *Gumbis* preserve cooked with sugar or honey is mentioned many times in its medical manifestation.

One of the best preserved recipes for the turnip-based preparation can be found in Theodore Zwinger's 1696 *Theatrum Botanicum*, a medical herbal published in Basel, Switzerland, and which served as the basis for an herbal published by Christopher Sauer of Germantown (now part of Philadelphia) during the 1760s and 1770s—the herbal was published in annual installments in Sauer's almanac.[3] While Sauer did not cite Zwinger's recipe for *Gumbis*, which appeared under a broad discussion of the health value of turnips, he did refer to its benefits, such as using the brine for medical remedies. Zwinger's recipe was essentially this: small, pared turnips were placed in brine with barberries and sloes or some other dried fruit and then allowed to undergo the same type of enzyme change as Polish cucumber pickles.[4] The result was a sweet-and-salty pickle that could either be eaten as a snack with bread and wine or administered as a botanical remedy for certain medical conditions.

It was evidently called *Gumbis* by the rural poor (also *Kumpis* or *Kumbish* in Zwinger) because it conformed to the original Latin idea: a composition, a mixture, or more commonly a mixture arranged in layers. When it was combined with shredded cabbage and baked in an earthenware pot, it became *Gumbistöpfel*, literally "pot *Gumbis*" (*Gumbistopp* in Pennsylfaanisch), and dried pears rather than sloes were preferred ingredients doubtless because they were cheaper and easier to find. In Pennsylvania dried Seckel pears or some similar type of dried butter pears were also preferred ingredients, although dried peaches and apples were often used as alternatives. Availability and economics played roles in choices of ingredients, but the basic concept of combining meat, cabbage, and fruit remained fairly consistent until the advent of the cast-iron cook stove, which pushed aside many old traditional dishes. While *Gumbis* declined as a preferred one-pot dish for Sunday dinner prior to the Civil War, other preparations rose up to take its place. Enter chicken and waffles.

FIGURE 17. Cover of a Pennsylvania Dutch menu created for Miller's restaurant in Ronks, Pa., in 1954. Written completely in Pennsylfaanisch, the menu uses Amish decorative themes to promote its chicken-and-waffle dinners. Roughwood Collection, Devon, Pa.

CHAPTER 8

Waffle Palaces

There is an old Pennsylvania Dutch saying: *weeche Waffle sin Dudelarewet ferlore,* which means "soft waffles are love's labor lost." In the Pennsylvania Dutch universe, there is probably nothing worse than a soft waffle, a bedroom euphemism for male dysfunction. So ingrained are waffles in our culture that less-than-perfect specimens are ready objects of contempt.

The German Reformed minister Peter Seibert Davis (1828–1892) was one of the first to remark on the prevalence of chicken and waffles among the Pennsylvania Dutch, and by Dutch I am speaking here of the "church" Dutch, not the plain sects. While living in Norristown, Pennsylvania, Davis published a novel called *The Young Parson,* which first appeared in 1861 and was reprinted in 1863. The book followed the fortunes and misfortunes of a young minister who came to live as a guest in the homes of several members of his congregation while they decided whether or not they liked him. In the course of discussing the sort of hospitality he received, the minister mentioned chicken and waffles as the "stereotypical" Sunday supper dish among the people in that area.[1] I think this was also the first time that a particular food was associated with the term "stereotype" in a Pennsylvania Dutch context. Whatever, the marriage of chicken and waffles was already a culinary institution in parts of the Dutch community by the 1860s, although to this day few people think of it as particularly Pennsylvania Dutch. To further confuse the issue, the dish was prepared in several different ways (and not always with chicken), the two basic forms being chicken-based gravy served over waffles and some form of chicken served beside the waffles. In either case the waffles were not sweetened, and when cooked to a turn, they were served crispy and hot.

However, there was an implicit framework for Davis's story: the novel's setting was urban; thus there may be a presumed difference between the dietary habits of people living in towns and those of residents in the countryside—a dichotomy that is evident from other period material and even within living memory. For example, Miriam Smoker Brendle, who grew up in an Amish household near Atglen, Pennsylvania, recalled during an interview that many country people were too poor to own waffle irons, so they made pancakes instead and ate them with chicken gravy. Truly frugal households used fried mush. There was a descending order of choices depending on economic circumstances. Just the same, chicken in any form was considered a special treat prior to the advent of large-scale poultry farming in the 1950s, and that is why chicken and waffles could attract such large crowds when served at country hotels and specialty restaurants.

In spite of this, the modern culinary explorer must become an intrepid traveler when it comes to seeking out chicken-and-waffle suppers in the Pennsylvania Dutch countryside. An early frost one October weekend brought the official end of summer to the hills south of Kutztown, and all the trees were ablaze with brilliant fall colors. The contrast between that backdrop and torrential rains mixed with fog and low-hanging clouds added a strangely wild and unpredictable note to my expedition to a chicken-and-waffle dinner being held at the Lutheran church in a quaintly named village called New Jerusalem.

Intimidating weather aside, the dinner was well attended, mostly by locals, a mix of elderly farmers and young families. Many came from other Lutheran churches in the area. It would seem that the dinners now have quite a following, with pork and sauerkraut one weekend and perhaps fried oysters at another church the next, as the locals move in round-robin fashion throughout the fall and winter from one event to the next. This is a form of migratory feasting not well advertised to the outside world but certainly well known through word of mouth.

The book on Pennsylvania Dutch chicken and waffles has not yet been written, but it will be a very thick tome to be sure because this regional favorite among fire halls and church suppers enjoys a long and colorful history in southeastern Pennsylvania. While it is a dish that comes to the table in many varied forms, chicken is a latecomer to the culinary story, because in the early nineteenth century—and perhaps even before that—other creatures were stewed and poured over waffles.

The first known references to this concept emerged in Philadelphia during the early 1800s in the form of catfish-and-waffle dinners served by hotels along the Schuylkill River and especially along Wissahickon Creek, which prior to its incorporation into Fairmount Park was considered one of the best catfish creeks in the region. The Schuylkill Hotel (1813) was one such resort, and so was the more famous Catfish and Waffle House at the falls of the Schuylkill, which by 1848 had a well-established reputation that continued into the early 1900s, although it was demolished and rebuilt several times by different owners to accommodate changing architectural tastes and ever-increasing patronage.

The typical menus for all these waffle palaces consisted of fried catfish with pepper hash, fried potatoes, fried chicken, beefsteaks, stewed catfish, stewed chicken, and of course waffles to accompany the stewed dish of your choice. Strong coffee came with the meal; waffles as a dessert, sprinkled with sugar and cinnamon, were extra. These basic dishes were then arranged into price categories from relatively cheap and simple to a full spread with everything on the menu. Guests reserved whole tables and could arrive as a group and create a shared menu to fit their inclinations or budgets.

Since each category had its fixed price, these eateries appealed to people of modest means who knew in advance what they would get for their money. But the festive atmosphere of the hotels (there was often a band playing popular tunes), the lack of pretension that otherwise characterized high-class restaurants and hotel dining rooms of that period, and the woodsy locations situated near scenic outlooks along the water also attracted the wealthy as a way to indulge in local color. What set the catfish-and-waffle houses apart from restaurants was their seasonality, for they operated only from May or June to October. This changed as blue-collar tourism moved into the countryside and small hotels sprouted up along the railroad and trolley lines. Why limit the menu to summer catfish when chicken can be served all year?

Whether the Pennsylvania Dutch hotels borrowed this menu format from Philadelphia or something like it already existed in the Dutch Country is yet to be determined, but the evidence seems to suggest that Philadelphia was indeed the epicenter. Certainly in the case of Davis's 1860s novel set in Norristown, keep in mind that Norristown is situated on the Schuylkill River and since the 1820s had been connected to Philadelphia by a canal. That canal, which went to Reading and somewhat beyond, may have been the conduit for the waffle dinners that soon spread into the upcountry. One thing is clear: by the late 1800s chicken and waffles were considered by many writers to be emblematic of Pennsylvania Dutch cookery and cultural identity, at least on the local level. The Pennsylvania Dutch version in home cookery may have started not with catfish or with chicken but rather with pot pudding, a meaty pork-based pâté that was commonly melted in a skillet and poured hot over bread, over noodles, over potatoes, and yes, even over waffles—unsweetened of course.

Regardless of these folk origins, Elsie Singmaster published a story in 1906 that mentioned chicken and waffles as a local iconic food. The setting was her fictional Millerstown (in reality Macungie, Pennsylvania) in Lehigh County, and the heroine of her story was a Dutch maiden named Jovina, who endeavored through her cookery to acquire a husband: "Jovina could make yeast beer and root-beer and half a dozen fruit vinegars. Her chicken and waffles, her *schnitz und knöpf,* her *latwerk* (apple butter), were the envy of all the other women."[2]

It may not be coincidental that by 1906 when this story appeared in a national magazine, hotels catering to tourists from outside the Pennsylvania Dutch area listed all of these local foods on their menus, although not always together. Thus Singmaster was both creating culinary expectations in the minds of readers intent on visiting the Dutch Country as well as reflecting a reality already in place in local cookery. Singmaster's promotion of these dishes was probably drawn from her personal experiences in country inns, not the least being Beidelman's Hotel in her native Macungie. Recipes from that now-demolished hotel are highly prized and still in use by local groups promoting Pennsylvania Dutch cookery, chicken-and-waffle dinners among them.

Pennsylvania Dutch families I have interviewed about their food habits have been unanimous in confirming that most rural people did not eat out, especially prior to the 1960s when fast foods and supermarkets began to penetrate the countryside. The question then arises: who were the people who packed the country hotels on weekends and traveled many miles to partake of chicken-and-waffle dinners? One answer is affluent urbanites. In the early 1900s these were the people who owned touring cars. They were the people with disposable incomes, and in towns such as Reading and Allentown, they had enough family connections to Pennsylvania Dutch culture to enjoy its homey rusticity in small weekend doses.

This brings us to the flip side of the waffle story—if I may be permitted the pun. The other type of guest who visited the Dutch Country to eat local cooking and to take in the fresh rural air was the urban working class. Before the advent of labor laws, these people did not have vacations as we know them today. Many workers had only Sundays off, so their leisure time was defined by how far they could travel by train or trolley in one day. The local train line brought people out from Philadelphia to the Pennsylvania Dutch hotels in the Perkiomen Valley of Montgomery County on Saturday after work. They stayed the night, dined on a large country meal the next day, and returned in the evening so that they could report to work on Monday morning. As the local folklorist and historian

Isaac Clarence Kulp pointed out in an interview, most of the hotels along this scenic river specialized in chicken-and-waffle dinners. This type of urban-rural exchange was relatively short-lived in the Perkiomen Valley because the Depression brought an end to its hotel trade, and the automobile shifted tourism to areas much farther afield, especially Lancaster County and its Amish community.

The earliest reference I have found to a waffle palace in the Dutch Country comes not from a location close to Philadelphia but rather from York County. This means that this type of seasonal hotel was already an integral part of the culture of the Pennsylvania Dutch countryside, and like the Philadelphia originals, it too was located along a river. The Accomac Hotel (now known as the Accomac Inn) at Wrightsville on the west side of the Susquehanna River published a brochure for the summer season dated June 6, 1892, in which chicken and waffles were listed as a specialty. This rare document is framed and hanging on the wall of the present inn and quoted on its Web site. Chicken and waffles became the hotel's signature dish and remained so for the next sixty years. The hotel was purchased in 1915 by Norman Pickle, former owner of the Wild Cat Falls Inn across the river at Marietta, Pennsylvania, in Lancaster County. The Wild Cat Falls Inn also specialized in chicken-and-waffle dinners, as well as catfish and waffles, with the catfish coming from the Susquehanna River.

One of the puzzling aspects of the chicken-and-waffle story is the absence of recipes for the dish in most Pennsylvania Dutch cookbooks; only Ruth Tyndall provided detailed instructions in *Eat Yourself Full*. However, the novelist Elsie Singmaster placed the dish emphatically in the Pennsylvania Dutch cultural camp, and yet there is no discussion of it in any book devoted specifically to Pennsylvania Dutch cultural identity. This suggests that Pennsylvania Dutch culinary identity was already coalescing around a cluster of nostalgia foods such as *Schnitz-un-Gnepp* and that the process of choosing what was emblematic of the Dutch was highly selective and shaped largely by the forces of tourism. Given that shoofly pie was a hybrid creation introduced at the United States Centennial

FIGURE 18. Interior of the Wild Cat Falls Inn at Marietta, Lancaster County, Pa. Postcard view, 1906. Roughwood Collection, Devon, Pa.

and that the ubiquitous chow chow pickle on Pennsylvania Dutch tables originated not only outside the culture but from India, why did the selective process accept them as iconic dishes and yet stop at chicken and waffles? For one thing, shoofly pie and chow chow are models of frugality that were quickly integrated into the post–Civil War farmhouse cookery of the Pennsylvania Dutch. Chicken and waffles were always a special-occasion dish, even if that special occasion was Saturday evening supper. They did not normally represent a dinner dish, the focal point of a big sit-down meal. They were therefore a satellite dish, food that played a secondary role in the structure of meals, especially since they utilized leftovers.

Another possible explanation is that chicken and waffles were not symbolic relics of the Old World German peasant life glorified by the early Pennsylvania German Society and the Germanists who followed that line of thinking. The dish did not come here on a boat; it had no ennobling (patriotic) cultural associations. Like *Lulu Bapp*

(LuLu paste, a soft pretzel beer-cheese dip popular in the Pennsylvania Dutch hill country), it was a local innovation too popular across class and cultural lines to pass as something uniquely Pennsylvania Dutch. Perhaps more important, it was never a true poverty dish, given the cost of the basic ingredients and the somewhat special-occasion context in which it was consumed. More to the point, it was not a common dish among the Amish and thus never fully coattailed on the dynamics of Amish tourism (Miller's in Ronks being one exception; see discussion below). Like the Christmas tree, chicken noodle soup, hash browns, and the pretzel, chicken and waffles quickly lost its Pennsylvania Dutch associations, and by the 1930s the dish had joined a long line of foods and customs incorporated into mainstream American culture—especially that of African Americans, who today have embraced the idea as their own.

However, the regional penchant for chicken and waffles did not go unnoticed. One of the earliest sources to provide a good look at the chicken-and-waffle situation in Pennsylvania was the 1941 edition of Duncan Hines's *Adventures in Good Eating*, although it was limited by the fact that Hines listed only places in Pennsylvania that did him favors or offered some type of unique price break. Shankweiler's at Fogelsville, one of the most famous of all the chicken-and-waffle palaces, was never mentioned. Yet he listed the Hollyhock Tea Room at Bushkill in the Pocono resort area, which catered mostly to summer tourists. He also singled out the Downingtown, Pennsylvania, Tea House, a historic stone building in which chicken a la king was served over heart-shaped waffles— my grandmother ate there often. In Harbor Creek, Pennsylvania, Johnny Knolls served chicken-and-steak versions of the dish, with the thinly chipped steak and onions prepared the same way they are cooked for steak sandwiches in Philadelphia. At New Hope in Bucks County, a famous artist colony at the time, the Old Cartwheel Inn served chicken, duck, and steak variations, with the duck-and-waffles idea coming directly out of the Berks County heartland. For reasons quite his own, Hines avoided the German Village (by then called simply the Village), a bus-station restaurant that stood at the hub of Lancaster's Pennsylvania Dutch food tourism until the Hotel Brunswick assumed that role in the early 1950s.

Whether approved by Duncan Hines or not, the waffle palaces of rural Pennsylvania attracted people not only from nearby cities but from neighboring states as well. Most of these hotels were not located near the Amish, so the chicken-and-waffle dinner and perhaps a day of antiquing before it competed with the Amish for the attention of outsiders. It provided an alternative reason for making a trip into the Dutch Country, and even to this day most of the establishments that keep chicken and waffles on the menu lie outside areas affected by Amish tourism, such as the Molly Pitcher Waffle Shop in Chambersburg, Pennsylvania, which may be considered a lineal descendant of the old waffle palaces that once lined the Schuylkill River in Philadelphia.

The acknowledged promoter of chicken and waffles in connection with Lancaster County Amish tourism was Miller's on the Lincoln Highway (Route 30) in Ronks, east of Lancaster. Now known as Miller's Smorgasbord, the restaurant opened in 1929 as a truck stop operated by Enos and Anna Miller. Since the truckers had nothing to eat while the mechanics made repairs, Mrs. Miller decided to serve chicken and waffles as an added inducement to business. The idea took off, and soon the Millers were serving more than just truckers; the place eventually blossomed into a full-scale family restaurant with chicken and waffles as the signature dish.

In the early 1950s the Millers retired and sold the restaurant to Thomas Strauss, who continued the name and the signature chicken and waffles. One of his menus from 1954, which was written entirely in Pennsylvania Dutch and featured an Amish buggy on the front, offered waffles served nine different ways, including with a sauce of chicken giblets, ham gravy, and the standard chicken fricassee. In those days all the food at the restaurant came from local farmers, including the chickens, which were supplied by Martin Brendle, a poultry man in nearby Strasburg.

While the Amish rarely ate in restaurants unless traveling and were not large consumers of chicken and waffles, the connection came together at Miller's, which lies in the heart of Lancaster's Amish belt. Thomas Strauss was also a great booster of local tourism, and it was he who first allowed African Americans to eat in his restaurant—a bus full of hungry and discouraged churchgoers who had come to Lancaster on an excursion. He is still remembered for his generosity and how he single-handedly shamed the other restaurants in the area into serving people of color, because until then they had no place to eat once they got to Lancaster County.

The popularity of chicken and waffles was not limited to southeastern Pennsylvania alone: a careful study of menus from the 1920s and 1930s will uncover the dish all over the state, but especially along the major highways favored by tourists. The dish leapfrogged its way west along the Lincoln Highway and even followed more roundabout roadways. At Newlonsburg (now part of Murrysville) on the William Penn Highway in Westmoreland County due east of Pittsburgh, the House by the Side of the Road featured chicken and waffles on its 1938 menu, the chef's specials being chicken and waffles deluxe for $1.35 (the gravy contained mushrooms) and for $1.50 chopped roast turkey on waffles. The restaurant was a well-known locale for bridge parties, and the extensive wine and liquor list suggests that the "exclusive clientele" (to quote the menu cover) mixed serious drinking with their card playing.

While automobile tourism seems to have spread chicken and waffles rather evenly across the state by the 1930s, the culinary heartland always remained in the Dutch Country. Yet history is never as clear-cut and as simple as a diffusionist approach might suggest. Ideas circulated in many directions at once, for one of the moving forces in popularizing chicken and waffles emanated not from the catfish houses along the Schuylkill River but from Erie, Pennsylvania, more specifically from the iron foundry of Erie's Griswold Manufacturing Company. This company made and sold high-quality cast-iron kitchen utensils, among them the 1908 American Waffle Iron, which was patented on December first of that year for use on wood- and coal-burning stoves. Many of these hand-turned Griswold waffle irons are still in use today, not only because they are easy to operate; they are completely off the power grid and thus appeal to environmentalists as well as campers.

More important, the owners of the company were well aware of the popularity of chicken-and-waffle dinners. Griswold's publicists made the following claim in an advertising campaign promoting the new invention in the March 1909 issue of the *Ladies' Home Journal*: "You can attend a chicken and waffle supper right at home any time you have the notion if you are the owner of a Griswold's American Waffle Iron." If there were any doubt about the effortless manner in which chicken and waffles could be incorporated into home cooking, the firm issued a booklet titled *Laying and Serving the Table* and prepared by Boston Cooking School's Janet McKenzie. Miss McKenzie was one of the early advocates of chicken and waffles as a dish worthy of the attention of home economists if for no other reasons than the gravy could use up leftovers or even canned meat and the waffles could be made with baking powder instead of eggs.

This low-cost approach takes us down a different path from old-time Pennsylvania Dutch saffron waffles that tasted of the homemade butter used to oil the irons, or the fragrance of Berks County–style sweet potato waffles covered copiously with sautéed smoked duck. McKenzie set the stage for the onslaught of electric waffle irons in the 1920s and doubtless helped to spread the popularity of the dish into other parts of the country. Today the situation is quite different: the chicken-and-waffle palaces faded with the passing of the old country inns. The culinary tradition has shifted to churches, fire halls, and Masonic temples, and now even truck stops and diners serve this dish, or one of its many variations, all across the Keystone State. Indeed, chicken and waffles can now be found in just about every state of the Union.

FIGURE 19. Program cover for the fifth annual Versommling (general meeting) of Grundsau Lodge Number One, Allentown, Pa., February 3, 1938. Roughwood Collection, Devon, Pa

CHAPTER 9

Consider the Groundhog

THERE was a time not too long ago when eating groundhog was fairly common throughout rural America, and a reasonable argument could be made that it is probably a lot healthier as food than hamburgers, French fries, pizza, or even Chicken McNuggets. For certain groundhog has better flavor. Groundhog dinners were once dependable money makers for local fund-raising projects—one of the most popular in Pennsylvania was held by the Liberty Fire Company in Friedensburg—but they are now history. Just the same there are still a few holdouts, such as the Boyertown Rod and Gun Club, which gathers every August in a park near Frederick, Pennsylvania, to celebrate an annual groundhog cookout. Over the course of the year, club members hunt groundhogs, clean them, and then freeze them for this now legendary but highly exclusive event. The member who brings in the most groundhogs earns a much-coveted prize, but it is the cooked groundhog, the cold lager beer, and the festive nature of this dinner that draw game lovers from far and wide.

This is one of the last remnants of the old Pennsylvania Dutch shooting fests that were often the highlight of country tavern life, especially around the holidays. Of course the gun club event is a private "male thing" with talk centering on guns, target practice, and hunting yarns and with a pretty good flow of alcohol, and yet the pepper hash served with the meal and the fresh peach-crumb pies, not to mention the groundhog, remind us of the true regional character of the menu. Until recently, before the passing of the older generation, it was also a good place to hear some spoken Pennsylvania Dutch in the form of off-color jokes and stories.

From the standpoint of charcouterie, groundhog is difficult to clean because the skin is sometimes tough and there are sweat glands in the armpits (locals call them "the patches") that must be removed with surgical precision; otherwise the flavor of the meat is rendered unpalatable. Yet properly dressed, groundhog is indeed an underrated American delicacy, and smoked groundhog is an unsung luxury—I do not exaggerate. The meat of young groundhogs is mild, not fatty, with excellent texture that many people liken to veal. The Schuylkill County butcher Samuel Laubenstein, who has cooked many groundhogs over the course of his ninety-one years, recommended that they not be larger than about eighteen inches counting the tail, adding that the small ones are excellent when spit roasted. MaryAnn Lovell (née Elstrodt), who grew up in the Stony Brook area of York County, described how her mother prepared roast groundhog: stuffed with bread filling, wrapped in cheesecloth, and basted while it cooked. The drippings made excellent rich gravy.

The cooks at the hunt club boil their groundhogs in highly flavored stock, then cut them up "chicken style" and brown them in butter, real country butter. All the cooking is done right there in the park, so it is possible to follow the culinary process through each step. As picnic attendee Roy Hartman assured me, groundhog is cleaner than pork because groundhogs are vegetarian; hogs will eat anything. On that point he is absolutely right, because groundhogs taste of their own *terroir*, not at all gamey if butchered when young, and they have none of the strong flavor of wild rabbit. But stay away from the late-season adults because they pack on fat for winter, and this bulking up makes them greasy—not to mention that as groundhogs age, their meat grows tough and stringy.

Among the rural poor—the Buckwheat Dutch—this problem was overcome by marinating the carcasses in buttermilk for one or two days and then stewing the meat in a little vinegar or beer along with wild ramps or top-set onions from the garden. This was unapologetically strong-tasting fare no matter how one prepared it, so an abundance of *Hooriche Gnepp* ("hairy" dumplings) came to the table to "cut the grease." Good old-time apple schnapps or hard cider helped digest it.

The Berks County housewife Grace Henninger (1915–2011) commented during an interview that her husband once shot a very large adult groundhog for Thanksgiving dinner (that would be in the 1940s, during war-time food shortages), but the meat was so tough and rank (remember the "patches") that they had to throw the whole thing out. They had been warned this would happen, but they could not afford to buy a roasting chicken, so their holiday dinner that year consisted of homemade mincemeat pie and little else. Just the same, groundhogs have been such an integral part of rural life in the Dutch Country that they have evolved into a cultural icon, an identity badge for the Groundhog Lodges that meet to perpetuate the Pennsylvania Dutch language.

The earliest Dutch conversation clubs were the hiking clubs that developed after the Civil War during the early years of the dialect revival movement. Henry L. Fisher (1822–1909) of York, Pennsylvania, was prominent in that movement and published a large body of poems, many of them collected into books that he also illustrated with scenes of old-time farm life. Perhaps one of the most singular of his poems was a four-page salutation devoted to Kuechler's Roost on Mt. Penn overlooking Reading. Fisher composed it as a Christmas and New Year's greeting sent in December 1884 to his friends and acquaintances. It was dedicated to Reading's Alsace Hiking Club, which used Kuechler's Roost as a place to pitch camp and picnic in the days prior to the construction of the Gravity Railroad in 1889. Until then hiking to the top of Mt. Penn was the only way to get to the Roost. Perhaps more important, the club eventually organized annual dinners at the Roost, and the menus as well as table conversation were completely in Pennsylvania Dutch.

The backstory to Fisher's poem is that by 1884 the Roost was already well known throughout the Pennsylvania Dutch region.

German-born Jacob Ludwig Kuechler established a popular wine house on Penn Street in Reading during the 1870s. In 1882 he aban-

FIGURE 20. Jacob Kuechler at the Roost. Cabinet photograph, 1893. Courtesy of the Historical Society of Berks County, Pa.

doned his temperance-minded and anti-mother-in-law wife and moved to Mount Penn—along with his doting mother, who won the feminine battle of affections and became his stalwart *chef de cuisine*.

This quirky, artisanal, cook-to-order food laid the groundwork for the clientele who frequented Kuechler's bar—mostly male, mostly Pennsylvania Dutch, and mostly well-to-do. Governor Pennypacker was one of his most enthusiastic patrons and mentioned his good times there in his memoirs. The Roost did not morph into a popular restaurant until after 1905, when it became more readily accessible to the public under the stewardship of Karl August Schaich. Until then it was a rustic and secluded male-only destination where Pennsylvania Dutch townies (such as lawyers, bankers, businessmen, and an occasional governor) could don hiking gear, take in the fresh mountain air, and then convene to smoke cigars, drink Kuechler's delightful red wines and champagne, dine on Dutch cooking, and tell off-color jokes and stories in Pennsylvania Dutch. Their wives or girlfriends were not part of the equation. In this respect Kuechler's Roost might be considered a forerunner of the Grundsau Lodges that sprouted up in the 1930s to promote Pennsylvania Dutch culture and especially the spoken dialect.

In his book *Groundhog Day,* Dr. Don Yoder investigated the evolution of the Grundsau Lodges—*Grundsau* means groundhog in Dutch—and the parallel development of Groundhog Day as a national observance, and yet little research has been done on the lodge menus and what steps, if any, the lodges have taken to preserve the culinary aspects of Pennsylvania Dutch culture. Most of the menus are indeed written in Pennsylfaanisch, but the foods are usually mainstream American dishes found anywhere in the United States. The reason is logistics: the annual banquets are normally held in fire halls or places that offer standardized catered meals; thus it is too expensive to create special menus. Furthermore, Lee Haas, titular head of all the lodges in Pennsylvania, pointed out that if they served something such as *Schnitz-un-Gnepp,* perhaps only half of the members would like it, so the choice of food is based on a compromise—in short, simple dishes that will appeal to the largest number of members. It is also widely accepted that most caterers are not proficient in Pennsylvania Dutch cooking; thus it would be a gamble at best to expect them to rise to the occasion and prepare something as simple as onion pies, much less something as technically demanding as *Hasenpfeffer.* However, eating is part of the camaraderie of the lodges, as important a component as the stage skits and dialect banter. Serving up good traditional cookery might be one way to draw in more members.

Pumpernickle Bill Spawns a Movement

It was the dialect writer William S. Troxell (1893–1957), a Dutch language columnist for the *Allentown Morning Call,* who started the lodge movement in Pennsylvania. Troxell, whose pen name was

"Pumpernickle Bill," was also a great organizer of Dutch events, such as the Apple Butter Festival at Dorney Park near Allentown, which later served as one of the inspirations for the Kutztown Folk Festival. Troxell called together some like-minded buddies who were concerned about the state of the dialect, and they held their first organizational meeting on March 13, 1933, at Joseph Trinkle's Keystone Trail Inn in Allentown. This restaurant was known at the time for its $1.50 chicken-and-waffle dinners, frogs' legs with sauerkraut ($0.90), and the unique handheld Lehigh County corn pies (they resembled Welsh pasties)—a culinary reputation it shared with Trinkle's other eatery, the Cetronia Hotel, whose corn pie recipe is on page 210. The underlying reason for organizing the lodge was a general uneasiness about Germany and about Hitler in particular, not to mention a growing need in the Dutch community to emphasize its essential American character and to distance itself from what was happening in Europe. At the 1933 planning session it was agreed that they would hold a general meeting the following year; some three hundred dialect speakers showed up. From there numbers grew quickly until as many as eight hundred people would attend annual meetings. There are now seventeen lodges in various parts of the state.

Rather than promote the food of the Pennsylvania Dutch, the Grundsau Lodges have concentrated on the language and have created workshops in which Dutch is taught over the course of fourteen weeks. Some five thousand people have graduated from these courses, and there seems to be a flowering of interest as more and more local organizations follow suit with language programs of their own. The shortcoming of the workshops is that once armed with Pennsylvania Dutch, the graduates often have no one with whom to chat, so perhaps this is where a culinary linkage might fill the void. Cooking clubs based on making Pennsylvania Dutch dishes with instruction and conversation solely in dialect might offer a practical and entertaining way to perpetuate and revitalize the language, especially since food terms provide direct access into the mind-set of the culture.

A question often asked is, "why groundhog?" Nearly all of the lodge members I have interviewed mention the fact that the groundhog fits neatly into Pennsylvania Dutch culture because it was a common denizen of the countryside, a ready symbol of farm life, and long associated with weather prognostication, an important point in the days when farmers spent the late winter poring over almanacs. The first groundhog club was established in 1887 at Punxsutawney in Jefferson County, a Pennsylvania Dutch enclave in northwestern Pennsylvania. The club evolved out of a groundhog hunt and now acts as official handler for "Punxsutawney Phil" in what has become an annual winter ritual on national television. This club had nothing to do with the lodge movement, with preserving Pennsylvania Dutch culture or the dialect, although Ida Fetterman's excellent recipe for a Dutch-style spice cookie served at early 1900s club dinners has come to light and is included on page 250.

FIGURE 21. Rare 1911 postcard spoofing Groundhog Day at Punxsutawney, Pa. Roughwood Collection, Devon, Pa

The Slumbering Groundhog Lodge of Quarryville, Pennsylvania, was established in 1908 along similar lines as the Punxsutawney club, and it holds a competing event on Groundhog Day. Again its purpose was not to speak Pennsylfaanisch, although most of the members were indeed Pennsylvania Dutch. The early menus for the banquets, which were printed inside the programs, reveal an interest in local food products such as pickles from Providence Township, turkey from Colerain, Drumore peas, and Martic sweet potatoes— all of these names referred to townships in Lancaster County where members resided. The meals were held in the Quarryville Hotel until it burned down on Christmas Eve 1921, the victim of a Christmas tree lit with candles. The club then moved its banquets to other nearby hotels and continued a similar menu, with roast turkey the inevitable main course. There was no special effort to eat groundhog or Pennsylvania Dutch foods, aside from an occasional pickled egg or a side dish of dried corn. The only unique foods at these meals were the "Wedding Buns," a local colloquial name for a type of fine white dinner roll that came in pairs, baked so that they were attached to one another. Other than that, the primary purpose of the club was camaraderie with a mix of humorous hocus-pocus surrounding groundhog lore.

Both of these two preexisting groundhog clubs, whose activities were well publicized, provided the lodge movement with an invaluable cultural symbol. In short, Troxell and his colleagues reinvented the groundhog for their own purposes and, given the political climate of 1933, discovered in the groundhog a perfect choice: it was a distinctly American creature. More important, it was sectarian neutral; it did not favor any one particular Pennsylvania Dutch community. In that respect it was the opposite of Amish. To this day the worlds of the Amish and the Grundsau Lodgers do not cross, and they represent the symbolic polarities that have marked a cultural division slicing through the Pennsylvania Dutch worldview, social mores, and even diet.

Many Grundsau Lodgers have eaten groundhog privately, but they are almost unanimous in not eating it at a lodge event: "We don't cook our mascot," one member quipped. So the question remains: will the lodges have any effect on the future development of Pennsylvania Dutch cuisine? Has food tourism altered their ideas about food? To date the lodges have been solidly male organizations; cookery is not their normal sphere of interest, and there has been no attempt to treat food with the same reverence as the spoken dialect. Yet things are changing. Lucy Kern of East Greenville, Pennsylvania, established the first female Grundsau Lodge in 1984, and another female lodge has been organized since then. During a recent interview, Lucy offered some thought-provoking insights about the long-term convergence of dialect and cuisine and efforts to keep them alive.

She was quick to point out that the only way she could facilitate her event, which features a covered-dish supper and dialect entertainment supplied by members of male Grundsau Lodges in the area, was to hold it in a local fire hall and not use the fire hall kitchen. Since the women attending make a small donation to cover the cost of the event rather than the food, Kern was able to circumvent health board regulations because the meal was essentially free. On the other hand, fire halls want to make money from their catering services and as a rule do not permit customers to bring in their own food, so she had to come to an understanding with the inhouse cooks. As it turned out, the Greenville fire hall was catering the dinner for a local male Grundsau Lodge that weekend; she could hold her dinner on the Tuesday or Wednesday before because after that the kitchen would be tied up with prepping for the weekend meal; the fire hall cooks were happy enough not to have to clean the fire hall kitchen twice in one week. These complicated negotiations that had to take into account the annual dinner of the male lodge members more or less placed the women's event in a satellite position that required a clear line of communication between the male and female lodges. As Lucy Kern reiterated several times, the real purpose of the women's lodge was to spoof the male clubs and to have a good time; food was only one element of the mix.

Is there an effort to supply the ladies' event with Pennsylvania Dutch foods? Some women bring traditional dishes, but most do not. Lucy Kern's larger concern is that there is no one to carry on after her, and she is not optimistic about the long-term viability of her lodge. In addition, while the Pennsylvania Dutch housewife represents the front line of the culture's traditional cookery, the younger women are not as interested in the hard work involved in making some of the classic dishes. As Kern observed, this was the case not just with the women's Grundsau Lodge but with church suppers as well. Many local churches that years ago featured sauerkraut dinners or pork and oyster suppers have now turned to pizza, hamburgers, and ice cream. Some of the other Dutch speakers who were present when I interviewed Mrs. Kern thought this was a sign of declining interest in Pennsylvania Dutch cooking, that the cuisine was dying out. But is it? Just because a familiar pattern changes, this does not necessarily mean that it is also heading toward a dead end.

Perhaps what we are witnessing is fallout from a major shift taking place within the culture itself. While churches and Grundsau Lodges represented a focus for social interaction in the past, declining membership, a more culturally diversified community, and the fact that local organizations are no longer the social anchors they once were are factors working together to redefine the cuisine. Just as many family-style restaurants and with them a type of large-scale commercialized Pennsylvania Dutch cookery have passed from the scene, the rather solid, plain home cooking that provided the blue-collar Dutch with nostalgic touchstones from the past is also disappearing.

Just as the younger generation who never knew or heard a word of spoken Dutch is now embracing dialect classes in impressive numbers, so too will the classic cuisine of the *Hasenpfeffer* Dutch fascinate an upcoming generation of cooks. They will see it through different eyes uncolored by the stigmas of the past. In short, the regional cookery in all its forms will undergo reinvention as an expression of a new form of social identity. This is not a prediction: this shift has been under way for many years, launched by the Society of Pennsylvania German Gastronomes in 1926 but held hostage during most of the intervening years by the mythic Amish table.

CHAPTER 10

The Amish Table Goes Dutch

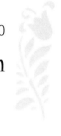

THERE are several Amish tables. One represents the sum total of what real Amish families eat on any given day of the week. Aside from such traditional foods as scrapple and sauerkraut, it is here that we find plenty of Bisquick, Crisco, instant pistachio pudding, Jell-O, Dream Whip, Velveeta, and dishes such as Rice Krispies pie, Chickenetti, Yumzetta, and more pizzas than one can count. Amish kids would eat pizza every day if their mothers would let them; pizza is often one of the culinary fixtures of the biweekly social gatherings of each Amish congregation. Deacon Beiler's wife explained it this way: "We have about 40 families in our district, so that makes about 80 to 90 pizzas. We send out for them because we can't cook that many in the ovens we use; sometimes five delivery trucks arrive all at once. There's no waste. Our people take home the leftovers and we feed the crusts to the horses." She paused a moment and then added, "Yes, we do like our pizza!"

Another Amish table consists of the sort of food the Old Order Amish prepare for weddings: the invariable *Roascht* and its side dishes of stewed celery, carrots cooked in brown sugar dressing, Spanish cream (an old-time dessert), wedding tapioca, red velvet cake, and chocolate mayonnaise cake, to mention just a few. Most of the dishes prepared for weddings represent extra work, but since there are many couples involved in assembling the dinners, there is a great deal of culinary variation from one event to the next; it is

FIGURE 22. The Amish table as interpreted by Weaver's Lebanon Bologna, a sausage and meat company in Lebanon, Pa. The Amishman is shown slicing the company's product. Advertising pamphlet, ca. 1955. Roughwood Collection, Devon, Pa

here that new or novel dishes are introduced. Pickles and preserves abound because they are easy to transport in buggies.

Then there is the other Amish table, the ersatz menu that evolved into the symbolic Pennsylvania Dutch meal and that has been replicated in one form or another in restaurants catering to the tourist industry since the 1930s. The way this menu took final shape is the story now before us. It is a tangle of opposing philosophies, subject to the shadowy workings of international politics, no small amount of business pragmatism, and a bending of the Amish mystique to conform to fixed notions about Pennsylvania Dutch culture as it was interpreted by a few influential individuals.

In 1942 the historian Ralph Wood published one of the best surveys of Pennsylvania Dutch culture yet assembled. In his preface Wood raised some issues that I think deserve repeating here:

> It may be a good thing to point out to the naïve, that the Pennsylvania Germans, a staunch old American stock, have less connection with modern Germany than New England has with England. And anyway, a group like the Pennsylvania Germans, who in the nineteenth century were anything but in complete accord with the growing power of the state over the individual and the community, would hardly be in sympathy with any system where the state is in control of all things. If America should ever go Fascist or Communist, the stubborn Pennsylvania Germans would be the last to fall in line.[1]

This in a nutshell is the answer to the question of why the Amish became such a ready symbol of Pennsylvania Dutch culture during the 1930s. Looming over the horizon, far removed from the local issues that I will discuss shortly, was Nazi Germany, and the perverse influence of that new cultural phenomenon shaped what happened in Pennsylvania. Without a doubt, Ralph Wood's book was published to counter any lingering ideas in public discourse that the Pennsylvania Dutch might be accessories to Hitler's grand designs—and this brings us back to the Amish.

Every discussion of the Amish must begin with one important qualification: the Amish are not a homogeneous group. Several different yet closely affiliated sects call themselves Amish; some, such as the Beachy Amish, drive automobiles; some do not. The variations are many due to theological and lifestyle disputes and divisions even within any given congregation. Furthermore, while tourists mesmerized by the Amish way of life may lump all Amish groups together regardless of their outward differences, the locals who live among them do not see them in a special light. Set aside the dress code and the buggies, and the Amish are just like other American families struggling with the challenges of raising children, paying bills and taxes, and dealing with the basic realities of life. Where the Amish differ is in their appreciation of a cohesive local community: they take care of one another. In addition, while they openly resist any system in which the state is in control of all things (to requote Ralph Wood), they have submitted to an existence in which their church is in control of all things. But these theological issues are not really central to how the Amish are portrayed in food tourism.

For better or for worse, the Old Order Amish, one of the most conservative of the many Amish sects in terms of dress code and lifestyle, have been exploited by the forces of tourism through no choice of their own. On the other hand, they have also deftly turned this to their advantage by branding their products as Amish; thus the tourist is also being exploited via a strategy of supply and demand. Just the same, the visitor's attempt to experience a taste of Amish culture is generally vicarious, more often than not an experience processed for them through a third party, be it a souvenir shop, a video presentation, or a Dutch diner.

The murky distinctions between reality in the flesh and the "fakelore," to use a term coined many years ago by the American folklorist Richard M. Dorson, were not carried into the Dutch Country by the tourists as many writers contend; rather they were sent out from the Dutch Country as the intentional inventions of entrepreneurs marketing Pennsylvania Dutch culture and by local journalists such as Ann Hark who created a livelihood by packaging the idea of the

Pennsylvania Dutch in wrappings of fictional lore. The blue gate, the hex sign as a protective device against witchcraft, the seven sweets and seven sours, Amish friendship bread, the four-square garden, the spirit window—the list is long and totally divorced from well-documented indigenous material such as Mountain Mary, the hoop snake, the *Elbedritsch* (a mythical bird), the *bucklich Mennli* (an elf who plagues households with pranks), the folk saint Genevieve, or even Groundhog Day, although the latter has morphed into something much more mainstream and pop culture than the local folk observance it once was.

The Emergence of the Amish Theme

Early inklings about interest in the Amish surfaced in nineteenth-century writings such as those of Phebe Earle Gibbons, but in that period the Amish were not considered as picturesque as the Dunkards, otherwise known today as the Church of the Brethren. The American illustrator Howard Pyle (1853–1911), founder of the Brandywine School of painting, was particularly taken with the Dunkards who still lived at Ephrata Cloister during his lifetime. He published a beautifully illustrated article on this sect in *Harper's New Monthly* magazine in October 1889 under the title "Peculiar People." In it he described life at Ephrata, a visit to a Brethren church service, and his fascination with the primitive material objects housed at the Cloister.

This article is perhaps one of the clearest evocations of nostalgia for an age when the Cloister served as a hospital during the Revolution; Pyle created imaginary scenes of wounded soldiers, interior views of the Cloister with Dunkards dressed in their ancient habits, a world delineated in the soft colors of fragile innocence. Yet in a backhanded way his narrative was also patriotic by linking the sect with the Revolution and its role in it: a pacifist sanctuary from the terrors of war. These are the same basic themes that later came into play when the Amish emerged as ready symbols of Pennsylvania Dutch culture.

On the other hand, late nineteenth-century interest in the Dunkards did not exist in a vacuum; fascination with Pennsylvania's coal miners also piqued the curiosity of tourists, especially in connection with the railroad tourism that developed around the mountain resorts of central and eastern Pennsylvania—Mauch Chunk among them. If we look at other areas of the country, the poor mountain people of Appalachia, the fishermen of the New England coast, and the cowboys of the High Plains were all being discovered about the same time. The common thread was a picturesque lifestyle and a disappearing, preindustrial source of livelihood. This theme of rediscovering agricultural roots is well explained in Amish terms by David Walbert in his *Garden Spot: Lancaster County, the Old Order Amish, and the Selling of Rural America* (2002).

Popular, mass-market food literature of the 1880s and 1890s was remarkably silent on Pennsylvania Dutch cooking, whether Amish, Dunkard, or otherwise, with one exception: the Moravians. The communitarian lifestyle of the Moravians was largely history by the later nineteenth century, and yet interest in their old buildings and the persistence of a number of single members paralleled interest in the Dunkards at Ephrata Cloister. Julia Davis Chandler's "Moravian Domestic Life," published in the *Boston Cooking-School* magazine in 1906, recounted her visit to an old Moravian sisters' house at Bethlehem, Pennsylvania. Like Pyle at Ephrata, she discovered quaint old ladies, historic connections with the Revolution, and more important for her readers, recipes from authentic sources. Both authors were looking for a new sort of authenticity, something indigenous derived from the land.

In glances through Philadelphia's *Table Talk* magazine, the *Boston Cooking-School* magazine, and similar journals with a national circulation, the term "Moravian" emerged time and again as a catchall label for anything vaguely Pennsylvania Dutch. The list of recipes from this period that are called Moravian is long, and it is under that rubric that one must look for foods associated with Pennsylvania Dutch culture. In fact the term filtered down from food journalism and even appeared in local cookbooks claiming the distinction of authenticity.

A case in point would be Emma Alder Giger's *Colonial Receipt Book,* published in Philadelphia in 1907 as a fund-raiser for the hospital of the University of Pennsylvania. It included a number of Moravian recipes with the connotation that "Moravian," at least in this case, implied old-family or blue-blood origins—the general tenor of the cookbook itself, which was assembled by the wives of leading university physicians. Granted, this type of culinary literature was a product of an era when the bald nationalism exhibited at the Jamestown Exposition in 1907 and again during the Henry Hudson Tercentennial in 1909 focused American attention on colonial roots and by extension on the first families who were part of that story. Yet the general appeal of this cookbook, like several others issued in Pennsylvania at that time, was its evocation of a rich regional culinary heritage, a contrast to the reformist cookbooks that had dominated the market since the 1890s.

Reformist cookery spearheaded in Pennsylvania by Sarah Tyson Rorer and her Philadelphia cooking school was a middle-class movement that took little interest in anything Pennsylvania Dutch beyond what could be reinvented as "delicate dishes" and thus so transformed from its land-based identity as to be unrecognizable. Rorer was of Pennsylvania Dutch heritage, which may have presented a problem for her given the steady flow of "dumb Dutch" literature then appearing in books and magazines—not to mention that she considered herself scientific and therefore at philosophical odds with traditional fare in general. When book commissions demanded that she turn her pen to history, as she did in her *Colonial Recipes* in 1894, traditional dishes were passed through the filter of Colonial Revival, nothing farmish at all, only the sorts of foods that would have been eaten by costumed people in powdered wigs.

Yet in an odd twist of history, it was the Colonial Revival movement that eventually led to the rehabilitation of Pennsylvania Dutch culture and ultimately the discovery of the Amish. The massive buildings erected by the Moravians at Bethlehem and Lititz and by the

Dunkards at Ephrata and Snow Hill were seen in a new light. By the 1920s wealthy collectors of Americana moved beyond the popular colonial re-creations that had typified earlier taste and wholeheartedly embraced a new type of authenticity that included Pennsylvania Dutch material culture, especially the decorative arts. Francis Henry DuPont was one of the leaders, but so were Titus Geesey, whose collection is now at the Philadelphia Museum of Art, and most surprising perhaps, Dr. Albert C. Barnes, who displayed Pennsylvania Dutch folk art as a side-by-side counterpoint to his world-famous collection of impressionist paintings. Edith Thomas's *Mary at the Farm* was written with this new perspective in mind; she even illustrated it with pictures of old culinary relics. By that time automobile tourism was clearly changing the way people viewed the countryside and the Pennsylvania Dutch in general, and it was no coincidence that Thomas's cookbook was reissued in 1926 for the United States Sesquicentennial.

The Beginnings of Amish Tourism in Lancaster County

In 1913 Isaac Steinfeldt, owner of a tobacco shop and newsstand in Lancaster, Pennsylvania, began publishing a series of Amish postcards that became standard fare for all the tourist shops in the area. A lack of Amish willing to pose for such pictures resulted in the recycling (and retouching) of the same images over and over. Most of the popular myths connected with the Amish, such as blue gates as signs of marriageable daughters living within and hex signs on barns to frighten away witches, can be traced to the Steinfeldt publications or to tracts sold in his shops. While Steinfeldt and his daughter Berenice did not invent the seven sweets and seven sours, they presented them as Amish customs, and these foods have been associated with the mythic Amish table ever since.

David Weaver-Zercher has traced the evolution of the Amish tourism industry in Lancaster County, and his book *The Amish in the American Imagination* is probably one of the most meticulous analyses to date. However, like Walbert's book, Weaver-Zercher's was written from the inside looking out, a Lancaster County perspective that placed emphasis on local events rather than holding up the Amish story against larger changes then occurring in the United States. Furthermore he did not follow the theme of food tourism or its role in this process, which in some ways was far more basic and pervasive than the more visible forms of tourism promoted by the Steinfeldts and other Lancaster entrepreneurs.

While Weaver-Zercher fingered the 1937 Amish schools controversy (the refusal of certain Old Order Amish families to allow their children to be bused to public schools) as the tipping point in directing national attention toward the Amish, many other forces were at work, not just this one localized dustup. While the 1937 school controversy was everywhere in the national media and may have served as the ulterior reason for the publication that same year of Berenice Steinfeldt's brochure *The Amish of Lancaster County, Pennsylvania,* an Amish image also appeared in 1936 on the cover and as decorative elements in the *Pennsylvania Dutch Cook Book of Fine Old Recipes* republished by the Culinary Arts Press of Reading (the first edition by J. Levan appeared in 1934). That artwork was not inspired by the Steinfeldts. Just the same, Steinfeldt images were adapted as vignettes on the menus of the German Village restaurant in Lancaster as early as 1935. Those first tentative menu ornaments, the same two Amishmen depicted on a 1920s Steinfeldt postcard and reissued on the cover of the 1937 Steinfeldt brochure, evolved into full-blown menu covers by 1937, the first evidence we have of a total shift to Amish imagery for a restaurant promotion of Pennsylvania Dutch foods. This was in some ways an odd shift because up to that point the German Village had promoted itself as a Bavarian rathskeller and late-night party spot. Thus its German character slowly transmogrified.

The 1937 Amish school controversy does not explain why the restaurant's name was abruptly changed to the Village in 1939 or why other images were also competing as icons of Pennsylvania Dutch culture. Furthermore, Weaver-Zercher did not realize that in 1933 images of Amish had already been equated with Pennsylvania Dutch

FIGURE 23. The Apfel & Wenrich die-cut cookbook in the shape of an Amish girl. Lancaster, Pa., 1933. Roughwood Collection, Devon, Pa

in the form of a die-cut cookbook by Mrs. T. Roberts Apfel and Mrs. Calvin N. Wenrich called *Old Pennsylvania Recipes*. It was published in the shape of an Amish girl standing at a gate; however, there is no direct mention of the Amish in the text. The 1939 name change and the 1933 cookbook (and the establishment of the first Ground-hog Lodge that same year) are evidence of something much more fundamental than the public schools issue: they are symptomatic of pervasive Pennsylvania Dutch concerns about changes then taking place in Nazi Germany, as Ralph Wood intimated in his preface to *The Pennsylvania Germans*. Hitler came to power in 1933; he invaded Poland in 1939; and these dates frame the period during which the Amish table took shape, focusing on *Schnitz-un-Gnepp*, chicken potpie, the seven sweets and seven sours, shoofly pie, fried apple fritters, and the connoisseur's anathema, deep-fried scrapple.

Paul Heine, the owner of the German Village restaurant, also operated the local bus company located next door. Heine's business model was to cater to tourists coming into the area and to provide them with scenic tours of the countryside followed by meals in his rathskeller-style restaurant. The backside of his later menus depicted a map of the county and all the scenic places to visit as well as views of the restaurant and its gift shop, where Amish memorabilia could be purchased, including the Apfel and Wenrich cookbook, Amish dolls, cast-iron Amish bookends, and other Amish-themed souvenirs. The cookbook included a number of tourist standbys, such as apple butter, chicken corn soup, shoofly pie, *Fastnachts* (Shrove Tuesday fat cakes), a rich array of cookies, Moravian mints—the same recipe featured by Julia Davis Chandler in her 1906 article on Bethlehem Moravians—and *Gnepp* (dumplings) for stewing in sauerkraut or with meat.

By contrast, the standard German Village menus included the typical American foods from this period, such as egg salad sandwiches, fried chicken, French-fried potatoes (as opposed to traditional potato fingers, recipe on page 187), and the like, with a small box set off with a few Lancaster County "specialties." These included sauerbraten with dumplings, frankfurters and sauerkraut, and *Wiener Schnitzel,* none of which is even vaguely Pennsylvania Dutch. To emphasize that point, while interviewing some Old Order Mennonites recently, one of the elderly ladies said to me that she had seen *Wiener Schnitzel* on a diner menu near Allentown and did not know what it was. She is fluent in Pennsylfaanisch but had no clue what the word *Schnitzel* meant. "Sausage with a little piece of apple," she asked? "What kind of a meal is *that*!"

The only real Pennsylvania Dutch dish on the entire German Village menu, aside from chicken-and-waffle specials, was *Schnitz-un-Gnepp*, which was

FIGURE 24. Menu cover with an Amish motif, the German Village, Lancaster, Pa., 1937. Roughwood Collection, Devon, Pa.

available on a daily basis. The blurring of distinctions between
Pennsylvania Dutch and German American rathskeller cookery
was common in Pennsylvania at this time because rathskellers with
their inevitable speakeasies were popular party spots in the 1920s
and 1930s. The food was familiar to people living in large cities
where dance clubs and nightlife carried forth in spite of Prohibition.
Given that, it should come as no surprise that the German Village
was designed to look like an Old World rathskeller, complete with
German-style chairs, half-timbered architectural details, leaded
glass windows, and lighting fixtures imitating beer steins. In spite
of its innocuous tourist facade during the day, the German Village
evolved into quite a different place at night (it was open twenty-

FIGURE 25. Interior view of the German Village showing a mix of rathskeller themes and
murals depicting scenes from local Lancaster history. Tinted postcard, ca. 1939. Roughwood Collection, Devon, Pa.

four hours): it became a notorious hot spot even though it was situated across an alley from Lancaster's police station (or as some local
wags have mused, it thrived under the nose of the law *because* of
this convenient location). Ladies of the night worked the bar well
into the wee hours, and the bus station provided an ample flow of

traveling businessmen. This was the birthing ground for the tentative beginnings of Amish food tourism.

Recognition of the Amish as an emerging symbol of Pennsylvania Dutch culture can be found in Cornelius Weygandt's 1939 *The Dutch Country*, a book published with full awareness of the problem that Hitler's Germany would present for the Pennsylvania Dutch. Weygandt explored the Amish issue under a discussion of the Amish folk art he had bought in the Lancaster bus terminal gift shop: "these non-belligerents do not strut it on parade," he wrote in reference to the Amish. The world had already seen Hitler take the Sudetenland; the *Anschluss* with Austria was complete; and intelligent people knew even then that it would not stop there.

Some critics of Weygandt's treatment of the Amish have depicted him as a maudlin old man fretful that the Amish would eventually lose their plainness and go the way of the world. Wishful thinking; he was more fretful about the growing threat to Pennsylvania Dutch and traditional American culture in general, not the loss of Amish picturesqueness. The Amish were in any case a peripheral part of the larger Pennsylvania Dutch community; they had been changing by degrees ever since they were founded in the 1600s and continue to this day to change in piecemeal fashion. What Weygandt realized at the time, doubtless with a certain degree of Pandora's horror and probably as the first scholar to admit it, was that the Amish were *preferable* as an image of the Pennsylvania Dutch at that moment in history because they were not Germans; they were the extreme opposite of goose-stepping Nazis. Specific references in *The Dutch Country* have placed him squarely on the premises of the German Village restaurant; thus he saw firsthand what was happening to Pennsylvania Dutch culture and its newfound Amish iconography, and in hindsight, the comically odd setting where it all came together.

This new development placed the term "Pennsylvania German" on precarious ground and gave strength to the faction who all along had preferred the term "Pennsylvania Dutch." This shift to the use of "Dutch" was picked up in culinary literature, the most influential spokesman being J. George Frederick (1882–1964), a New York advertising mogul who had grown up in Reading, Pennsylvania. His *The Pennsylvania Dutch and Their Cookery*, published in 1935, became the first nationally marketed Pennsylvania Dutch cookbook. Frederick's book received considerable attention in the press because of his Madison Avenue connections and his leadership role in New York's elite Gourmet Society and also because this was more than a simple cookbook. Frederick included chapters on the decorative arts, by then well known in national museum collections; on the Revolutionary War record of the Pennsylvania Dutch; and perhaps most important, material on Pennsylvania Dutch character and accomplishments. His book was an unabashed apologetic that attempted to place the Pennsylvania Dutch firmly within the American tradition and to divorce them completely from what was then transpiring in Germany. Frederick was largely successful in accomplishing his goals, and he helped make the term "Pennsylvania Dutch" more fashionable, perhaps even preferable. Yet he made no correlation between the terms "Pennsylvania Dutch" and "Amish." That conflation had emerged in fits and starts somewhat earlier in the century but did not come together as a popular notion until the pen of the Pennsylvania journalist Ann Hark committed it to print.

Ann Hark and the Amish Table

Hark set the stage for what followed in her 1938 best-selling collection of essays, *Hex Marks the Spot*. Written as fictionalized first-person narratives, each set piece took up an aspect of Pennsylvania Dutch culture. Hark did in fact travel around the countryside and observe local customs, but her take on the Pennsylvania Dutch was colored by her own upbringing as a Moravian, and thus skewed by a condescending attitude toward the Pennsylvania Dutch in general. The Moravians have always considered the other Dutch as cultural inferiors; they do not see their own group as a product of American soil but rather as an enlightened continuation of the high Pietistic culture of eighteenth-century Germany. Near the end of *Hex Marks the Spot,* Hark included a chapter called "Dinner at Smoker's," which was one of the most revealing and lasting testimonies to her fictionalization of the Amish—in fact, to her mastery at creating Pennsylvania Dutch stereotypes.

Following the literary artifice of *Mary at the Farm* (a visit to the country), Hark created an unlikely plot whereby she too traveled into the Dutch Country and finally found acceptance by an Amish family—false, but as a result of this fictional epiphany, she was invited to supper. By being accepted into this imaginary household, she established herself as an authorized observer, an "authentic source." Let us not forget that Hark arrived at this picturesque meal in rural Lancaster County accompanied by a chauffeur with whom she carried on a long, glib discourse about the Amish before arriving. This was part of the setup of the plot so that Hark could inform the reader about the Amish, or what she thought she knew about the Amish. It may not be coincidental that *Hex Marks the Spot* was also dedicated to this unnamed chauffeur, whose shadowy presence remains intriguing for what was suggested but not said. The known facts about him are these: in real life he was her secret lover, and he committed suicide, all of which adds a dark, murky veneer to Hark's narrative and perhaps also something telling about her manipulative personality.

No Pennsylvania Dutch family, plain sect or otherwise, would overlook the opportunity to comment out of earshot about her relationship with a good-looking *Dudelbu* (boy toy/male companion), because no matter how fancy the car or how strenuously the chauffeur exhibited the rules of servant decorum, to the Dutch mind of the 1930s, single women gallivanting about the countryside with unmarried men were fair targets for the worst sort of gossip, and if the chauffeur were married, even more so. Hark's artifice would have invited a plausible cover had she arrived with another female in tow. This little subplot may not seem so startling today because mores have changed, but when the book came out, it must have raised some eyebrows, although none of the reviewers picked up on this. Then again, the reviewers lived in New York or Boston or somewhere else far removed from the Dutch Country where dalliances with chauffeurs were hardly breaking news.

It is not my intention here to rake over Ann Hark's tumultuous personal life, which is probably worthy of in-depth biography—better than what has been written about her to date—yet she exerted an enormous influence on popular literature, in part because she was articulate and well-connected in the world of mass-market journalism. She found a literary niche in the Pennsylvania Dutch cultural revival of the 1930s and traveled in the same circles as Joseph Hergesheimer, a writer of historical novels, and R. Brognard Okie, a Colonial Revival architect who incorporated Pennsylvania Dutch motifs in his decorative vocabulary. Okie not only re-created Hergesheimer's house to better fit the oral history surrounding its imaginary colonial origins (Hergesheimer wrote *From an Old House*, describing this transformation); he also used architectural details of the Millbach Room at the Philadelphia Museum of Art to define the staid character of many Philadelphia Main Line colonial-style mansions. Hark, Hergesheimer, and Okie all shared a common passion for transforming vague oral traditions into reality: Hark accomplished it through essay form; Hergesheimer did it through fiction; Okie gave it meaning in architecture, even to the extent of inserting real date stones from demolished buildings to confirm the historical credentials of his retro renovations.

Hark could reinvent cultural history with similar fictions because she was part of this same milieu of people who used history as ornamental wallpaper or stage sets for social-register entertainments. Okie's fly painted on a wavy pane of artificially aged purple glass inserted in the window of a colonial renovation was meant to titillate the eye and remind us that history is artifice; believe whatever details you like. Thus throughout her visit to the Amish Smokers, Ann Hark indulged in similar artifices, punctuating her observations with sentences such as "yet clinging still to customs of two hundred years ago"[2] or "there wasn't one more picturesque in dress and customs than the Amish!"[3] She even arrived at the remarkable conclusion that they still dressed and lived in the same manner as

FIGURE 26. The Millbach Room at the Philadelphia Museum of Art. Real Photo postcard, 1928. Roughwood Collection, Devon, Pa.

when they resided as Swiss refugees in Alsace during the 1600s, in spite of the well-known fact that Amish bonnets are borrowed from the Pennsylvania Quakers, to mention but one glaring anachronism. Just the same, this type of embroidered nostalgia was precisely what the Germanophiles thought about the Pennsylvania Dutch in general: a culture preserved like living "fossils" of Old Europe. This appealed to Moravian sensibilities, since Old Europe was their cultural anchor.

Hark took her enthusiasm for living fossils one step further with her 1943 children's book, *The Story of the Pennsylvania Dutch*. This handsomely illustrated full-color history used figures of the Amish throughout as though they were the only authentic representations of the Pennsylvania Dutch people. Hark created this same linkage in her nationally circulated magazine articles, public lectures, and newspaper essays. Her article "Who Are the Pennsylvania Dutch?" in the June 1941 issue of *House & Garden* told her readers that the answer was, the Amish. The exposure this article received was enormous and helped to solidify the Pennsylvania Dutch–Amish equation.

FIGURE 27. The Amish table becomes the Pennsylvania Dutch table in Ann Hark's children's book *The Story of the Pennsylvania Dutch* (New York: Harper & Brothers, 1943). The room is based on the Millbach Room at the Philadelphia Museum of Art. Roughwood Collection, Devon, Pa.

From the standpoint of food tourism, one image from Hark's children's book has had a long-lasting effect: a dinner scene showing an Amish family seated at a table in what was clearly a stylized version of the Millbach Room at the Philadelphia Museum of Art. The falsification of historical fact in this one picture alone is fairly representative of what transpired in the rest of the book. First, the Millbach house was a rustic German-style baroque residence in Lebanon County. It belonged to a *Bach Adel*, a wealthy miller; an Amish family never lived there, and the Amish never lived in such highly ornamented houses in any case. Even today their houses are stripped to bare essentials. Second, the *Kich*, or kitchen, which is what the Millbach Room was before its removal to the museum in the 1920s, was the area of the Pennsylvania Dutch house deemed the most public, akin to a hall so that cross ventilation would carry out smoke and keep the room cool during hot weather. People did not eat in the *Kich* unless they were poor and this was the only room in the house. In spite of this, Hark's artist depicted her Amish family eating in the Millbach *Kich*. The anachronistic image of an Amish cook using an open hearth was perpetuated in myriads of ways in the literature of food tourism.

Furthermore none of the elaborate decorative arts and furniture displayed in the museum's reinterpretation of the Millbach kitchen was crafted by the Amish (no one even knows what eighteenth-century Amish furniture was like), nor did little Amish girls wear bright crimson red dresses like the one in the foreground of the picture. Most important, the spread of food on the table was an idealized depiction of a table d'hôte or "family style" method of food service employed in restaurants such as Haag's Hotel in Shartlesville, Pennsylvania, by then a well-known eating destination. The fact that Hark transposed this onto home cookery, complete with a loaf of sliced *Faektribrod* ("factory bread"), makes the scene all the more artificial because this is supposed to represent a meal for one family, not for twenty or thirty tourists who might be arriving in a bus.

Yet the groaning table overloaded with food was just another Pennsylvania Dutch stereotype disseminated by writers such as Ann Hark and then embraced by the tourist industry as a living reality—if only in restaurant settings. Furthermore the all-you-can-eat family-style restaurants that proliferated throughout the area relied heavily on two predetermined expectations of their customers: that the food be cheap and that it be bland because a large portion of the clientele was elderly—as much of the clientele still is to this day. There is an unkind word in Pennsylfaanisch for this type of food with its abundant reliance on poultry seasoning, garlic salt, and parsley flakes as the sole sources of flavor. Establishments such as the Fuddergang Restaurant (now closed) near Ephrata were at least honest to their name. A *Fuddergang* is the passageway along the stalls in a traditional Pennsylvania barn; it was used to shovel fodder to the livestock, hardly flattering to either the food or the customer.

John Fisher, who grew up Old Order Amish, offered some insightful comments on the Amish view of the Amish table as presented in tourist restaurants. His parents, Amos and Naomi Fisher, along with the whole family, were invited by the owners of two Intercourse, Pennsylvania, "Amish" restaurants (Plain and Fancy and Good 'n Plenty) to eat there and to critique the cooking. This attempt to give tourist fare a stamp of authenticity by vetting it with Old Order Amish who rarely ate in such places backfired. No Amish family would make critical remarks about a free meal. More to the point, when pressed for their personal reactions, John said that eating in these restaurants made his parents feel like tourists: "We were strangers in our own homeland."[4]

In 2007 I interviewed Crystal Koch, until recently chef-owner of the Willows Restaurant in East Texas, Pennsylvania, and well known for her Pennsylvania Dutch cuisine—honest home cooking at its best. Crystal objected to the style of cookery in the big family restaurants because of the massive waste: platters of food once placed on the table cannot be served to someone else, even if the food goes untouched. Just how much control do you have over quality and flavor when you must multiply every important ingredient by five hundred or a thousand, she asked? Fresh food suffers; many basics start coming out of plastic tubs and cans. Customers in her restaurant were often amazed by her black raspberry pies: the berries were picked in her garden the day they were baked. Crystal's food exuded real *Boddegeschmack* (taste of place). Cooks do not create that kind of authenticity. They evolve out of it.

In 1950 a similar complaint about mediocre all-you-can-eat cookery at places such as the Shartlesville Hotel in Berks County,

Trainer's in Quakertown, and other family-style restaurants of that genre surfaced in *The Pennsylvania Dutch,* a collection of essays by Frederick Klees:

> In recent years a few country hotels north of Philadelphia have loaded their tables with as much food as they can carry. Forty or fifty dishes are set out to stupefy a public that queues up for the privilege of gorging itself. There is no style, only food, and often indifferently cooked. The old country hotel set a more modest table, but sometimes the cooking was superlative. Earlier in this century the Black Horse Tavern at Reinholds Station served meals that were good plain country cooking yet an epicure's delight. Today there is no restaurant or hotel anywhere in the Dutch Country with cooking to match that of the Black Horse Tavern of the past. By and large Pennsylvania Dutch restaurants are almost as poor as those elsewhere in the United States. Many restaurants serve local dishes, but the cooking is seldom more than fair. There is better food served at church suppers than in hotels and restaurants.[5]

Clara Bowman's legendary chicken-and-waffle dinners at the Black Horse Hotel left a lasting impression on Klees, but he also could have mentioned the excellent food prepared by the Carversville Christian Church in Carversville, Bucks County, which has served its annual pork-and-oyster suppers since 1871, the oldest continuous church suppers in the country. Even more important, the church prepares most of its food from local farm produce, and the rich homey flavor of the cooking draws crowds from as far away as New York City. Unfortunately the Carversville church is an exception, and alas Frederick Klee's lament is as valid today as it was in 1950, except that in Lancaster County under the guise of Amish or Mennonite the same indifferent cooking has taken on new life.

Perhaps an ominous lesson in tourist demographics lies hidden in the fate of the Shartlesville Hotel, now closed; Walp's, formerly an

Allentown institution and now the site of a Wawa fast-foods store; and Trainer's, now a shopping mall. As my grandmother's generation passed away—the folks who just wanted a Sunday after-church trip to the country and a five-dollar dinner—younger people have sought out different authenticities, especially after sensibilities about food and dining out evolved to a more sophisticated level during the 1970s and 1980s. The new authenticity is farm-fresh rustic "peasant" cooking, and that is where Pennsylvania Dutch cuisine has an extremely bright future.

My own fieldwork has confirmed time and again that traditionally most Pennsylvania Dutch ate very frugal one-pot meals. Prior to the 1940s most meals centered on homemade bread (or bread from a local Dutch bakery), which served as the sop for everything else eaten with the food. It was not rare for rural families to serve themselves fondue-style out of a large common bowl. Several Dutch informants have described their "need" for gravy bread (*Dunkesbrod*) to clean up the leftovers after a wedding or some other special-occasion dinner. This inner desire to feast on the forbidden dips into one of those old Pennsylvania Dutch customs by which food belongs to the guest; but when the guest leaves, the remnants revert to the hosting family, which then makes a ritual meal that many informants have confided was more fun than the actual dinner that preceded. With shoes kicked off and shirts unbuttoned, not to mention a few half-empty wine bottles to kill, this meal might last well into the night.

Chunks of bread were used as sponges to wipe clean leftover serving dishes from a wedding feast and then eaten by the cleanup crew or shared with little children who swarmed into the kitchen for free tidbits. In other cases bowls of leftovers were passed around the table for each person to sample; generally this was practiced among friends and close family after the guests had departed. Some of these one-pot dishes still survive in living memory under the name *Schlappichdunkes* ("slop pot" gravy), with each family member impaling a piece of bread on a fork and then dipping this into the common bowl of stew, pureed vegetables, or anything that might double as a dip. Nonetheless, one-pot meals aside, Ann Hark's overabundant table

FIGURE 28. The Dutch Haven restaurant and gift shop in Ronks, Pa. Color postcard, ca. 1955. Roughwood Collection, Devon, Pa.

became the iconic image of Pennsylvania Dutch cookery. It has been replicated over and over in food advertising to this day, even to the extent that most people have forgotten what old-style Pennsylvania Dutch bread was like and how its crusty fresh-from-the-oven flavor was one of the high points of Pennsylvania Dutch cuisine and the absolute cornerstone to any good meal, be it dinner for company or the cleanup party that followed.

Mainstreaming the Amish Table

Dienner's (with bus parking in the back) is only a stone's throw from the Dutch Haven, a gaudy yellow windmill along Route 30 in Ronks, Pennsylvania, specializing in "Amish Stuff." This windmill is considered by non-Lancastrians to be the true crown jewel of Lancaster County Amish kitsch: it is one of those must-see experiences; otherwise who would believe it? Modeled after a better-known 1930s windmill diner in Clearfield County, the Ronks knockoff is not as architecturally ambitious but is brilliantly effective in grabbing attention. Its original builder, the late Roy Weaver, imagined that his Mennonite ancestors came from Rotterdam instead of Zurich; thus the oddly out-of-context Holland Dutch motif. He was no practicing Mennonite, and after several brushes with the law, he eventually found Jesus and joined an evangelical church.

The garish Dutchification of the Haven with decorations by the Reading cartoonist Roy Gensler and its "world famous" shoofly pies are counterbalanced by Dienner's Country Restaurant next door, with its bare-bones decor and wall plaques bearing provocative religious messages in much the same spirit as mosques hung with large blown-up quotes from the Quran. In its own way Dienner's offers a philosophical antidote to "Amish Stuff."

Under the triune hat of ethnographer, anthropologist, and food critic I sought out Dienner's Beachy Amish cuisine and its Christian ambiance because it was important to me to establish a point of reference regarding the other culinary experiences available in the Dutch Country. After all, this was yet another one of the Amish tables, and it might speak volumes about the way this table is changing today. I went there with a cousin, and we took copious notes, which did not seem to sit well with our Amish waitress. There was not much on the menu (which is available online) that could not be found elsewhere in the United States: no special twists to the cooking; nothing exceptional beyond low prices and an Amish waitstaff. This must be its saving grace among travelers with low culinary expectations because they tend to rate the place highly. Just the same, for nonlocals who venture in unforewarned, the culture shock can be unnerving because the mix of missionary outreach and unimaginative cooking leaves a lasting impression on the palate. The casserole of canned string beans baked in canned mushroom soup topped with broken potato chips was something I would have expected in an elementary school cafeteria. It was difficult to find items on the menu that were both healthful and appealing.

Yet Dienner's is important because it represents a new shift in the way things Amish are being handled by Lancaster tourism, a shift that can be seen in all of the family-style restaurants in the Amish belt: a gradual disappearance of foods that might be considered iconic of the Amish table. The emphasis is now on the marketing of "the Amish experience"; thus food is secondary to a message promoting a simple Christian way of life. There is now a long list of Amish and Mennonite cookbooks constructed around this core doctrine, although it is not clear who buys these books, since the recipes read like material out of 1950s *Good Housekeeping* or some similar mainstream publication of that era. What makes them special? How do Dienner's customers find moral atonement in cherry Jell-O or potato-chip casseroles?

It is possible to observe occasional Old Order Amish families eating at Dienner's, perhaps because some of the waitstaff are relatives or belong to the same congregation. Conversations often lapse into Pennsylvania Dutch in order to cut out eavesdroppers because that way they can discuss some of the strangers in the dining room—as my cousin and I witnessed firsthand, never revealing that I knew exactly what they were saying. If mixing cookery with a dash of missionary zeal does not engender your idea of peaceful digestion, salvation can be attained in other ways, because Miller's Smorgasbord is right down the road. It serves local wine and plenty of it and offers a respectable menu based on locally grown ingredients. Just the same, by putting Jesus in the orange juice, Dienner's represents Amish food tourism taken to a new level of intensity. How this has evolved into the strange culinary mutation we know today goes back to the political milieu of the late 1930s and, of course, to the war-time propaganda churned out by Ann Hark and other journalists of that ilk.

Ann Hark's 1941 article on the Amish in *House & Garden* was not the only nationally circulated story: it would seem there were hundreds. David Weaver-Zercher's premise that the 1937 Amish school controversy lay at the heart of the rise of Amish tourism is in fact overshadowed by a much larger and pressing issue that is often brought out in the articles: American isolationism. That political stance set against the rise of Hitler in Europe and the rumblings from Japan and coupled with the peaceful Amish became a primary theme once Hitler invaded Poland. Isolationism came in many shades, but perhaps the most unambiguous was Guy McConnell's "The Peace People of Pennsylvania," which appeared in the June 1940 issue of *Family Circle*. McConnell made the point that the Amish had not gone to war for over 250 years, "so perhaps the world might do worse than to emulate them."[6] This was a definite appeal to isolationist sentiments, and as a result of articles such as this, the Amish became a mantra for staying out of the war in Europe right up to the attack on Pearl Harbor.

In the July 1941 issue of *National Geographic* magazine, Elmer C. Stauffer published "In the Pennsylvania Dutch Country," a long and richly illustrated article about the Pennsylvania Dutch, focusing largely on Lancaster County. His coda was "people from another world" and the theme of William Penn's Peaceable Kingdom, an agricultural paradise planted in the wilderness of North America and now representative of the best of Main Street American values. His photo-essay captured the lives of hardworking farmers, colorful hometown scenes, and an abundance of Amish. Stauffer was a Chicago expatriate Dutchman from York County whose nostalgia for his Pennsylvania homeland was relieved only by immersing his readers in the rich details of local color captured in what was then top-of-the-line photography. Stauffer's text consisted of material reworked from earlier sources, including elements borrowed from J. George Frederick, Cornelius Weygandt, Ann Hark, and even the Steinfeldts of Lancaster. He was obviously well read. What set his article apart as singular and haunting (given the hindsight of history) were the unspoken yet fundamental idealizations of American isolationism and a wide-eyed innocent view of rural America as the embodiment of peace and plenty.

Five months later the Japanese shattered this overly complacent American ideal by attacking Pearl Harbor. Military historians have depicted the attack as pointless since the United States already had contingency plans for war with Japan, and social historians have described how this so-called "shock" (which the government had anticipated) changed American views about the world at large. Lost in the initial turmoil of the times was the discussion about the Pennsylvania Dutch and the Amish and where they might fit into this reordering of cultural perceptions.

It was probably a good thing for the Pennsylvania Dutch that the attack on Pearl Harbor came from Japan rather than from Germany. It was the Japanese who became demons overnight, and as a result Americans of Japanese descent were herded into internment camps regardless of their political sympathies. This terrifying fate was precisely the kind of hysterical response that the Pennsylvania Dutch community had feared, having already experienced virulent anti-German sentiments during World War I and the virtual shutdown of nearly all the traditional German-language newspapers in the state—even the Pennsylvania German Society disbanded annual meetings during that troubling period. Cornelius Weygandt was exceedingly wise by prognosticating that the Amish would make a useful symbol of Pennsylvania Dutch culture given the context of those emotionally charged times. Indeed the Amish image became the culture's inadvertent salvation.

If tourism during the 1930s planted scores of long-standing misrepresentations about the Amish and the Pennsylvania Dutch, it also confirmed their essential American roots. That core idea pervaded everything written about the Pennsylvania Dutch between 1918 and 1941. During the war years (1941–1945) the image of the Pennsylvania Dutch remained positive and appropriately patriotic. Many Dutchmen returned home war heroes, as in the case of Carl Snyder, whom I interviewed before his death about his role in the Grundsau movement. And let us not forget General Dwight Eisenhower, who was of Pennsylvania Dutch ancestry and not at all afraid to don an apron to demonstrate his culinary prowess in Mamie's famous kitchen.

On the other hand, many of the real war heroes never left our shores; instead of the bulwark of peace and plenty, the Pennsylvania Dutch farmer became an agricultural hero in the popular press, the man feeding the home front while the nation was at war. Thus even during the 1940s when the political situation was looking fairly bleak, the Amish and the Pennsylvania Dutch in general

FIGURE 29. Cover of a 1943 Lancaster County almanac depicting the Amish farmer. Roughwood Collection, Devon, Pa.

weathered the war as positive symbols of America rolling up its sleeves and doing its bit for democracy. That is the subliminal message hidden in the picture of the Amish farmer on the 1943 almanac in Figure 29.

The year 1949 witnessed the founding of the Pennsylvania Dutch

Folklore Center at Franklin and Marshall College in Lancaster. This marked a new phase in the evolution of Pennsylvania Dutch tourism and indeed in all things connected with Pennsylvania Dutch culture. The choice of the term "Pennsylvania Dutch" was decided by the center's founders, Dr. Alfred Shoemaker (who had been a prisoner of war), Dr. J. William Frey, and Dr. Don Yoder. "Pennsylvania Dutch" was what the common man used to describe his language and who he was. The Folklore Center was all about the "folk," as slippery as that word may be even today, not about the perpetuation of labels created by self-appointed cultural elites. The term "Pennsylvania German" was out for good because every Pennsylvania Dutch soldier who returned from the war knew in his heart of hearts that he was not a German. He was Pennsylvania Dutch and as thoroughly American as shoofly pie.

FIGURE 30. The Country Kitchen at the Kutztown Folk Festival serves food free to visitors selected on a random basis. Original photo, 1965. Roughwood Collection, Devon, Pa.

CHAPTER 11

The Kutztown Folk Festival

T HE origin of the Kutztown Folk Festival is fairly straightforward, and I was fortunate to interview one of its cofounders, Dr. Don Yoder, who revealed much about the way in which Pennsylvania Dutch food was brought into that event. In a sense the festival was born out of necessity because in 1949 Professors Alfred L. Shoemaker, J. William Frey, and Don Yoder joined forces to establish the Pennsylvania Dutch Folklore Center at Franklin and Marshall College in Lancaster, Pennsylvania. In order to fulfill the educational mandate of their newly formed center, they realized that they would need a venue to promote Pennsylvania Dutch culture as well as a plan for raising money to further research. Thus in 1950 the Pennsylvania Dutch Folk Festival was born. Not only was it the first folklife festival in the United States, but it has also taken on a life of its own by surviving a bankruptcy and several managerial upheavals over the course of the past sixty years. If its positive long-term contributions can be described as spotty, its overall effect on Pennsylvania Dutch culture was earth-shifting, although for the most part those results were unintended.

The key difference between the Kutztown festival and other American folk festivals held before 1950 was that the earlier festivals were mostly stage performances of folk dance and music with little emphasis on folklife. The Kutztown festival focused on one single American regional culture, the Pennsylvania Dutch, in all of its aspects, from religious diversity to food. Furthermore the purpose of the folk festival was to bring this culture before the American public in ways that could not be explained through books or museum exhibits. This new concept emphasized living history using real people from the culture, including farmers and their wives, craftsmen, and cooking demonstrators, to illustrate their cultural origins and way of life. In this respect the Kutztown Folk Festival was visionary with no real counterparts even in Europe.

The festival was established at a time when there was a growing local and national interest in Pennsylvania Dutch culture; even the label "Pennsylvania Dutch" had been rehabilitated as a positive antidote to the old "dumb Dutch" prejudices of the past.[1] Nationally much had already been written about Pennsylvania Dutch decorative arts, and the well-known Water Gate Inn in Washington, D.C., had been showcasing an upscale form of Pennsylvania Dutch cookery throughout the 1940s; it was heavily patronized by wartime government officials. Thus the time was ripe for creating a venue where the public could come face-to-face with the Pennsylvania Dutch themselves. Furthermore the opening of the eastern portion of the Pennsylvania Turnpike in 1950 not only provided motorists with a novel driving experience (it was the first major highway of its kind in the United States); it allowed them to reach Kutztown without the inconvenience of long drives and backcountry roads. This new highway and the unusual concepts featured at the festival provided the right mix of elements to give the festival the initial financial boost it needed to succeed.

The choice of Kutztown, Pennsylvania, was Alfred L. Shoemaker's and was based on his long-term plans to create an open-air museum on the Swedish Skansen model to showcase Pennsylvania Dutch culture. Shoemaker's peasant village never materialized, but the choice of Kutztown proved fortuitous because of accessibility, available fairgrounds, and the cooperation of several local organizations with previous experience in organizing similar, although much smaller, events. The apple-butter festival organized by William Troxell at Dorney Park near Allentown and held throughout the 1930s and 1940s may be viewed as a direct antecedent of the Kutztown festival. The old hotel in Dorney Park had been one of the famous dining spots for Pennsylvania Dutch cookery in the early 1900s, so food and regional cooking were destined from the start to become important components of the Kutztown experience.

Standing behind the local festivals and the sponsorship of their activities was the Lehigh Valley Grundsau Lodge. It was one of the strongest of the lodges, and many of its members collaborated with the festival to help launch it. The lodge exhibit, with its giant effigy of a groundhog, has been a feature of the festival since the beginning. Lodge member Carl Snyder explained to me that one reason the lodge exhibit remained at the festival all these years was the opportunity to recruit new members, since this was the only direct contact the lodge had with the general public.

Alfred Shoemaker's grand design was to use the money earned from the festivals to provide cash for research among living informants and thus create an archive of first-person accounts, to collect material on historical ethnography, and then to publish the findings in various scholarly formats. This innovative idea worked to a degree. By 1958 enough money had been accumulated that the Folklore Center was incorporated as the Pennsylvania Folklife Society and began publishing books and monographs under that name.

Under this new identity, the center's newspaperlike periodical, the *Pennsylvania Dutchman,* became a quarterly journal called *Pennsylvania Folklife,* a distinguished regional publication under the editorship of Alfred Shoemaker (until 1961) and Don Yoder (1961–1978) that had no equal in the United States. No scholarly magazine has been able to pick up where *Pennsylvania Folklife* left off after its demise in the 1990s. Both the *Pennsylvania Dutchman* and *Pennsylvania Folklife* were filled with material about Pennsylvania Dutch foods and foodways, and there is now a pressing need to create a master index for the entire series.

According to Don Yoder, when the festival opened at Kutztown in July 1950, it was a modest financial success. Festival events were broadcast from the fairgrounds on local radio stations, and they were soon picked up by national media. Newspaper clippings from the 1950s only hint at the kind of excitement in the press that developed around the festival and its activities. Maynard Owen Williams, a well-known correspondent of *National Geographic* magazine, came to the festival in 1952 and published a major article about it that same year.[2] Although his piece was of high quality and gave national stature to the event, a large amount of inaccurate information about the Pennsylvania Dutch found its way into print through the pens of other, overly enthusiastic journalists. On the other hand, while the festival organizers fretted about that sort of coverage, the festival garnered so much publicity that in 1960 it was the largest in the country, attracting over one hundred thousand people during the festival week.

This huge onslaught of tourists provided a bonanza for local businesses selling foods and Pennsylvania Dutch products, and they were quick to pick up on many of the themes featured at the festival. The Amishman as a Pennsylvania Dutch symbol was already evolving into a popular icon, and as much as the festival organizers tried to keep Amish culture in perspective, the very fact that the Amish were discussed gave them the credentials of authentic symbols of the culture. Furthermore, while in hindsight it may seem to have been highly counterproductive, Alfred Shoemaker hired the Reading, Pennsylvania, cartoonist Roy Gensler to create cover illustrations for all the Folklore Center's publications. These gaudy designs, which mixed Amish with hex signs and distelfinks, went to the very heart of the meaning of "Dutchified," and even today their garish inaccuracies stand out as a monument to Shoemaker's poor judgment and managerial shortcomings.

The effect of Gensler's folksy art was almost immediate because food companies involved with the festival and hotels and restaurants throughout the region began to employ similar Amish motifs on their packaging and menus. The equation of Amish with Pennsylvania Dutch was not what the festival organizers intended; it was a grassroots response to marketing opportunities given tourist interest in all things Amish. However, it is clear that the festival became an unwitting disseminator of this type of advertising iconography,

FIGURE 31. Amish-themed paper napkins by York Craft of York, Pa., 1960s. The Amish sayings in strange English were based on the "Dutch talk" created by Helen R. Martin in her novels. Roughwood Collection, Devon, Pa.

FIGURE 32. Many of the worst clichés of Pennsylvania Dutch tourism come together on the cover of this brochure published by the Pennsylvania Dutch Folklore Center in 1956. Roughwood Collection, Devon, Pa.

and as the festival programs became more and more elaborate over time—and increasingly Dutchified under the creative imagination of Roy Gensler—the artwork provided businesses throughout the region with a new advertising vocabulary. The festival programs, especially the early ones, also set in motion another curious and unintended spin-off: the rise of a new hex-sign mythology. It started in a restaurant as the brainchild of Johnny Ott (1891–1964), the chief cook and owner of the Deitsch Eck Hotel in Lenhartsville, Pennsylvania, only a few miles northwest of Kutztown.

Hex Signs Run Amok

Ott was an outsider from the start. A Roman Catholic, he had no immediate sense of connectedness to the rural and mostly Protestant Pennsylvania Dutch, and yet he embraced their culture with the enthusiasm of a convert—and eventually took it many steps farther. Ott was a self-taught folk artist, and folk art was his first love, but the reality of his situation demanded that he cook in order to support himself because selling folk art was not a secure livelihood. Thus he bought the old Lenhartsville hotel in 1941 after learning the basics of cooking at hotels in nearby Reading. He painted the interior with Pennsylvania Dutch motifs, designed menus and postcards, and promoted a number of old regional foods that were fast disappearing, among them beer cheese soup, one of his signature dishes (recipe on page 189). Ott's colorful life story has not been assembled from the many scattered articles that featured him in the 1940s and 1950s, but Steven Stetzler, the present owner of the hotel, has created an archive of Ott materials that is a rich source of information on the man and his work.

Ott began painting hex signs on old hubcaps in a shop attached to his restaurant and selling them during the first few seasons of the Kutztown festival. Eventually the hubcap idea evolved into the flat wooden disks that became Ott's signature art form. Ott created his own type of nontraditional hex sign that was given special themes and meanings, or as he called them, "powers." Jacob Zook

FIGURE 33. Johnny Ott promoting hex signs at the Deitsch Eck Hotel in Lenhartsville, Pa. Color postcard, ca. 1960. Roughwood Collection, Devon, Pa

of the Hex Place in Paradise, Lancaster County, began mass-producing Ott's designs by silk screen and selling them throughout the region, a business partnership that lasted until Ott's death in 1964. Rather than painting the hex signs on the sides of barns, as was done with the traditional designs of the past, Ott painted them on disks that could be hung anywhere. Ott had an eye for marketing, so he created designs for every conceivable situation and culture, such as Irish hex signs with shamrocks or "Christian" designs that would appeal to customers cautious of associations with witchcraft (a false assumption often repeated in popular lore). Ott also disseminated the art of painting traditional hex signs by training a number of barn painters. Some, among them Johnny Claypoole, became well known regionally for their own distinctive and much more historically based styles.

So dismayed was Alfred Shoemaker by Ott's inventions that in 1953 he responded with a pamphlet distributed by the Folklore Center called *Hex No!* (again with a Gensler cover design). However, the seeds for Ott's newfangled hex signs had been planted, and they have become one of the most common types of hex sign seen today in the Pennsylvania countryside. Furthermore, Ott's distinctive hex signs were widely adapted as motifs on menus, napkins, place mats, tablecloths, and other souvenirs connected with food tourism, not to mention labels on commercial food products. Ott continued to

FIGURE 34. Paper coasters with Johnny Ott designs were sold in gift shops throughout the Dutch Country. Roughwood Collection, Devon, Pa.

operate the Deitsch Eck until his death, but his role as country hotel keeper was effectively superseded by that of "hexologist." A corpulent figure in an odd costume of Amish broad-brimmed hat and black swallowtail coat, he was a "must see" for anyone attending.

From Virginville to Funnel Cake Queen

Another inadvertent spin-off from the festival was the popularization of funnel cakes and the idea that they were something quintessentially Pennsylvania Dutch. Grace Merkel Henninger (now deceased) once told me that not only did she know who first brought them to the festival but also she was there herself cooking the funnel cakes as fast as the ladies could sell them for twenty-five cents apiece. In fact she had the original recipe. Emma Miller and Stella Heinly, two now-deceased members of the Virginville Grange, to which Grace belonged, came up with the plan whereby they would sell funnel cakes and turn a good profit, since the batter was easy to make and relatively inexpensive.

Emma Miller had fried funnel cakes for her own family during Christmas and New Year's, so she was able to provide a good working recipe plus the necessary expertise. Thus in the summer of 1950, during the first festival, these two ladies along with Grace Henninger, Viola Miller (Emma's daughter-in-law), and a few others worked in the back of the concession stand using deep fryers for French fries and turned out thousands of cakes over the course of a few days (Grace said she worked fast, making four funnel cakes at a time). The runaway success of this idea provided a financial windfall for the grange, and it was quickly copied so that within the course of ten years, funnel cakes became a standard feature of every event claiming a connection with the Pennsylvania Dutch. One of the great disseminators of funnel cakes was Alice Reinert of Maidencreek Township, Berks County, who helped to make them at the festival during the 1950s. In 1961 she set up a business of her own and began selling the cakes at the Reading Fair. During the 1970s she bought a funnel cake truck complete with its own kitchen and service counter and began circulating among the fairs and festivals throughout the region, thus giving the funnel cake exposure far beyond the Berks County heartland. She has received a good deal of press for her creative marketing and is now dubbed the uncontested queen of Pennsylvania Dutch funnel cakes.

This is not to imply that funnel cakes were unknown in Pennsylvania Dutch cookery before the Kutztown Folk Festival, although one would be hard-pressed to find funnel cake recipes in most regional cookbooks published before 1950 (they do appear from time to time in old manuscript cookbooks and in German-language cookbooks published in Philadelphia). For one thing, this was mostly an urban holiday food until fresh eggs became inexpensive during the

1930s and 1940s—you cannot make puffy funnel cakes with the old-style winter eggs stored in isinglass. Furthermore most of the nineteenth-century German American recipes call for a specialized funnel with three spouts. As soon as the cakes were scooped from the hot fat, they were laid over rolling pins so that they would stiffen into a curled shape. They were often served with wine sauce. This is all somewhat more elaborate than what most upcountry Dutch attempted to make at home.

Some of the earliest published Pennsylvania Dutch funnel cake recipes appeared in the 1934 *Globe-Times Cook Book of Old-Fashioned Recipes* printed in Bethlehem. This cookbook was intentionally nostalgic in its backward look at local heirloom recipes sent to the newspaper by its readers. Judging from the *Globe-Times* food columns, it is evident that funnel cakes were a traditional Christmas food in the Bethlehem area and may have spread from there to other parts of the Pennsylvania Dutch region. For certain there are no recipes in Edith Thomas's *Mary at the Farm*, which is where we would expect to find them, or in J. Levan's 1934 *Berks County Cook Book of Pennsylvania Dutch Recipes* (later issued as *Pennsylvania Dutch Cook Book of Fine Old Recipes*), which was Berks County's response to the *Globe-Times* recipe collection. But we do find them on occasion in charitable cookbooks. For this reason I have included Lizzie Weinhold's 1916 recipe on page 216. Nonetheless I am suspicious that her recipe may trace to a ladies' magazine rather than to a Weinhold ancestor: the same ingredients and proportions appear in too many disparate recipes to be coincidental.

Just the same, Elsie Singmaster, borrowing on local custom, mentioned funnel cakes in her short story "The End of the World," which appeared in her 1925 collection *Bred in the Bone*. In that story Eleazer Herr, a self-designated prophet, determined that the world was coming to an end, but an old spinster, Tilly Shindledecker, left a tempting dinner of sausages and funnel cakes at his house, which he ate and which caused him to fall asleep and therefore miss his presumed appointment with Judgment Day on the top of Shankweiler's Hill. Thus with funnel cakes and sausages, Tilly unwittingly prevented the end of the world and more directly the humiliation of the lonely old bachelor.

Several writers on Pennsylvania Dutch culture have used this passage from Singmaster to justify the Dutchness of funnel cakes, with Ann Hark going a step further by inferring that they were essentially Amish, a point now embraced by the boosters of Lancaster County tourism. While Singmaster's story is a back-porch spoof of *Tillie the Mennonite Maid* and the none-too-prophetic origin of the Reformed Mennonites (allegedly over a bad horse deal), the characters are not Amish, and the fictional hill in question was actually in Lehigh County. It would not be surprising in the least if the insider joke set up in the name Shankweiler's Hill was for Singmaster a pyramid of waffles, for the name Shankweiler is still to this day synonymous with chicken and waffles even though the old family hotel has long since closed.

In any case three essential features of Pennsylvania Dutch tourism came out of the Kutztown Folk Festival within a few years of its establishment: the rapid dissemination of the Amish as a symbol of Pennsylvania Dutch culture; the popularization of nontraditional disk hex signs; and the morphing of an unusual holiday treat into a common fairground snack. The festival's ability to send mixed signals about Pennsylvania Dutch culture backfired on the organizers in other ways as well, because pictures of the Amish, Johnny Ott's hex signs, and funnel cakes were only parts of the story: among the main drawing points of the festival were the meals, but they have missed the mark to such an extent that even today many visitors to the event leave with only the vaguest impression of what Pennsylvania Dutch cuisine is like.

Food Tents, Heat Waves, and the Country Kitchen

From the very beginning the food situation at the festival was a compromise that worked against attempts to depict the regional cookery in a positive light. One of the persistent issues has been that the community organizations preparing the food have fixed ideas about what is representative of the cuisine; certainly very few of the sixteen hundred or so documented regional foods ever make their appearance on festival menus. Part of this is due to class perceptions about authenticity, since most of the concessions are operated by farming organizations that place a nostalgic emphasis on old poverty dishes that may have played a special role in their own daily lives as children. Dried apples and dumplings (*Schnitz-un-Gnepp*) and chicken potpie stand at the very top of this list. Both of these dishes were traditional one-pot meals served boardinghouse style to work hands during the week to dispose of leftovers from a big Sunday dinner. Historically they were not in any way special-occasion foods as was butchering day stew (*Metzelsupp*), although they are now presented as culinary icons at the festival. The other issue concerning the food is about the time and place: limitations imposed by logistics and weather.

In order to feed the public for the duration of the week-long festival, several community organizations were invited by Alfred Shoemaker in 1950 to set up tents for serving meals. This included several church groups and local granges. One church has participated since the opening in 1950: Zion's Windsor Castle Church (Hamburg, Pennsylvania), which was successfully recruited because Shoemaker's sister was married to Reverend Harper Schneck, minister of the church at that time. An interview with the present church committee that handles the festival tent filled in many blanks about what happened and why.

The main reason for the continued participation of this church (many of the other churches and organizations eventually dropped out) is not the promotion of Pennsylvania Dutch foods but rather the tent idea's success as a church fund-raiser. As many as twenty-five hundred people are served during the course of the festival. Zion's Church has the largest food concession still operating at the festival and provides visitors with full sit-down meals for a fixed-price ticket. Meals are served continuously, and visitors are reminded of the tent's presence by the periodic ringing of a large farmhouse dinner bell.

As odd as it may seem, when the various church groups were invited in 1950 to cook for the festival, the initial reaction from the ladies' committees was resistance to the idea of serving Pennsylvania Dutch food to the public: *War daet sel alt Schtoff esse?* (Who would want to eat that *old* stuff?) was the most common response. Furthermore, in spite of the educational mandate of the Folklore Center, no one running the festival actually sat down with any of the participating organizations and suggested a general menu that would best reflect Pennsylvania Dutch cookery. Essentially the solution settled on the lowest common denominators, a simplified menu that the groups were most comfortable preparing on a large scale in tents on a sweltering hot day. This rather than an eye for ethnography shaped the way regional food was presented at the festival.

While the menus were modeled on the type of family-style, all-you-can-eat arrangements that had proven popular at such well-known local restaurants as Haag's in Shartlesville, Pennsylvania, the selections were even further simplified to reduce the number of dishes that needed to be cooked at the fairgrounds (much of the actual cooking is still done off the premises). The mythic seven sweets and seven sours proved extremely well adapted to this practical requirement because the pickles and preserves could come directly out of jars. Dishes such as crumb-dumpling soup (*Riwwelsupp*), noodle soup (*Nudelsupp*), and browned flour soup (*Gereeschte Mehlsupp*) could be cooked ahead or assembled in the morning prior to the festival opening, even though technically speaking, these are not typical summer dishes. In fact, if a generalization can be made, much of traditional Pennsylvania Dutch cooking is cold-weather fare because in the summer people ate very light meals and relied on smoked meats, fish (especially catfish or suckers), fresh fruits, and cold milk dishes.

Many of the festival concessions also chose to serve their food according to a platter format (meat and a side of vegetables served on one plate) with an overabundance of entrées. This is how meals were condensed into a form familiar to anyone who has eaten in a diner. In either case, whether family style or platter style, the festival menus did not reflect the reality of Pennsylvania Dutch eating habits but rather mirrored the fictional groaning tables conjured up by Ann Hark and other travel journalists. In spite of this, the stereotypical menus created at the festival are the ones that have persisted longest and are the ones most widely replicated by other fund-raising organizations. Another irony is that this type of meal is now imitated in private homes, particularly those specializing in home-cooked meals for tourists, so that today the old fictions have assumed the guise of a new reality.

A well-known local folk artist who has exhibited at the festival for many years once commented to me about the food situation at that event: "I don't eat one single thing all week long. I take my own food. It makes me really sad that the food isn't better than it is. I am Pennsylvania Dutch. I cook. I know what good food tastes like."[3] Those sentiments are shared by a lot of people, but of course everyone brings to the festival his or her personalized definition of authenticity. The artist also pointed out that there is a category of visitor who attends primarily because the prices are cheap and the quantity of food abundant regardless of quality or its ethnographic context. The festival cultivates the atmosphere of an old-time country fair minus serious alcohol consumption, so there is a level of light-hearted fun that makes up for many deficiencies.

One way the festival has responded to the food issue is through its Country Kitchen, where cooking demonstrators prepare meals on a cast-iron stove. The stove provides a visual allusion to the fictive kitchens of the Amish (which incidentally operate mostly on bottled gas), and to the days when many Pennsylvania farmhouse kitchens were furnished with the once-popular "Penn Esther" stoves or some other local brand. Yet cooking on a cast-iron stove does not prove much about the Dutchness of the food; *Riwwelsupp* is the same whether prepared over glowing wood ashes, coal, gas, or electricity. This is just a novel way to rivet the attention of the tourist on a hot and bothersome method of cooking that has passed out of living memory, even for most grandmothers.

The range of dishes prepared on this stove is large, although due to health board regulations, these dishes cannot be sold to the public. However, the food can be given away free, so every day certain members of the public are invited to sit down and taste-test Pennsylvania Dutch fare. This popular idea has been copied by other festivals in the area. Then again there is no vetting of the recipes prepared in this kitchen; what goes out on the table is more or less up to the whims of the cooking demonstrators, none of whom have any professional training in food preparation or even coaching in the basics of classic Pennsylvania Dutch cuisine. I asked one of the demonstrators what made the fried chicken Pennsylvania Dutch. She said it was in the way it was prepared. I said I was not aware of this technique; could she show me? "Well, it's Dutch because I am Dutch and I cooked it." This takes us back to the old bugaboo of ethnic peculiarities: that you can taste Africa in food prepared by black hands or the Amishness in shoofly pie.

Mrs. Heller Saves the Day

The organizers of the folk festival were always aware of these shortcomings and the touchy diplomacy of dealing with a corps of well-meaning volunteers on whom the outcome depended. However, when the festival first opened, food studies did not exist, food ethnography was only a budding science, and for the most part cookery was still viewed as the sphere of women, and so a woman was recruited to act as point person for the festival. J. William Frey, one of the festival organizers, invited Edna Eby Heller (1914–2009) to serve as the festival spokesperson on matters of cookery. Mrs. Heller accepted her charge with great enthusiasm. Through her prolific food columns in the *Pennsylvania Dutchman* she eventually exerted a huge influence on the way Pennsylvania Dutch foods and foodways were perceived. An inveterate recipe collector and referee of lively letter exchanges about Pennsylvania Dutch food, she quickly accumulated material that was organized into pamphlet cookbooks that were published and distributed by the Folklore Center.

In spite of her amazing ability to get up on a stage and speak with conviction to hundreds of people at a time, Edna Heller was privately a quiet, retiring person who did not fully appreciate the profound influence she exerted on her listeners and on Pennsylvania Dutch cookery in general. She became the ad hoc contact person for all matters pertaining to Pennsylvania Dutch food, and journalists all over the country sought out her advice and recipes. Furthermore the little pamphlet cookbooks published under her name by the Folklore Center gave festival visitors something tangible and useful to take away as mementos of their Kutztown experience. In this way her influence

FIGURE 35. Edna Eby Heller at the Kutztown Folk Festival promoting her newly reissued cookbook, 1974. Original photo. Roughwood Collection, Devon, Pa

lingered on long after the festival closed for the season. Her pamphlet cookbooks also constitute a very good record of the material that Heller discussed during her public food presentations into the late 1960s. She covered a broad range of seasonal recipes, including many with sauerkraut, so for the adventuresome cook there was plenty to try out on the family.

Heller's training in home economics at Penn State University was a plus inasmuch as she was able to create recipes that were clear and efficient. On the other hand, her training also worked against the "art" of Pennsylvania Dutch cooking, as she later called it in her final cookbook. The home economics program at Penn State was not designed to encourage regional cookery or for that matter the use of fresh, local ingredients, although it did publish a pamphlet dealing with Pennsylvania Dutch cookery in 1968. In general the Penn State philosophy was to champion processed food and culinary shortcuts. Thus Heller's take on Pennsylvania Dutch cookery

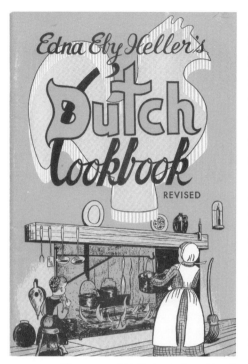

FIGURE 36. The cover of Heller's 1974 cookbook further strengthens the Amish–Pennsylvania Dutch equation. The Amish girls are cooking on an open hearth that is in reality a faux hearth in the museum of the Historical Society of Berks County, Pa. Roughwood Collection, Devon, Pa.

introduced a certain leveling or sanitizing of the fare so that many of the richly flavorful and quirky regionalisms that made the dishes interesting, especially the old emphasis on fresh herbs and greens, were more or less edited out.

This homogenized Pennsylvania Dutch cookery is what Heller included in her 1968 *Art of Pennsylvania Dutch Cooking*. While the book was an attempt to represent the sum total of her previous pamphlet cookbooks and to allow her to rest on her laurels as spokesperson for the festival, its colorless presentation worked against it. This was especially the case given the dubious success of Ruth Tyndall's *Eat Yourself Full*, which had come out the year before and made great claims about authenticity that were mostly wind and yet seemed to define what New York publishers imagined the Pennsylvania Dutch cookbook market was like. Heller could have saved the genre from fakes, but she was too nice. What her text lacked was the kind of rich contextual information that is now demanded of cookbook writing (something that was present in the 1950 Hark and Barba cookbook), narratives and cultural framework that reassure the reader that the material is derived from authoritative sources. There was ample research of that kind in the archives of the Pennsylvania Folklife Society, but by 1968 due to bankruptcy those files had been dispersed or wantonly destroyed. Edna Eby Heller was more or less left to her own devices. This same disconnection between the food and its story still lurks in most of the culinary vignettes found at the Kutztown festival today.

However, Edna Eby Heller's story places her squarely in the same class of entrepreneurial women who managed to accomplish in Pennsylvania Dutch culture what women in other segments of American society have only recently come to enjoy: positions of importance as business leaders in the food community. The restaurateur and cookbook author Betty Groff took Heller's food advocacy even further. Alice Reinert has done the same with funnel cakes, and more recently Anne Beiler's Auntie Anne soft pretzels have become well known nationally. Yet it was probably Lottie Kettering's Dutch Pantry, first established near Selinsgrove, Pennsylvania, in the 1920s, that did the most to spread the Amish table into far-flung parts of the country. Her chain of restaurants in the South and the Midwest featured Amish goods (canned foods and menu selections) that embraced all the unintended culinary lessons of the Kutztown Folk Festival.

FIGURE 37. Marjorie Hendricks standing by the hearth of the Water Gate Inn. Advertisement from the *Washington Star*, 1964. Roughwood Collection, Devon, Pa.

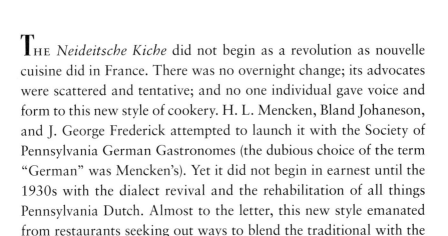

CHAPTER 12

New Dutch Cuisine and the Greening of the Amish

THE *Neideitsche Kiche* did not begin as a revolution as nouvelle cuisine did in France. There was no overnight change; its advocates were scattered and tentative; and no one individual gave voice and form to this new style of cookery. H. L. Mencken, Bland Johaneson, and J. George Frederick attempted to launch it with the Society of Pennsylvania German Gastronomes (the dubious choice of the term "German" was Mencken's). Yet it did not begin in earnest until the 1930s with the dialect revival and the rehabilitation of all things Pennsylvania Dutch. Almost to the letter, this new style emanated from restaurants seeking out ways to blend the traditional with the changing times.

Although she never used the term, in 1942 Marjorie Hendricks launched her well-known Water Gate Inn in Washington, D.C., at the suggestion of Eleanor Roosevelt as a trial ground for this new cuisine. Hendricks was keenly interested in elevating Pennsylvania Dutch cookery out of the doldrums of chicken potpie, and her menus reflected this. Her 1953 pamphlet cookbook compiled by the food consultant Flora Orr recorded recipes for many of the dishes developed for the restaurant, but on the whole, the truly experimental cookery was often treated as a "special" and thus was off the normal printed menus. Much of that experimentation has vanished without a trace. It is also fair to point out that Hendricks operated in a cultural universe far removed from the Pennsylvania Dutch heart-

FIGURE 38. Interior view of the Water Gate Inn. Black and white postcard, 1953. Rough-wood Collection, Devon, Pa.

land. Her cozy restaurant decorated with fine Pennsylvania antiques relied on the novelty of down-home farmhouse cookery reinvented for a cosmopolitan audience. She had little influence on the culinary scene in the Keystone State.

Closer to home, popular eating spots such as the Hotel Easton and the Cetronia Hotel near Allentown attempted to advance a more experimental type of Pennsylvania Dutch cookery during the 1940s. This is evident from surviving menus featuring interesting fusions, for example the Trinkle family's sauerkraut and frogs' legs and their handheld corn pies (already mentioned in Chapter 9). Other dishes from this era are pickled summer sausage with okra (recipe on page 239) and sweet buckwheat bread (recipe on page 270). The latter moved from a rural poverty dish to something quite acceptable to high-end chefs (it has been served in a number of Philadelphia restaurants in more recent times).

Throughout the 1970s and 1980s, as part of the general revival of interest in American regional cuisines, Pennsylvania Dutch dishes often appeared on menus in many parts of the country, although the chefs trying to reinvent the cuisine had little or no training in its culinary foundations. Much of the food was unrecognizable, cartoonish, and rather than truly creative an indulgence in short-lived gimmickry. Furthermore much of it focused on the Amish table as though this alone is the purest fountainhead of culinary epiphanies.

On that point, the Amish derivations might be considered inevitable since the tourist industry has pushed the Amish to the front of everything else. After the late 1940s and especially after the establishment of the Kutztown Folk Festival in 1950, the Amish image held Pennsylvania Dutch cuisine hostage to the propaganda of the Lancaster County Tourism Bureau and the missionary zeal of the mainstream Mennonites who own a large number of the tourist-oriented businesses in Lancaster's Amish belt. How could Pennsylvania Dutch cuisine evolve beyond Whoopee Pies, a junk food invented in New England and named for a 1928 Broadway tune that since the late 1960s has become a local symbol of Amish culture?[1] How could Pennsylvania Dutch cuisine with its extraordinary cultural traditions look toward this type of industrial food as a culinary model?

In spite of the Amish culture's picturesque appearance to the outside world, there is nothing in Amish religious beliefs that prohibits them from eating as other Americans do; there are no unspoken rules that they must preserve culinary tradition in the same manner that they preserve certain aspects of late nineteenth-century dress or farming practices. Perhaps it is a good thing for the Amish that the focus is now shifting away from them, at least in terms of Pennsylvania Dutch cuisine, because it takes away the burden of false expectations laid on them by an outside world that does not understand their philosophical underpinnings. However, there are other forces at play that in some ways have muted this conversation and created dynamics of their own. The equation of the Amish with environmentalism and "green cuisine" is one of them. It is not necessarily a new phenomenon, and it plays into other sets of myths about Amish life.

In the 1934 Radnor, Pennsylvania, cookbook *Old Family Reci-*

pes from St. Martin's Parish, there is a full-page advertisement for the Rosemont Farmer's Market (now defunct). The market promised to deliver the following: "Mennonites, Dunkards from Lancaster, 70 farmers with hour-old produce. Absolutely NO cold storage."[2] Can food get any fresher than that? The theme of this advertisement touches on another one of the Amish cultural equations: food raised and sold by the plain sects is more natural, more pure, more honest, and by extension more healthful than commercial produce of the same sort shipped in from other locales. This has given rise to labeling foods as Amish in order to convey a range of subjective values and, as in the case of the old Rosemont Farmer's Market, to populating farm markets with plain people as a sign of authenticity of both the food and its presumed origins. The Lancaster Farmer's Market in Strafford, Pennsylvania, owned by S. Clyde Weaver Meats of Lancaster County and a lineal continuation of the Rosemont market, still promotes itself as a true farm market by using Amish people to work behind several of the counters. Aside from the meats and poultry sold by Montgomery County Mennonites who are not plain dressed, a good portion of the other produce does not come from Pennsylvania. Its rural connectedness is highly scripted, and the prices are sometimes double what you would pay if you bought from Amish farmers directly.

This use of the Amish trademark is so pervasive today that it would be a burden to the reader to list all the food products using it. The Lancaster Brewing Company, which is located in Wilkes-Barre, Pennsylvania, many miles from Lancaster County and well outside the Dutch Country, produces an Amish Four Grain Pale Ale. This flavorful beer, which is not bad from a drinking standpoint, seems to suffer rather than benefit from the

FIGURE 39. Lancaster Brewing Company's Amish beer. Photo by Rob Cardillo.

branding. The government warning on the side label of each bottle advises against drinking and driving cars or operating machinery, so we must presume that the warning was not meant for buggy-driving Amish eyes in spite of the fact that the Amish do drink on occasion—and some more than they should.

The Amish never owned breweries, and just because this beer is "brewed naturally" without preservatives, the label Amish is no guarantee of either claim. If the beer is intended as a tongue-in-cheek joke on the weird range of foods called Amish (such as Amish Polish pickles, Amish curry, and Amish pizza, for example), then the laughs are on us. To be honest, I would not have bought the beer were it not for the fact that the label and the product inside were so blatantly at odds with one another. Can anyone take it seriously?

This line of trademark manipulation follows the same evolutionary curve as products sold as Quaker in the nineteenth century, the idea being that the name assured purity and integrity of product. There was at one time some truth to this in terms of Quaker merchants and their dealings, but as Quakerism declined and the big merchant families such as the Macys sold their companies to other people, the term "Quaker" assumed a vague marketing value. This is the same fate that awaits the Amish as soon as they begin to drop their visible customs of dress code and mode of transportation. Their religious ideas are irrelevant to the world of business; new faces will appear on the horizon.

One of those new faces is already among us. In April 2007 an electronic news release was sent to me, evidently due to my dual position at the time as a contributing editor to both *Gourmet* and *Mother Earth News*. It was sent from Holmesville, Ohio, a heartland of Amish settlements even more extensive than those in Pennsylvania. It announced the formation of a new company called Amish Naturals, and the firm's mission statement explained what it was all about: "Amish Naturals' mission is to increase shareholder value through the sale and distribution of organic, Amish food products to the exploding market for organic and wholesome foods. Last year, the U.S. market for natural/organic foods was estimated to have totaled approximately \$13.8 billion. Building on generations of traditions, the Company has created foods that reflect the wholesomeness and purity of the Amish people and their culinary customs." This rings the same patriotic bells as the early 1900s Pennsylvania German Society invocations of the moral virtues of Pennsylvania Dutch peasant roots, and in a moment of déjà-vu it transports us back to the Kutztown Folk Festival and the woman who attempted to explain the inherent Pennsylvania Dutchness of her fried chicken. It echoes the hollow claims of Troyer's Dutch Heritage restaurant in Sarasota, Florida, whose menus of "Amish style cooking" contain not one dish of Pennsylvania Dutch origin. In short, the wholesomeness and purity of the Amish people, the ambiguous taste of Dutchness, are all imaginary ethnic peculiarities transferred to food.

Amish Naturals was founded by David Skinner Sr., who is not Amish and whose corporate team brings together experience from ConAgra and Hebrew National, about as far afield from sustainable agriculture as agribusiness can get. Those connections may impress Wall Street, but even the investment analysts pooh-poohed the new corporate concept as a "buggy ride" on dubious penny stocks. Lost in the hoopla was the Amish Naturals equation that organic equals Amish. This corporate greening of the Amish to package them as a Good Housekeeping Seal of Approval for the firm's tomato basil spaghetti or whole wheat fettuccini, untouched in production by Amish hands, follows the same kind of image expropriation used by Quaker Oats in the nineteenth century. If the company were Amish owned and operated, it might invite a shred of credibility, yet I doubt any practicing Amishman would feel comfortable proselytizing his religion in this manner.

The Amish-equals-organic equation is more of an anomaly for the community in terms of actual farming practices—like food consumption, Amish religious beliefs do not cover fertilizers, pesticides, or GMOs, although there are pockets of counterculture Amish where natural foods are indeed an important focal point of their personal lives. One of the leaders of this minority in Pennsylvania is Miller's Natural Foods of Bird-in-Hand, which began in 1968 as a small shop on the family farm well ahead of the mainstream American health-food movement. This shop has morphed into quite a large store with an amazing array of organic food products, much of it locally grown and better in quality than some Whole Foods products. The family was initially drawn into the movement not by agricultural politics or religion but rather by a health crisis followed by an exploration of alternative medicines, all of which eventually led to homeopathy, herbal cures, and a gradual shift to diet as preventive medicine. Tourists who manage to find this store (it is pretty well hidden on back roads) jump to the conclusion that it represents something typical about Amish lifestyle, when in fact it does not, at least not yet.

We are going to see more and more appropriations of the Amish-equals-organic equation in the coming years, and at times it may run countercurrent to New Dutch cuisine. In the end, like Quaker Oats' William Penn, who over the course of time lost his identity to corporate retouching and who now serves as a meaningless and archaic symbol on countless numbers of boxed and packaged products, the Amish symbol will also lose its holding power. In fact, trademarking it will probably debase its effectiveness. New Dutch cuisine was never derived from a religious symbol; it cuts across all segments of the Pennsylvania Dutch community simply because it is religion-neutral. That is one reason it will eventually flourish without predetermined restrictions.

Pennsylvania Dutch food and culture are undergoing a rapid transformation that thirty years ago could not have been foreseen. Large family-style restaurants are disappearing rapidly. This is taken as a sign that the cuisine and the culture are in decline, which is not the case—in terms of moving Pennsylvania Dutch culinary arts to another level, the passing of those restaurants is probably a welcomed funeral. Perhaps more important, there has been a refocusing of emphasis on the agricultural roots of the culture and how this—in pure economic terms—will safeguard the family farm, where Pennsylvania Dutch culture is still alive and well.

At the forefront of this new perspective is the Pennsylvania Association for Sustainable Agriculture, which has not only become an advocate for organic farming, niche farming, and the establishment of innumerable new farm markets—not to mention a model for similar movements in other states; this organization has also brought together diverse elements of the Pennsylvania Dutch community to engage in a common conversation. This mutual concern for the state of the farm, the type of produce it yields, and the more environmentally informed lifestyle it suggests is the dialogue of the younger generation, whether Amish, Mennonite, Lutheran, or some other segment of the community.

In the world beyond Lancaster County, the young Pennsylvania Dutch farmers are now less interested in the old cultural icons than in niche farming with organic crops and produce. High-end chefs such as Daniel Stern of Philadelphia are turning to Pennsylvania Dutch foods as a source of inspiration for this new type of regional cuisine. I have often seen it written that Pennsylvania Dutch cooking is nothing but a faded facsimile of German cuisine. For certain, the basic dish categories evolved out of a southwest German tradition, but the cuisine moved on long ago. For example, while our bread soup is a true *Schlupper* (a word few Pennsylvania Dutch use anymore), nothing in Germany resembles the way we make ours. Likewise sauerkraut half-moon pies, shoofly pie, chicken potpie, potato potpie with saffron, frogs' legs with sauerkraut, chicken and waffles, peach and yellow tomato recipes, pickled okra with summer sausage, beer cheese soup, Amish *Roascht*, and pig stomach stuffed with potatoes cannot be found in the Old World. Pennsylvania Dutch cookery has created its own New World persona, and it is now as different from German cuisine as Mexican cooking is from Spanish.

Hopefully the historical lessons contained in the preceding pages will drive a stake through many old and persistent myths. These same lessons should give the Pennsylvania Dutch a new sense of pride in their extraordinary ability against all odds to create a distinctly American style of cooking that draws its strength directly from the people and their innate love of the land that sustains them. It is my hope that, after so many years of cultural marginalization by the state of Pennsylvania, as a culture that has existed here longer than the state itself, each of us can continue to be who we are with enough internal grace to hold up our heads against conformity and declare: *Der Geischt fun meine Leit geheert zu mir* (The spirit of my people belongs to me).

Recipes

Tʜᴇ recipes in this section are arranged alphabetically according to their English names. Beginning on page 278 there is a list of recipes divided into categories, such as soups or poverty dishes, so that you will have a better sense of where they best belong when assembling a menu. Otherwise, key recipes may be found in the table of contents. In addition to English, recipe titles are rendered in Pennsylfaanisch in order that non-Dutch speakers can better familiarize themselves with our culinary language. Beyond that, most recipes are accompanied by introductory material that will hopefully add a fuller understanding of each dish and its cultural context.

Almond Fingers (*Mandelschnidde*)

Like chocolate pretzels and Snickerdoodles (a type of cookie), almond fingers were very much a Reading, Pennsylvania, Christmas tradition. The city's confectioners were famous for their remarkable inventions, and during December the old-time shops overflowed with culinary riches. A bag of *Mandelschnidde* under the Christmas tree was certainly a welcome Christmas Day treat because the *Schnidde* could be dipped in coffee much like Italian biscotti or served at dinner with a variety of fruity dishes. Even though the idea of serving neatly sliced bread or pastry with soup may hark back to the table niceties promoted by Christian Friedrich Germershausen in the 1700s, this recipe comes from J. Levan's *Berks County Cook*

Book of Pennsylvania Dutch Recipes, a 1934 treasure trove of local culinary classics.[1] Properly served à la Germershausen, the *Schnidde* should be arranged on a plate in an ornamental pyramid. They are also excellent for dunking in coffee. If your oven bakes hot, set the temperature at 325°F (165°C) and bake for 30 to 35 minutes instead of the cooking temperature and time given below.

Yield: 18 pieces

¾ cup (90g) pastry flour
½ teaspoon baking powder
2 large eggs, room temperature
½ cup (125g) sugar (preferably superfine or bar sugar)
Juice of ½ lemon
2 tablespoons (30ml) ice water
1 cup (140g) sliced almonds
2 tablespoons (30g) coarse granulated sugar

Preheat the oven to 350°F (175°C). Sift together the flour and baking powder, then set aside. Beat the eggs until lemon color and frothy, then fold in the sugar and beat vigorously until well dissolved. Add the lemon juice and cold water, and beat again. Break up the almonds with your hand, squeezing them to make small pieces. Reserve ¼ cup (35g). Add the almonds and then sift in the flour, folding it in gently until fully mixed. Pour this into a well-greased 7½ by 11 inch (19cm by 28cm) baking pan and scatter the reserved sliced almonds over the top. Sprinkle the coarse sugar over this. Bake in the preheated oven for 25 to 30 minutes or until golden. Remove and cool on a rack. Once cool, cut into 3 inch (7.5cm) strips about 1 inch (2.5cm) wide. Store in an airtight container.

Comment: Professional bakers in Reading normally ornamented these cookies with decorative icing. It was applied in a zigzag pattern with rose hip jam mixed with the icing glaze on page 224.

Amish Roast (*Amische Roascht*)

This recipe is used by Old Order Amish Lavinia Blank when she is called upon to serve a large number of family or friends. Most published Amish *Roascht* recipes call for "bread crumbs" (*Grumme*), which is in fact the Amish term for crumbled bread or diced bread from the inner part of the loaf—a point easy to misinterpret if you are not familiar with Amish parlance. Furthermore the quantity here using one chicken is not the norm. For a wedding, 30 to 40 chickens are required, and the day before the wedding they are brought alive to the groom's house. It is his traditional role to butcher them, and there is a certain amount of machismo involved in how well he does the job.

The chickens are then dressed, and the first stages of the recipe are prepared. The couples involved in the wedding—those who are helping with the food preparations—then each take a few chickens home, stuff them with some of the *Roascht* mixture, and roast them in their ovens. The stuffing is removed and the birds are deboned. Early the next day, this stuffing and the meat are brought to the site of the wedding and assembled there for final cooking. In this manner two days of preparation are spread out over many hands because no one family has ovens large enough to cook that many chickens. As Lavinia pointed out to me, it is particularly important to incorporate the stuffing from inside the roasted chickens: this gives added flavor to the dish and provides another texture since it is dense and moist.

This important piece of advice does not appear in recipes; it is part of the oral lore surrounding the dish. I have tried to incorporate some of those "silent" steps into the recipe below because they really do affect the outcome. One of the most important points mentioned is that the *Roascht* should develop a crispy brown crust, especially on the bottom. This is considered by most Amish to be the very best part, as I was reminded by Lavinia's little son Phares, who commented with a shy grin that he always looked forward to weddings for this reason. Leftover roast will resemble very dense meat loaf when cold. It can be sliced and fried for breakfast just like scrapple.

Yield: Serves 6 to 8

1 cup (275g) chicken giblets and livers (see note)
1½ cups (250g) celery, diced very small
10 ounces (315g) unsalted butter
4 quarts (2½ pounds/1.25kg) diced sourdough bread, white part only
   (reserve the crusts for crust pancakes, page 195)
4 large eggs
1 tablespoon salt
1 tablespoon coarsely ground pepper, or to taste
2 tablespoons celery seeds (optional)
1 roasting chicken (about 4 pounds/2kg) with giblets and neck
1 cup (20g) chopped parsley and celery leaves
½ cup (125ml) giblet broth

Put the giblets, livers, and chicken neck in a small saucepan and cover with 3 cups (750ml) water. Simmer over low heat until the ingredients are well cooked (about 20 minutes). Strain the giblet broth and reserve. Remove the meat from the neck and chop it into small pieces with the cooked giblets and livers.

Put the cooked giblets and livers in a food processor with the celery and pulse until this forms a coarse paste. Heat 8 ounces (250g) of butter in a heavy skillet or sauté pan, and once it is melted, add the giblet mixture. Cover and sweat over medium heat for 4 minutes, then pour this over the diced bread and mix thoroughly. Beat the eggs until light and lemon color, then pour this into the bread mixture and combine well. Season with the salt, pepper, and the celery seed.

Stuff the chicken with part of the bread mixture and rub it down with butter and salt. Set the remaining bread mixture aside and store in a cool place until needed. Roast the chicken in an oven preheated to 400°F (200°C) for 30 minutes, then reduce the temperature to 350°F (175°C) and continue roasting until tender (about 35 to 40 minutes).

Remove the chicken from the oven and cool. Take out the stuffing and set aside. Debone the carcass and chop the meat into small pieces or shreds. Grind the skin and add it to the reserved bread mixture. Reserve the bones for chicken stock or soup. Chop the cooked stuffing into small pea-size pieces and combine this with the uncooked *Roascht* mixture and add the parsley. Adjust seasonings. Work this together with the hands in a squeezing motion so that the mixture acquires the texture of thick sticky paste.

Melt 2 tablespoons (30g) butter in a medium-size casserole pan measuring approximately 8 by 12 inches (20 by 30cm) or slightly larger. Coat the entire bottom of the pan. Add the bread and chicken mixture and press it down to fill the pan, patting it smooth on the top. Pour ½ cup (125ml) of the giblet broth over this, then chop the remaining butter and scatter it over the top. (Use the remaining giblet broth to moisten the roast from time to time should it bake too dry.)

Bake in an oven preheated to 325°F (165°C) for 1 hour and 20 or 30 minutes or until the mixture is set and developing a golden crust on the sides and bottom. Serve hot directly from the oven or, when cool, cut it into squares, cover with cling wrap, and freeze in sealed containers. Reheat in a microwave oven as needed.

Note: When purchasing the chicken, buy some extra giblets and livers if they are available. For added flavor, you can double the amount of giblets called for in the recipe.

Watch Point: Freshly baked bread is sometimes too soft to dice easily even with a sharp knife. Use sharp kitchen scissors instead.

Apple *Schnitz* and Dumplings (*Schnitz-un-Gnepp*)

I think it goes without saying that for every sliced apple in Pennsylvania (note that the singular of *Schnitz* is *Schnutz*) there are two or perhaps three recipes for *Schnitz-un-Gnepp*. This is the most broad-based, most idiosyncratically variable, and most warmly loved iconic dish of the Pennsylvania Dutch. As one old-timer said to me, off the record of course, *far die wenige Ludderische die in der Himmel aakumme duhne, dess Engels Schmaus soll ihre erschte Esse sei!* (for those few Lutherans who manage to get into Heaven, this "banquet of the angels" will be their first real meal). I will not take sides in that contentious argument; yet it is said that when St. Peter was confronted by this same Pennsylfaanisch conundrum, all he was able to exclaim was *Gerada so!* (But of course).

I have discussed the common wash-day origins of this dish elsewhere, and no amount of spleen and finger wagging from me will alter the Dutch love for this stew. The important assignment here is to provide a typical working recipe. The Hamm family in New Tripoli (Lehigh County) assured me that they made *Schnitz-un-Gnepp* only with stock recovered from boiled pig feet. Thus the apples were stewed in what anyone else would consider liquefied pork aspic, but to the hearty-eating Hamms this was a meatless meal and more power to them.

On the other hand, the Troyers out in a highly rural corner of Lancaster County never considered the dish savory, meaning that they ate it as dessert (no meat at all), stewed apple *Schnitz* cooked with brown sugar and little else—well, perhaps one or two healthy scoops of homemade butter and a dash of cinnamon or nutmeg; the dumplings might even include a few raisins. Some people added dried cherries to their *Schnitz* or cooked it up with dried pears instead of apples. My point is that *Schnitz-un-Gnepp* is as varied as the imagination, so perhaps there is no single classic representation of the dish. Yet we can say, at least, that there are two basic types, the savory (meat based) and the fruity (sweet). The recipe below strikes a balance between the two. If you like your *Schnitz-un-Gnepp* juicy (*saftich*), then use 2 quarts (2 liters) of stock; if you prefer it thick (*schlappich*), cut the cooking stock in half. Otherwise add what you like and put on those wings: have a good *Engels Schmaus*!

Yield: 4 to 6 servings

Schnitz
Two 2-pound (1kg) meaty ham hocks
2 quarts (2 liters) ham or pork stock
2 cups (500ml) hard cider or Perry (preferable)
4 cups (250g) sweet apple Schnitz
1 cup (175g) dried sour cherries
1 recipe dumplings (see below)

Cover the ham hocks in a deep stewing pan with the ham or pork stock and hard cider or Perry. Simmer 1 hour or until the liquid is reduced and the meat is falling from the bones. Remove the hocks, trim away the fat, and chop the meat into small bite-size pieces. Measure out 2 cups (300g) of the coarsely chopped meat and reserve.

Put the stock and reserved meat in a deep stewing pan and add the dried apples and cherries. Cover and simmer 35 minutes or until the fruit is soft. Add the dumplings (see below) and cover. Simmer an additional 15 minutes and then serve immediately

Dumplings

After these dumplings are boiled, they can be chopped into smaller pieces and used to make *Gnepplin*, small pea- or bean-size bits of dough.

Yield: 4 to 6 servings

1 cup (250g) cottage cheese
1 large egg
1¼ cups (155g) flour
1 teaspoon baking powder
1 teaspoon salt

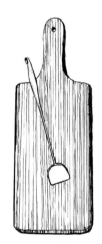

FIGURE 40. *Gnepp-linbrett* with *Gneppschpatz* for chopping the dumpling dough.

Put the cottage cheese, egg, 1 cup (125g) of the flour, the baking powder, and the salt in a food processor and pulse intermittently until the mixture forms a smooth paste. Scatter the remaining flour over a clean cutting board (preferably a *Gnepplinbrett*, one with a handle; see Figure 40) and turn out the dumpling paste onto it. Spread it out to about ¼ inch (½cm) thick. Bring a large kettle of salted water to a full boil, then turn back to a gentle simmer. Hold the cutting board in one hand and rest it on the rim of the kettle. Take a sharp knife or a *Gneppschpatz* (a small spatula made specifically for this purpose) and chop off small bits of dough from the dumpling mixture. Cook 10 minutes or until they float. Skim off with a slotted spoon and add to the stewed apples. Serve immediately.

Apple *Schnitz* Pie (*Ebbelschnitz Boi*)

Generally speaking the *Schnitz* pies served at the Kutztown Folk Festival are prepared this way: the cooked *Schnitz* are pureed with brown sugar and baked like apple sauce, sometimes with a meringue topping. Other than cloying sweetness, these pies generally lack flavor and character, which is not the case with the recipe that follows.

"Cousin Betty" Zook (my grandfather's niece who lived in New Holland, Pennsylvania), my intrepid recipe collector, took up my call for old-time dishes some forty years ago and over the ensuing decades sent me a number of treasures. Among them was this excellent recipe for apple *Schnitz* pie that came from Elma Landis Harnish (1899–1945), who lived near New Danville in Lancaster County. Techniques for making home-style apple *Schnitz* were often demonstrated in the early years of the Kutztown Folk Festival and were recorded in several issues of the *Pennsylvania Dutchman*.[2]

Yield: one 9- to 10-inch (23 to 25cm) pie

Pastry for one 9- to 10-inch (23 to 25cm) pie
3 cups (750ml) boiling water or cider
8 ounces (250g) tart apple Schnitz (pie Schnitz)
2 tablespoons (15g) potato starch
2 tablespoons (25g) brown sugar
1 teaspoon ground cinnamon
½ teaspoon ground allspice
2 cups (500ml) sour cream
½ cup (125g) sugar
1 tablespoon (15g) unsalted butter

Pour the boiling water over the *Schnitz*. Cover and let stand 4 to 6 hours or overnight until the *Schnitz* are soft. Drain and chop into lima bean–size pieces, then place them in a large work bowl. Combine the potato starch, brown sugar, cinnamon, and allspice, working the mixture with a fork to create fine crumbs. Take out 1 tablespoon of the crumb mixture and set aside. Line a 9- to 10-inch (23 to 25cm) pie dish with short pastry. Dust the *Schnitz* with the brown sugar mixture and then arrange the fruit in the pie shell, pressing down with a spoon so that the *Schnitz* fit together closely. Mix the sour cream and sugar and spread this evenly over the fruit. Combine the reserved tablespoon of brown sugar mixture with the butter and work this to a crumb texture. Scatter the crumbs over the top of the pie. Bake in an oven preheated to 350°F (175°C) for 40 to 50 minutes. Serve at room temperature.

Apple Soup for Christmas (*Ebbelsupp fer Grischdaag*)

There is something symbolic about this soup, like the wooden cherries on Pennsylvania Dutch Christmas trees and the menagerie of animals that figured in the language of cookie cutters. December 24 was Adam and Eve Day, a theme celebrated in Pennsylvania Dutch folk art and the reason for snakes appearing as decorative motifs on springerle cookies. Central to many old Fraktur drawings is the Tree of Life with Adam and Eve on each side, and hanging overhead are apples. Pennsylvania Dutch apple soup celebrated this age-old story by reminding everyone at the Christmas Day table just how good original sin can taste.

It is a great pity that Elsie Singmaster never wrote about this delightful Christmas Day treat in *The Magic Mirror*, but I suppose it was not an Allentown thing, so it dropped off the edge of the unique little culinary world that she captured in her novel. However, the soup surfaces in the more western reaches of the Dutch Country, in Franklin County and Mifflin County, and like Mifflinburg rose soup, which was served to belschnicklers before belschnickling fell into decline, it was carried over the Alleghenies into the Dutch settlements of Ohio. Belschnicklers were the teenagers who dressed up in costumes on Second Christmas (December 26) and went mumming from house to house begging for treats.

George Girardey included a recipe for apple soup in his 1841 cookbook, the same cookbook that published the earliest American recipe for *Gumbis,* and since apples figure in that dish as well as this one, it is Girardey to whom I have turned for inspiration.[3] The original proportions have been adjusted. For a little nouveau variation, float toast in it with sharp cheese grated over the top and bake like French onion soup.

Yield: Serves 4 to 6

8 large apples (about 3 pounds/1.5kg), preferably heirlooms such as
    Winesap, Stayman, or York Imperial
2 quarts (2 liters) ham stock
Juice and rind of 1 lemon (pith removed)
2 sticks of cinnamon
2 tablespoons (30g) unsalted butter
2 tablespoons (15g) flour
2 cups (500ml) dry hard cider
¼ cup (65g) sugar or to taste (depending on the apples)
1 teaspoon salt to taste

Pare and core the apples and cook the parings in the ham broth until the color is drawn out (about 25 minutes). Strain and discard the parings. Return the stock to the saucepan and add the apples, lemon, and cinnamon. Cover and stew the apples until soft (about 35 minutes), then remove the lemon and cinnamon. Mash or puree the apples in a food processor until smooth and creamy. Set aside. Clean the stewing pan and add the butter and flour. Cook over medium-high heat to make a blond roux. Add the cider and whisk until smooth and creamy. Add the reserved soup and continue whisking until it thickens. Add the sugar and adjust the seasoning. Serve with strips of fried bread or with an accompaniment of salt pretzels or *Mandelschnidde* (almond fingers).

Baked Potato Fingers
(*Schpeckgrumbiere odder Grumbiere Schniddlen*)
The name of this dish is not easy to translate into English because the Dutch name is a simple combination of two words: *Schpeck* (bacon) and *Grumbiere* (potatoes). Its Palatine equivalent

is *Blechgrumbiere* (potatoes baked in a tin *Schales* pan), which is perhaps a little more descriptive of the way the recipe is prepared. On both sides of the Atlantic this was a popular snack served during winter butchering, and in the Palatinate with new wine. It was also a typical accompaniment to alcoholic drinks in Pennsylvania Dutch Country taverns. Yet in spite of the fact that it was easy to make (or perhaps because of its rustic simplicity), not many recipes were written down. Fortunately during the 1930s the "potato baron" and well-known Lehigh County politician Mark W. Hoffman published a little potato cookbook at New Tripoli, Pennsylvania, and in it we find a recipe for baked potato fingers, or *Schniddlen*, as they are called in Dutch.[4] Incidentally, Hoffman was one of the original founders of the first Grundsau Lodge in Pennsylvania and spoke fluent Pennsylvania Dutch.

Yield: Serves 4 to 6

2 pounds (1kg) new potatoes, peeled and cut into thick "fingers"
4 ounces (125g) slab bacon, diced or coarsely chopped
8 ounces (250g) pearl onions or Catawissa onions
2 tablespoons (30g) cold butter, chopped
Salt and pepper to taste
2 tablespoons chopped parsley
1 tablespoon fresh marjoram, minced fine
1 tablespoon chopped chives

Preheat the oven to 400°F (200°C). Put the potatoes, bacon, onions, and butter on a broad baking sheet with raised edges. Sprinkle with salt and pepper and bake in the preheated oven for 35–40 minutes. Once the potatoes are turning golden brown, remove from the oven and scatter the herbs over them. Serve hot from the baking sheet.

Basic *Gumbis* (*Grundrezept fer Gumbis*)

Keep in mind that this is a fruit-and-vegetable dish; meat is only a garnish, so you can reduce it to a minimum if you prefer. Even though the basic idea is to use leftover meat or meat scraps, you can create the meat and stock for this dish by simmering two meaty ham hocks in 2 quarts (2 liters) of water for 1½ hours or until the meat is falling from the bones.

Yield: 6 to 8

10 cups (850g) finely shredded cabbage
6 medium onions cut in half lengthwise, then sliced paper thin
4 apples cored and sliced as thin as possible (do not pare)
1 pound (500g) cooked ham or ham hock coarsely chopped
2 tablespoons coriander seeds
2 tablespoons dried summer savory
6 fresh bay leaves
6 cups (1.5 liters) well-flavored ham stock
Salt and freshly ground pepper to taste

Preheat the oven to 350°F (175°C). Take a heavy 6-quart (6-liter) baking pan and line the bottom with shredded cabbage. Scatter a layer of onion over this, then a layer of apples, and then a layer of meat. Combine the coriander and savory and scatter half of this over the meat. Add 3 bay leaves. Make another layer of cabbage, a layer of onion, the rest of the apples, and then the rest of the meat. Scatter the remaining herbs over this and cover with the remaining onions. Make a top layer with the rest of the cabbage. Add the stock, cover, and bake for 1 hour. Once baked, stir up with a fork and season to taste. Serve hot from the baking pan or from a common bowl in the center of the table.

Beer Cheese Soup (*Bierkees Supp*)

Milwaukee may lay claim to beer cheese soup, but the Pennsylvania Dutch were making it in hotel saloons and country taverns long before Milwaukee existed. Furthermore our beer cheese soup is quite different from its midwestern cousins, which today are loaded with so many ingredients that reading through a recipe is like picking one's way through an Indian curry.

FIGURE 41. The Germania Palm Room, Reading, Pa., postcard view ca. 1906. Roughwood Collection, Devon, Pa.

Perhaps from a Pennsylvania Dutch standpoint the best place to begin is with Yuengling's amber beer, which is sold as lager. Lagering first started in the United States in Philadelphia, but those 1840s breweries are alas now long gone. Reading, Pennsylvania, was once famous for Lauer's (another local leader in lagering), and for a while that beer was the essential ingredient in the old-time beer cheese soups served in Pretzel City. The soup was also made in Pottsville, the home of Yuengling's brewery since 1829, and in all other major urban centers of Pennsylvania Dutch culture as well.

This brings us to Johnny Ott (1891–1964): hotel keeper, Pennsylvania Dutch cook extraordinaire, folk artist, and self-proclaimed hexologist. Johnny learned to make beer cheese soup while he worked as a line cook in Reading hotels, although oral tradition has it that his recipe originated at Hassler's Germania Palm Room, a Reading saloon where beer was sold by the "schooner" and ladies by the hour. Like chicken and waffles, beer soup was a popular standby on Johnny Ott's menu at the Deitsch Eck in Lenhartsville, Pennsylvania. Johnny never gave out his recipe in written form, but after interviewing a number of people who sampled his cooking, I have been able to reconstruct his famous soup, which was based on Old Reading Beer, a local brand that is now extinct. My recipe may not replicate Johnny's down to the last grain of salt, but it comes so close that it can pass handily for the original. Unlike the Milwaukee soup, the cheese in this case is recurdled and removed to make beer cheese dumplings (see recipe below). The resulting soup stock is rich and flavorful.

Yield: Serves 4 to 6 persons

Soup

1 pound (500g) Pennsylvania farmer's cheese or an equivalent Swiss-
   type cheese
2 tablespoons (15g) flour
¼ cup (65g) unsalted butter

FIGURE 42. Bottle label for Dutch Country Beer depicting the Millbach Room at the Philadelphia Museum of Art with realistic Pennsylvania Dutch men. Roughwood Collection, Devon, Pa.

¼ cup (30g) flour
2 cups (500ml) beer, preferably a Pennsylvania lager
2 quarts (2 liters) hot pork or chicken stock
2 teaspoons smooth Dijon mustard
Ham-and-cheese or onion-and-cheese dumplings (see recipe below)
Salt to taste
Crumbled fried bacon or a mixture of chopped chives and marjoram
    for garnish

Shred the cheese on the large holes of a vegetable grater and reserve this in a separate work bowl. Dust the shredded cheese with 2 tablespoons (15g) flour.

Melt the butter in a large stewing pan over medium-high heat until it foams. Add the flour and stir constantly until you attain a nutty roux about the same color as peanut butter. Add the beer and whisk vigorously until thick and creamy.

Gradually add the cheese, whisking at intervals to blend the cheese into the thickened beer. Add the hot stock and continue beating to create a smooth, creamy consistency. Once the stock is boiling hot, the cheese will curdle and gather into large clumps on the bottom. Remove the curds with a slotted spoon and while still warm combine with the dumpling mixture (see below).

Once the curds are removed from the soup, add the mustard. At this point you should have a thick, creamy, yellow, cheese-flavored stock. Add the dumplings and continue cooking no more than 10 minutes or until they float. Adjust seasonings, garnish with crumbled fried bacon or chopped herbs, and serve with warm soft pretzels, *Zwiwwelkuche* (page 232), pickled okra and summer sausage (page 239), or hot potato fingers (page 187).

Ham-and-Cheese Dumplings (Gnepp fun Schunkefleesch-un-Kees)

These are fairly easy to make with a food processor. If you prefer to use onions instead, just substitute the 4 ounces (125g) of cooked ham with 4 ounces (125g) of finely chopped onion that has been sautéed in butter or with bits of slab bacon. Omit the 2 teaspoons of melted butter.

Yield: 28 mini-dumplings

4 ounces (125g) warm curds reserved from beer cheese soup (recipe above)
4 ounces (125g) cooked ham (or equivalent amount from a cooked ham hock), coarsely chopped
2 teaspoons melted butter
¼ cup (30g) bread crumbs
2 large egg yolks
1 tablespoon ground coriander
1 teaspoon coarsely ground pepper or to taste

Put the curds, chopped ham, butter, bread crumbs, and egg yolks into a food processor and pulse until the mixture is reduced to a smooth paste. Put the paste on a clean work surface lightly dusted with flour. Divide the dumpling mixture into 28 equal pieces and roll into balls, each about the size and shape of a chestnut (they should weigh about 10g each). Let stand 30 minutes so that the dumplings dry and mature. Then cook them in the simmering soup stock for 10 minutes or until they float. Serve immediately as directed in the soup recipe.

Note: The uncooked dumplings can be deep-fried for about 1 minute and served crisp and piping hot in the soup. The dumpling mixture can also be used as filling in half-moon pies, Dampfgnepp, *and* Mauldasche *or put in casings to make sausage. Smoked beer cheese sausage is an excellent addition to the soup, especially when a little hot pepper is added to the sausage filling.*

"Boys Bits" (*Buweschpitzle*)

These dumplings are called *Bubenschpitzel* in Palatine dialect and were just as popular among the Palatine segment of the Pennsylvania Dutch community as they were among those of Swabian descent. While the English translation of this seemingly indelicate

FIGURE 43. *Buweschpitzle.*

dialect euphemism may send old maids blushing (it literally means "pricks"), it is considered cute and humorous in Pennsylvania Dutch, a language with a heavy infusion of barnyard witticisms.

Just the same, the editors of Pennsylvania Dutch newspapers and almanacs were well aware of the obvious awkwardness, so they generally opted for the Pennsylvania High German term *Schupfnudeln* (from the Swiss verb *schupfen*, "to shove or shake"), and it is under this name that you will find the dish in many printed sources, including Mrs. Mahlon O. Rohn's 1912 *Lancaster County Tested Cook Book*. In Lancaster County Pennsylfaanisch (which incorporates a number of Swiss influences), the dialect verb *schuppe* literally means "to sauté"—shaking the pan while you fry, which is precisely what you do when you brown *Buweschpitzle*; that is why they are called *Schuppgnepplin* ("shake dumplings") in Lancaster dialect. Almost every subregion in the Pennsylvania Dutch world has its own euphemistic name for this dish.

All said, I suppose the underlying joke is that they are small (*Schpitzle* is diminutive), and while no one would question that they are delicate, they are just dumplings of a peculiar shape and yet are absolutely classic when eaten with sauerkraut or as a side dish with game. You can make them from just about anything; the most common form is made with mealy potatoes. Even though the traditional method was to brown them in a skillet, I think they are far better looking and tasting when deep-fried like French fried potatoes. Naturally you don't have to fry them at all; just eat them boiled like any other dumpling. They are best when fresh but can be frozen for later use. This same dumpling mixture can be used to make small dumplings for *Schnitz-un-Gnepp* (page 182) or for any of the recipes calling for dumplings.

Yield: About 40 dumplings (serves 6 to 8)

2 pounds (1kg) peeled, cooked mealy potatoes
2 large eggs
4 egg yolks
1 tablespoon grated nutmeg
Salt and pepper to taste
2 teaspoons baking powder
1 cup (125g) bread crumbs
¼ cup (30g) flour, more or less (depending on the potatoes)
Fat or oil for frying

Rice the potatoes and put them in a deep work bowl. Beat the eggs and yolks until lemon color and frothy, and add them to the potatoes, whipping them until smooth and creamy. Add the nutmeg and season with salt and pepper, then combine the baking powder and bread crumbs and add to the dumpling mixture. Work in only enough flour to form soft dough. Shape into dumplings about 3 inches (7.5cm) long and make them slightly pointed on both ends. They should resemble little cigars—well, you get the picture.

Heat a kettle of salted water to a rolling boil. Reduce the heat to a gentle simmer and add the dumplings. Let them float for about 3 minutes, then skim them off and set aside to drain on a warm platter. Once all of the dumplings are cooked, heat butter or bacon drippings in a skillet and sauté (*schuppe*) the dumplings until golden brown on both sides. Or better yet, deep-fry them, without parboiling, for about 1 minute in cooking oil brought to a temperature of 375°F (190°C). Serve immediately scattered over hot sauerkraut or serve together with smoked sausage fried with sliced apples and onions.

Bread Crust Pancakes (*Gruscht Pannkuche*)

According to the reminiscences of Kate Gingery Cronister (1859–1933), who lived on a farm near Martha Furnace in Centre County, frugal pancakes of recycled ingredients were often given out as *Rumleefer-Schticke* (tramp pieces), folded over sandwich style with a filling of apple butter—snacks for hobos and beggars who came to the door. They were also packed in this same fashion into the lunch pails of schoolchildren, along with a few apple *Schnitz* to tide them over until dinner.

The original recipe for this poverty dish may be found in an 1854 edition of *Der americanische Bauer,* an Allentown farm journal published for the Pennsylvania Dutch.[5] In spite of their intended purpose to help make ends meet, these griddle cakes are among the best I have tasted. One of the secrets to their excellent texture and appearance is to scatter small bits of chopped slab bacon on the griddle while they are cooking. This imparts more flavor and creates a smooth, crispy surface on the pancakes. If the cakes are laid on a plate to cool, spread them out rather than stacking. The cakes can be set aside and reheated in a toaster or frozen for later use and microwaved. It goes without saying that the bread crusts in this case are taken from a firm crusty farm loaf, preferably sourdough, similar to the leftover crust from the recipe for Amish roast on page 180.

Yield: 12 griddle cakes (serves 4 to 6)

6 ounces (185g) crust freshly trimmed from a loaf of bread
2 cups (500ml) buttermilk
4 tablespoons (30g) whole wheat or spelt flour
¾ teaspoon baking soda
2 large eggs

Soften the crust in the buttermilk for about 25 minutes, then puree this in a food processor to a fine batter consistency. Sift together the flour and soda twice. Beat the eggs until lemon color and combine with the batter. Sift in the dry ingredients, stirring thoroughly. Heat a large griddle or cast-iron *Schales* pan until smoking hot and grease it liberally or scatter bits of chopped slab bacon on it and render the fat (as suggested above). Dip out ¼ cup (65ml) scoops of batter and pour them on the griddle. Bake golden brown on both sides and serve immediately on a hot platter with molasses or apple butter. You will know when to flip them because the pancakes will develop numerous air holes on the top. They should cook no more than 4 minutes once turned over. Serve hot.

Note: The pancakes can be saved for later use in soups. As an addition to soup, roll up each pancake and slice into narrow strips. Drop into hot soup stock and serve.

Bread Soup or Wild Mushroom Casserole (*Brodsupp odder Morchelschlupper*)

This is one of those *Neideitsch* recipes that has been subtly reinvented; I say "subtly" because it adheres rather closely to tradition: it has the structure of a classic *Schlupper*. A *Schlupper* is a deep-dish casserole made with bread. By nature it is sloppy because it normally contains a lot of stock or sauce (or stewed fruit). This particular *Schlupper* is called a "soup" because it is served, like *Schlappichdunkes* (see Glossary for a description), in its own baking dish from the center of the table. While it is piping hot, it is indeed soupy, but once it cools, it shrinks and becomes more like a dense pudding, and it is just as good reheated the next day.

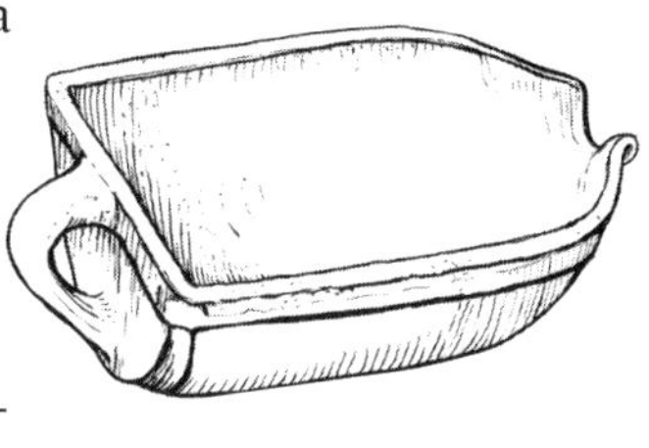

FIGURE 44. *Rutscher.*

In former times, when it was prepared in outdoor bake ovens, the "soup" was normally baked in an earthenware *Rutscher*—the radiant heat of earthenware gives the bottom and side crusts a very special crispy quality that is considered by some to be the best part. Do not hold back on the sage; it adds an important dimension to the flavor.

Yield: 8 to 10 servings

1½ ounces (25g) dried wild mushrooms
2 large onions (1½ pounds/750g), sliced
3 tablespoons (45g) unsalted butter or olive oil
3 tablespoons (45g) brown sugar
1 teaspoon salt or to taste
1½ pounds (750g) stale, thick crusted country-style bread cut into thick slices (sourdough bread is recommended)

*10 ounces (315g) Gruyère or Pennsylvania Dutch farmer's cheese
   shredded on the large holes of a vegetable grater
4 tablespoons (10g) minced fresh sage, or to taste
½ cup (65g) grated Parmesan cheese
1 teaspoon caraway seeds*

Put the mushrooms in a large jar and add 1 quart (1 liter) of boiling water. Cover and infuse 1 to 2 hours or until the mushrooms are fully reconstituted. Strain the infusion, reserving both the infusion and the mushrooms. Coarsely chop the mushrooms and set aside.

Put the sliced onions in a broad skillet or sauté pan with the butter and sugar. Cover and sweat over medium heat for 10 minutes or until the onions are soft and beginning to caramelize. Add the salt. Remove the onions and reserve. Pour any remaining pan juices into the mushroom infusion, using some of the infusion to deglaze the pan if necessary.

Preheat the oven to 375°F (190°C). Make a layer of sliced stale bread on the bottom of a large casserole pan measuring 2½ inches (5cm) deep and 9½ by 14 inches (23.5 by 35cm). Chop any remaining bread into small irregular pieces and reserve. Cover the bread layer with the chopped mushrooms. Combine the grated cheese and the sage and spread this evenly over the mushrooms. Cover this with chopped bread. Spread the onions over the bread, then add the mushroom infusion. Pat smooth with a wooden spoon. If there is not enough liquid to reach the top of the bread, add water. Sprinkle the Parmesan cheese over this, then scatter caraway seeds over the top and bake uncovered for 45 to 55 minutes or until set and crispy on the top.

Serve as a one-pot meal directly from the oven. The "soup" can be reheated in a microwave oven.

Browned Flour Soup (*Gereeschte Mehlsupp*)

This extremely easy-to-make soup is so universal among all the different Pennsylvania Dutch communities that written recipes are almost unnecessary. Just the same, here is the basic method, keeping in mind that the variations are seemingly endless and entirely a matter of personal taste.

Yield: Serves 4 to 6

2 quarts (2 liters) meat stock, such as pork, ham, or chicken
2 tablespoons (30g) unsalted butter
2 tablespoons (15g) flour
½ teaspoon grated nutmeg (optional)
Salt and pepper to taste

Heat the meat stock in a large saucepan until it is boiling gently. In another saucepan melt the butter over medium-high heat, and when it begins to foam, add the flour. Whisk until the roux attains the desired color (the darker, the nuttier the flavor). Add 2 cups (500ml) of the hot stock and whisk until smooth and creamy, then add the remaining stock and bring to a gentle boil to thicken the soup. Add diced cooked potatoes, meat dumplings, sausage, noodles, sliced bread crumb pancakes, or beaten eggs for "chopped soup" (see page 206). Season with nutmeg, salt, and pepper and serve.

Buckwheat Cakes (*Buchweetze Pannkuche*)

This old-fashioned breadlike buckwheat cake is very hard to come by these days. It was once considered an almost universal winter dish in the Dutch Country. In poor households the pancakes often took the place of wheat bread and were made in the same skillet in which bacon had been cooked in order to give them a faint, smoky, country flavor. Plain but good, they are delicious when served with dark buckwheat blossom honey.

Yield: Serves 8

2 cups (250g) whole wheat flour
1½ cups (185g) buckwheat flour
1½ teaspoons baking powder
½ teaspoon baking soda
1 teaspoon salt
2 eggs
3 cups (375ml) buttermilk
Cooking oil or bacon drippings

Sift together the whole wheat and buckwheat flours, baking powder, soda, and salt three times in order to combine all ingredients evenly. Beat the eggs until lemon color, then beat in the buttermilk. Form a valley in the middle of the dry ingredients and add the buttermilk mixture. Stir gently until a thick, ropy batter is formed. Let the batter rest a few minutes (bubbles should form on the top).

Pour a few tablespoons of oil into a large cast-iron skillet, just enough to coat the surface, and place over medium-high heat until the oil begins to smoke. Add about ⅓ cup (80ml) of batter, spreading it out so that it forms a nicely shaped round cake. Let it cook until golden brown on one side, then flip it over to brown on the other. Let the cake cook until fully risen and about ½ inch (1.25cm) thick. Transfer to a hot platter and reserve or serve immediately. Repeat this process until all the buckwheat cakes are cooked, adding more oil from time to time to keep the cakes from sticking to the pan.

Cabbage Dumplings (*Grautgnepp*)

When I first saw this recipe in the 1843–1890 recipe scrapbook of the well-to-do Berks County farmer Johannes Reisner, I thought it must be an anomaly—not something normally found in rural kitchens. Since then I have discovered it in various editions of the *Reading Adler* (a German-language newspaper), manuscript cookbooks, scrapbooks, marginal jottings in printed cookbooks, and even in the Lancaster almanac *Neuer gemeinnütziger Pennsylvanischer Calender* for 1908. All of this should underscore its perennial popularity among the culinary elites who relied on the wells of urban culture to sustain their lifestyle. In short, this is one of those dishes favored by the *Hasenpfeffer* Dutch and would find a welcome spot on the same table beside Mary Wacker's sour marinated rabbit (page 257).

Yield: 20 to 25 dumplings

4 cups (350g) finely shredded cabbage
¼ cup (5g) chopped chives
3 eggs, well beaten
3 tablespoons (25g) flour
1 cup (125g) bread crumbs
Salt and pepper to season
1 cup (100g) diced slab bacon cooked golden brown

Pour ½ cup (125ml) water in the bottom of a heavy stewing pan and bring it to a boil. Add the cabbage, cover, and simmer until the cabbage is heated through and wilted but not soft. Drain and press out any excess liquid. Set aside to cool.

Once the cabbage is cool enough to handle, add the chives and run it through a meat grinder or food processor to chop it as fine as possible, almost to paste consistency. Pour this into a work bowl and add the eggs, flour, and bread crumbs. Adjust seasoning with salt and pepper and work until smooth with a wooden spoon.

Scoop out 1-tablespoon lumps of the dumpling mixture and roll them into balls between the palms of your hands (or form into balls with two wet spoons). Set the dumplings aside to dry a few minutes while you prepare the boiling medium.

Bring salted water to a rolling boil in a large kettle or stewing pan, then reduce the heat to a slow simmer. Gently lower the dumplings into the water, doing only a few at a time since they will reduce the water temperature and stick together if too crowded. Cook uncovered until they rise to the surface. Once they float, the dumplings are done. Lift out with a slotted spoon or skimmer and drain. Then lay the dumplings in a buttered baking dish and sprinkle them liberally with the diced bacon. Set in the oven to warm a few minutes before serving. Garnish with additional chopped chives if you desire.

Catfish Gravy and Dried Corn Waffles
(*Katzefisch un Gedarrte Welschkarn Waffle*)

This variation on old-fashioned tomato gravy was one of several catfish recipes served at the Wild Cat Falls Inn along the Susquehanna River during the early 1900s. The inn also specialized in snapping turtle over waffles, crayfish over waffles, and duck over waffles. Serve with pepper hash and a side of three fried oysters during cold weather or three large fried clams during the summer.

Yield: Serves 4 to 6

Catfish Gravy
4 tablespoons (60g) unsalted butter
1 pound (500g) catfish fillets
3 tablespoons (25g) flour
1 cup (250g) minced onion or leek
1 tablespoon minced garlic
2 cups (400g) chopped vine-ripe tomatoes
½ cup (125ml) fish stock (made with trimmings from the catfish)
2 tablespoons chopped celery leaves (from the inner stems)
1½ cups (375ml) whole milk
1 to 2 tablespoons small capers, or to taste
1 teaspoon ground cayenne pepper, or to taste
¼ cup (65ml) heavy cream
Salt and pepper to taste
Chopped sweet basil

Heat 2 tablespoons (30g) of butter in a large sauté pan. Dry the fillets with paper towels and dust them with one tablespoon of flour, then brown lightly on both sides (about 5 minutes). Remove from the pan and set aside. Add the remaining butter and flour and cook vigorously, scraping the pan to deglaze it so that a light brown roux develops. Add the onion and garlic and cover. Sweat about 3 minutes or until the onions are soft and turning color, then add the tomatoes and fish stock. Cover again and simmer until the tomatoes are well cooked (about 8 minutes). Chop the fish and add it to the tomatoes along with the celery, milk, and capers. Simmer gently until the mixture thickens, then season with hot pepper (optional). Add the cream and season with salt and pepper to taste. Serve hot over crispy dried corn waffles, garnishing each dish generously with chopped sweet basil.

Variation: An alternative method was to serve a lightly browned fillet of catfish on top of each serving of waffles, then pour the catfish gravy over it. The catfish gravy is also excellent served over boiled new potatoes.

Dried Corn Waffles
Yield: Approximately 14 to 18 small waffles

1 cup (125g) dried sweet corn
½ cup (125ml) buttermilk
2 tablespoons (30ml) melted butter or vegetable oil
4 large eggs, separated
1½ cups (190g) pastry flour
1 tablespoon baking powder
½ teaspoon baking soda
½ teaspoon salt

Put the dried corn in a deep work bowl and cover with 2 cups (500ml) boiling water. Let the corn infuse for 2 to 3 hours until completely soft. Puree the corn and excess liquid in a blender or food processor with the buttermilk and melted butter to form a thick, smooth batter. Beat the egg yolks until lemon color and frothy, then fold them into the batter. Pour this into a work bowl.

In a separate work bowl, sift together the flour, baking powder, soda, and salt twice, then sift the flour mixture into the batter. Beat the egg whites until they form stiff peaks, then fold them into the batter. Let the batter rest for 5 minutes. While it is resting, heat the waffle iron.

Follow the instructions accompanying your waffle iron concerning how much batter will be required for each waffle. Since this batter is on the heavy side, make the waffles in small batches and cook slightly longer than normal (as much as 6 minutes). Once the waffle iron is ready, add the batter in half-cup increments, spreading it evenly with a spatula. Close the lid and cook until crisp and golden brown. Serve piping hot with the catfish gravy above.

Note: If your waffle iron bakes these waffles overly moist, finish them in an oven preheated to 350°F (190°C) for about 8 minutes or until crispy.

Chicken Gravy and Ham Waffles (*Hinkel un Schunkefleesch Waffle*)

This recipe follows fairly closely a similar recipe used at the Water Gate Inn in Washington, D.C. The restaurant served a house specialty called "Mennonite Chicken," which was chicken stewed in sour cream; this often doubled as gravy for waffles. Marjorie Hendricks (the restaurant owner) was not reluctant to introduce wine into her recipes since her Normandy Farm restaurant in Rockville, Maryland, used the grape abundantly in her French-style dishes. She understood that the best of the old-time Dutch cooking, à la Kuechler's Roost, also made use of local wines, and a good Pennsylvania wine is one of the defining features of this dish. The wine should be a little on the fruity side, such as a Gewürztraminer or a Riesling.

Yield: Serves 4 to 6

Chicken Gravy
1½ pounds (750g) frying chicken, preferably 2 boneless breasts
1 tablespoon (15g) unsalted butter
2 ounces (60g) country slab bacon, diced very small
1 cup (125g) diced cooked ham
1 cup (125g) chopped onion or leek
1 cup (75g) fresh morels or other wild mushrooms, sliced or quartered
    depending on size
2 tablespoons (15g) flour
1 cup (250ml) fruity white Pennsylvania wine
1 cup (250ml) sour cream
1 cup (250ml) hot milk or heavy cream

Salt and pepper to taste
1 tablespoon each of minced parsley and minced fresh thyme as
  garnish

Remove the skin and fat from the chicken and set aside (see note). Divide the breasts into 3 or 4 pieces. Heat the butter and bacon in a large, heavy sauté pan. Once the bacon is rendered (about 3 minutes), add the chicken and brown evenly over medium-high heat. Cover and reduce to low heat and simmer 25 to 30 minutes or until the meat is thoroughly cooked. Remove the bacon and chicken. Add the bacon to the diced ham and chop the chicken into small, bean-size pieces. Combine with the ham and bacon and set aside.

Add to the pan the onion or leek as well as the mushrooms, dusting them with the flour. Cover and sweat for 2 minutes, then add the wine. Boil briskly to deglaze the pan, then reduce the heat. Add the chopped chicken mixture, then add the sour cream and milk. Stir to thicken. Adjust seasonings and add herbs. Serve immediately over hot waffles (recipe below). Add more milk or hot chicken stock if you want the gravy to be extra runny.

Note: The chicken fat and skin should not be wasted. Cook them in a small saucepan until fully rendered of the fat. Pour the fat through a fine strainer or sieve into a jar and set aside to cool. Once cool, cover with a tight lid and use like butter in cookery, especially where savory (meat) dishes are called for. The flavor is unique and tastes better than butter.

Ham Waffles

Make the waffles ahead of the chicken and keep them warm in the oven heated to 200°F (90°C). Serve with side dishes of red cabbage and stewed celery.

Yield: Approximately 14 to 16 small waffles

4 large eggs, separated
1½ cups (375ml) buttermilk
¼ cup (65ml) vegetable oil or olive oil
1 cup (100g) finely ground cooked ham

1¾ cups (220g) pastry flour
1 tablespoon baking powder
½ teaspoon baking soda
½ teaspoon salt

Beat the egg yolks until lemon color and frothy, then combine this with the buttermilk and vegetable oil. Fold in the ground ham.

In a separate work bowl, sift together the flour, baking powder, soda, and salt twice, then sift this into the batter. Beat the egg whites until they form stiff peaks, then fold them gently into the batter. Let the batter rest 5 minutes. While it is resting, heat the waffle iron.

Follow the instructions accompanying your waffle iron concerning how much batter will be required for each waffle. Once the waffle iron is ready, add the batter in half-cup increments, spreading it evenly with a spatula. Close the lid and cook until crisp and golden brown (5 to 6 minutes). Serve piping hot with the chicken gravy above.

Chopped Soup (*Gehacktesupp*)

This was considered a good starter dish or a light meal for supper. It was often given to children or the elderly. Ora Cronister Yoder (1896–1974) used to beat eggs and add them to *Gereeschte Mehlsupp* prepared with diced potatoes, a popular variation in the Bald Eagle Valley region of Centre County.

Yield: Serves 4 to 6

2 quarts (2 liters) Gereeschte Mehlsupp (see recipe page 199)
1 or 2 eggs, depending on desired thickness

Bring the soup to a gentle boil over medium heat. Lightly beat the egg to stir up the yolks and whites, then drizzle this into the hot soup. Stir vigorously with a fork to create strands of egg. Once the egg is cooked, the soup is ready to serve. Garnish with chopped parsley or herb of your choice.

Christmas Preserve (*Grischdaags Siesses*)

This delightful green tomato recipe comes from the Pennsylvania Dutch community near Hagerstown, Maryland, although it appears to have been widely circulated in Pennsylvania Dutch charitable cookbooks during the early 1900s.

Yield: 6 to 7 pints

3 pounds (1.5kg) green tomatoes sliced paper thin
3 lemons sliced paper thin (remove seeds)
2½ pounds (1.25kg) sugar
1 cup (250ml) spring water
¾ pound (375g) fresh ginger root, pared and shredded

Wash and slice the tomatoes and lemons. Place the sugar in a preserving kettle with the water and dissolve over low heat. Bring the syrup to a hard boil, then add the lemon (well picked of seeds). Boil 2 minutes, then add the green tomatoes and ginger. Reduce to a moderate heat and boil gently until the fruit is transparent (about 20 minutes), stirring from time to time so that the bottom does not scorch or cook more than the top. Lift out the fruit with a perforated spoon and put into hot, sanitized jars. Reduce the liquid to thick syrup (test thermometer should read 230°F/115°C), then pour over the fruit and seal. Water bath 10 minutes.

Christmas Shoofly Pie or Honey Shoofly Pie (*Grischdaags Riwwelboi odder Hunnich Riwwelboi*)

One of the leaders in experimenting with new sorts of shoofly pies is Verna Dietrich of Dietrich's Country Meats in Krumsville, Pennsylvania—Verna sells a lot of homemade pastry from her store. A few years ago Verna began making honey shoofly pies, and this has resulted in a number of clever spin-offs. Using honey instead of molasses takes us back to the gingerbread origins of shoofly pie, to Jenny Lind pie, and to who knows what other variations that once lurked in early Pennsylvania Dutch kitchens? In that sense the recipe here is a revival, or at least a reinvention intended for Christmas morning or early New Year's Day. It is quite festive and calls for good strong coffee as an accompaniment.

Yield: One 10-inch (25cm) pie, or 8 to 10 servings (see watch point below)

1¼ cups (155g) all-purpose flour
¼ cup (65g) light brown sugar
½ cup (125g) unsalted butter
1 teaspoon ground cinnamon
1 teaspoon freshly grated nutmeg
½ teaspoon ground cardamom
¼ teaspoon salt
1 tablespoon baking powder
½ cup (75g) coarsely chopped walnuts
⅔ cup (160ml) warm water
¾ cup (180ml) honey
½ teaspoon baking soda

Preheat the oven to 350°F (175°C). Sift the flour before measuring—this is critical to the texture of the pie. Using a pastry cutter or food processor work the flour, sugar, butter, cinnamon, nutmeg, cardamom, salt, and baking powder to a coarse crumb texture. Add the walnuts and then take out ½ cup (75g) of the crumb mixture. In a separate work bowl, dissolve the warm water and honey and then add the baking soda. Combine this with the dry ingredients, then pour the batter into a prepared 10-inch (25cm) pie shell. Scatter the reserved crumb mixture over the top. For added appearance, you can scatter a few broken walnuts over the crumbs.

Bake the pie in the middle of the preheated oven for 45 to 50 minutes, or until the center of the pie is firm and cakelike. Cool on a rack and serve at room temperature.

Watch Point: If you do not have a 10-inch (25cm) pie dish, use one 9-inch (23cm) pan and one 6-inch (15cm) dish; otherwise the batter may overflow the crust.

Colonel Tilghman Good's Venison Cutlets
(*em Kernel Good sei Harsch Schnidde*)

Colonel Tilghman Good (1830–1887) was a member of the urban Pennsylvania Dutch elite—the *Hasenpfeffer* Dutch—who left a remarkable imprint on the food culture of the region. He began his career as a shoemaker but eventually turned to hotel keeping, becoming proprietor of the Allen House in Allentown and later the Central House in Reading. Because of him, both hotels became well known in their heyday for fine regional cooking. Good was elected mayor of Allentown three times, his political success due in part to his record as a Civil War hero. However, it is this delicious chafing-dish recipe for which he is remembered today. It is normally served with either a side of small boiled red potatoes, a mixture of butter-fried hominy and chopped hickory nuts, or freshly made potato *Buweschpitzle*. If venison is not available, use pork chops, lamb chops, or even breasts of chicken.

Yield: 6 servings

⅓ cup (50g) finely chopped carrot
1 cup (250ml) beef stock or bouillon
½ cup (125g) thick unseasoned tomato sauce
⅓ cup (80ml) tarragon vinegar
2 tablespoons (30g) unsalted butter
6 venison loin chops, each weighing about 12 ounces (375g)
⅔ cup (65g) finely minced onion
⅓ cup (35g) Zante currants
1 tablespoon minced parsley
6 fresh bay leaves, bruised
½ cup (125ml) sour cream
½ cup (125ml) dry red wine
2 tablespoons (30ml) pureed raw tomato
3 tablespoons (35g) old-style Dijon mustard
Salt and freshly ground pepper to season
Minced parsley as garnish

Put the carrot and beef stock in a saucepan and cook over medium heat until the carrot is tender (about 6 minutes). Pour the carrot and cooking stock into a blender or food processor and process until reduced to a thin puree. Add the tomato sauce and vinegar, then set aside.

Melt the butter in a large skillet or chafing dish and brown the chops on both sides over medium-high heat. Remove the meat and set aside on a platter. Add the onion and cook until the pan is completely deglazed (about 3 minutes). Add the reserved carrot and stock mixture along with the currants, parsley, and bay leaves. Return the meat to the pan, cover, and simmer over low heat until the meat is tender (about 25 to 30 minutes).

While the meat is cooking, combine the sour cream, wine, and pureed raw tomato in a mixing bowl. As soon as the meat is ready to serve, remove it from the pan and place it on a hot platter. Add the sour cream and wine mixture to the pan and bring this to a gentle boil, just enough to thicken the sauce. Add the mustard, adjust seasonings, then pour part of the sauce over the chops, garnishing them with the cooked bay leaves and minced parsley. Serve immediately and send the rest of the sauce to the table in a sauceboat.

Dried Corn Pie with Chicken and Saffron
(Gedarrte Welschkarn Boi mit Hinkelfleesch un Safferich)

This extremely attractive winter pie is a study in simplicity yet is fragrant with the rich sweet flavor of dried corn. The most traditional way to serve the pie, aside from simply eating it sliced and hot from the oven, was to eat it in a bowl of hot milk or cream, or to serve it with chicken gravy over the top, the same sort of giblet gravy you would use for chicken and waffles.

Yield: two 9-inch (23cm) pies

2 cups (200g) dried corn
4 cups (1 liter) well-flavored chicken stock
1 cup (200g) cooked, diced potato
1 cup (150g) shredded cooked chicken (see note)

½ cup (65g) bread crumbs
2 tablespoons minced parsley
3 eggs
¼ teaspoon powdered saffron
Salt and freshly ground pepper to taste
2 9-inch (23cm) unbaked pie shells
2 tablespoons butter (one per pie)

Preheat the oven to 375°F (190°C). Cook the dried corn in 3½ cups (875ml) chicken stock until the corn is tender (about 15 to 20 minutes). Reserve the remaining ½ cup (125ml) of stock. Put the corn in a deep work bowl and add the diced potato, shredded chicken, bread crumbs, and parsley. Beat two eggs until lemon color and add the saffron. Once the saffron is fully dissolved and the eggs have turned bright yellow, add this to the corn and chicken mixture. Season with salt and pepper and then scrape the corn mixture evenly into two 9-inch (23cm) prepared pie crusts. Pat smooth with a wooden spoon.

Beat the remaining egg until lemon color, then add the remaining chicken stock. Pour this evenly over both pies so that they are nearly filled with liquid. Dot the pies with chopped butter and bake in the preheated oven for 45 to 50 minutes or until the tops are turning golden and the pies have set. Serve hot or at room temperature.

Note: To shred chicken, take two forks and pull the meat apart in opposite directions until you have reduced it to the consistency of small threads or strings. The size of the shreds is a matter of personal taste.

Dunk Babies Christmas Cookies (*Dunke Bobblin*)

Dunk babies are a type of sand tart (crisp sugar cookie) with an unusual appearance. They start out looking fairly homely when they go into the oven but come out totally transformed into charming cinnamon swirls. The original recipe for this old-fashioned Christmas treat appeared as *Dingle Babbles* in the 1932 *Pennsylvania State Grange Cook Book*.[6] The name appears to be a bad transliteration of *dunke Bobblin*, literally "dunk-babies," a children's name for a cookie intended for dipping in coffee or cider. Long before the Pennsylvania Dutch accepted the custom of St. Nicholas, children left the *Bobblin* on trays beneath the table-top Christmas trees with the idea that the *Grischtkindel* (Baby Jesus) would leave gifts in their stead.

FIGURE 45. Dunk babies.

Yield: 4 dozen

½ cup (125g) salted butter
1 cup (250g) sugar
2 eggs
½ cup (125ml) full milk or sour cream
1 teaspoons cream of tartar
½ teaspoon baking soda
2¾ cups (340g) pastry flour
1 tablespoon sugar
1 tablespoon powdered cinnamon
½ cup (125g) coarsely granulated sugar

Cream the butter and the sugar until light and fluffy. Beat the eggs until lemon color and frothy, then combine with the butter mixture. Add the milk and whisk smooth. Sift together the cream of tartar, baking soda, and pastry flour twice, then sift this into the batter, stirring gently to combine the flour mixture evenly. Form into a soft ball of dough, cover, and refrigerate for at least 4 hours or until the dough stiffens.

Break the ball in half and on a clean, well-floured work surface roll out the dough to about ¼ inch (6cm) thick, forming it into a rectangle about 14 inches (35cm) in length and 6 inches (15cm) wide. Combine the tablespoon each of sugar and cinnamon in a small work bowl and spread half of this over the dough. Cut the dough into 4 equal pieces, then roll them up to form logs about 1-inch (2.5cm) thick. Set these on a plate or tin tray and return to the refrigerator to cool. Repeat these steps with the other half of the dough, taking care to keep the dough as cool as possible and well-dusted with flour.

While the logs are cooling in the refrigerator, preheat the oven to 350°F (175°C). Once the oven is hot, grease 4 baking sheets and remove one batch of logs. Slice the logs into ½-inch (1.25cm) pieces. Dip each one in the coarsely granulated sugar, coating both top and bottom, then set the cookies at least 2 inches (5cm) apart on each baking sheet—they will puff and spread a good deal, so allow about 12 cookies per sheet. Repeat this with the other logs until all the cookies are sliced and dipped. Bake in the preheated oven for 15 minutes. Remove and cool on racks. Store in airtight containers.

Filling (*Fillsel*)

This excellent recipe is actually a potato *Schlupper* meant to double as stuffing for roast chicken. It traces to Irene B. Arthur of East Mauch Chunk (now Jim Thorpe, Pennsylvania) in Carbon County, a border region whose distinctive local cookery is often overlooked. Carbon County is in the coal country; thus mining has brought together many different cultural groups in addition to the original Pennsylvania Dutch settlers. This interesting overlay has given rise to culinary borrowings in both directions.[7] For enhanced flavor, you may add 4 ounces (125g) of chopped fried ham or 4 ounces (125g) of smoked sausage, fried and chopped. This recipe can also be used to fill half-moon pies; just leave out the milk.

Yield: Serves 4 to 6

6 tablespoons (90g) unsalted butter
4 cups (250g) bread diced very small (¼-inch/6mm cubes)

2 cups (500g) warm mashed potatoes
½ cup (125ml) potato water (water in which the potatoes were boiled)
1 cup (250g) minced onion
½ cup (10g) minced fresh parsley
2 tablespoons chopped fresh sage
2 eggs, well beaten
Salt and pepper to season
2 cups (500ml) milk

Heat the butter in a broad skillet or sauté pan, and once it begins to foam, add the bread. Cook the bread over medium-high heat until golden brown, stirring often to keep it from scorching. Pour this into a deep mixing bowl. Add the potatoes, potato water, onion, parsley, and sage. Mix well, then add the eggs. Season with salt and pepper. Pour this into a well-greased baking pan and drizzle the milk evenly over the surface. Bake in an oven preheated to 350°F (175°C) for 40 to 50 minutes. Serve hot with fried bread crumbs over the top.

Fried Potato and Sauerkraut Sandwich or *Backet* Sandwich (*Gebrotne Grumbier Sandwich mit Sauergraut odder Backet Sandwich*)

While I was interviewing members of the Hamm family it came out that one of their favorite snack foods was a fried potato sandwich: good crusty farm bread lightly toasted, smeared with a little lard or bacon drippings, and then filled with a thick, golden brown slice of hot fried potato. The Hamms live near New Tripoli, which was formerly the uncontested potato capital of the Dutch Country. All sorts of potato recipes from that area are still found in local kitchens. In fact there are so many different variations of this basic idea, which evolved out of the old plate-stove *Backet* (potatoes browned on the top of the stove), that it would be possible to compile an impressive potato sandwich cookbook. Fried potato sandwiches even appear from time to time on the menus of local diners and restaurants. Back in the 1920s these sandwiches became popular among truckers who made their rounds in the countryside delivering produce or picking it up for market. Today you sometimes find the ingredients served in a long loaf much like a Philadelphia hoagie, but toasted sourdough bread or salt-raised bread is still the best.

Since this recipe also contains pot pudding, perhaps it is appropriate to point out that you will not get the right flavor or texture unless you use real Pennsylvania Dutch pot pudding. Its composition varies from one country butcher to the next. The saltier types, such as that made by Peters Brothers in Lenhartsville, Pennsylvania, resemble true *rilettes du Mans*, while others, like Dietrich's in Krumsville, contain more pork liver and thus have a texture and flavor similar to French country pâtés. Like any pâté, Pennsylvania Dutch pot puddings are rich and should be spread very thin in sandwiches—and do not forget that important side of applejack or hard cider.

Yield: Serves 4 to 6

One round 1¼ pound (625g) loaf of crusty sourdough bread or salt-raised bread
1 pound (500g) potatoes, preferably waxy fingerlings
2 tablespoons (30g) unsalted butter, lard, or cooking medium of your choice
3 medium onions
2 cups (350g) sauerkraut pressed of excess liquid
8 ounces (250g) pot pudding
Salt and pepper to taste

Cut the bread crosswise into 8 thick slices, then cut these in half down the center, yielding 16 half slices for 8 sandwiches. Leftover pieces of bread can be reserved for bread crust pancakes (page 195). Set aside.

Cut the potatoes lengthwise into ½-inch (1.25cm) thick slices. It is not necessary to pare them. Set the potatoes on a well-greased hot griddle and let them turn golden brown on one side, then turn them over and brown the other side. The idea is to create a crisp crust, so the cooking process is similar to that for cooking scrapple.

While the potatoes are browning, melt the butter in a heavy skillet. Cut the onions in half lengthwise, then slice into paper-thin pieces. Put them in the butter and cover. Sweat over medium-high heat until the onions begin to turn golden (3 to 4 minutes), then add the sauerkraut. Stir and cover. Sweat until the sauerkraut begins to brown lightly, then remove from the heat.

Toast the bread and cover each bottom slice with sauerkraut. Lay a piece of potato over this and spread it generously with pot pudding. Add more sauerkraut, season with salt and pepper, then cover with the top slices of bread. Serve immediately while the ingredients are still hot.

Comment: While these sandwiches are wonderfully flavorful as is, some locals like to add mustard or a few slices of pickled cucumbers or even pickled hot peppers. Raw hot peppers can be cooked with the sauerkraut.

Funnel Cake (*Drechterkuche*)

Funnel cakes were a nineteenth-century Christmas and New Year's novelty sold at church bazaars and holiday markets. Like *Fastnachts* (Shrove Tuesday fat cakes), they were once expensive to make because fresh eggs were in short supply during the winter months and eggs stored in isinglass (the only way to preserve eggs during cold weather) were worthless for use in cakes. Thus pre-1940s Pennsylvania Dutch recipes for funnel cakes are relatively scarce. This particular recipe dates from 1916 and was used by Lizzie Brendle Weinhold (1884–1958), whose husband, John Dridge Weinhold, was a well-to-do cigar maker in Lancaster County.[8] In other words, they were *Hasenpfeffer* Dutch.

Yield: About 24 large funnel cakes

Lard or oil for frying
4 eggs, separated
1 quart (1 liter) milk, lukewarm
4 cups (500g) sifted flour, more or less
2 teaspoons baking powder

1 teaspoon salt
Confectioners' sugar

Heat lard or cooking medium of your choice in a deep-fryer until it attains the temperature of 375°F (190°C). While the lard or oil is warming, beat the egg yolks until lemon color and frothy. Add the milk. Sift together 3 cups (375g) of the flour, the baking powder, and the salt. Then sift this into the milk and egg mixture. If the batter seems too thin, add some of the remaining flour until thick. Beat the egg whites until they form stiff peaks and gently fold into the batter.

FIGURE 46. Funnel.

Take about ½ cup (125ml) of batter and pour it into your funnel. Drizzle the batter into the preheated lard, starting at the center and moving in circles in an outward motion; this will create "coils" of cake. Work quickly since the cakes take only a minute or two to cook. You can become as creative as you like and make all sorts of exotic shapes once you learn to master the funnel. Continue filling the funnel and frying cakes in this manner until all the batter is used up. Depending on the size of your frier, you can cook as many as four cakes at a time; otherwise, cook them one at a time because the batter will lower the oil temperature and may make the cakes soggy.

Once the cakes turn crispy and golden yellow, lift them out with a slotted spoon and drain on a rack or paper towels. Dust with confectioners' sugar when cool and serve.

Grated Potato Soup (*Geriewwenesupp*)

This poverty soup is the picture of simplicity and yet is quite tasty, especially when 1 or 2 cups (250 or 500ml) of sauerkraut juice or liquid from sour pickles are added. When I have a jar of pickles that have been used up and there is a little sour liquid left, I always save it for soups such as this. If you do not have basic stock from *Hooriche Gnepp* (see recipe below), you can use the broth leftover from boiling dumplings or stuffed pig stomach or even the liquid remaining from boiled potatoes or beans. The idea is to waste nothing.

Yield: Serves 8 to 10

6 tablespoons (90g) lard or unsalted butter
6 tablespoons (45g) flour
2½ quarts (2.5 liters) cold Hooriche Gnepp stock
1½ pounds (750g) shredded raw peeled potato
Salt and freshly ground pepper to taste
Toasted pieces of hearth-baked potato bread
Chopped chives, parsley, marjoram, or savory (optional)

In a deep stewing pan heat the lard or butter, then add the flour, stirring until the roux attains the desired color (light peanut-butter brown). Add the cold *Gnepp* stock and stir well to incorporate the roux into the liquid. Once the soup mixture is hot, add the grated raw potato and cook until tender (about 20 minutes). Add seasonings to taste and serve with large irregular pieces of toasted hearth-baked potato bread. Scatter freshly chopped herbs over the top of the soup at the table.

"Hairy" Dumplings (*Hooriche Gnepp*)

Yield: Serves 4 to 6 (about 18 dumplings)

3 pounds (1.5kg) raw grated potatoes
1½ pounds (750g) peeled, grated, and mashed day-old boiled potatoes
2 to 3 tablespoons potato starch, cornstarch, or rice flour
1 tablespoon freshly ground pepper
Chopped marjoram, chives, or summer savory

Combine the grated and mashed potatoes in a deep work bowl with the starch and pepper. Knead the potato mixture until it becomes stiff, then mold into perfectly round dumplings weighing about 3½ ounces (100g) each. Set aside to dry for about 25 minutes.

While the dumplings are drying, bring 8 quarts (8 liters) of lightly salted water to a rolling boil. Reduce the heat and let the water boil at a gentle simmer. Add the dumplings about 6 at a time and cook for about 15 minutes. Lift out with a slotted spoon and drain on a platter. Repeat until all the dumplings are cooked. Reserve the cooking water for grated potato soup stock (see preceding recipe) or serve the dumplings hot in the cooking broth flavored with pickle juice, sauerkraut juice, herb-flavored vinegar, or sour cream. Garnish liberally with chopped fresh herbs.

Hot Bacon Dressing with Eggs
(*Heese Schpecksass mit Oier*)

Hot salads, usually made with wilted lettuce, are standard items at the Kutztown Folk Festival because they are easy to prepare in hot weather and can be served at room temperature. Many home cooks prefer this dressing with dandelion greens, but the best combination is to use a mixture of dandelion, corn salad (mâche), and a few mustard greens. Mustard in particular gives the salad that extra zip it needs. If corn salad is not available, use some chopped spinach or even a little lettuce. The bacon usually supplies enough salt, so there is no need to add more to the dressing. Sliced hard-cooked eggs and boiled potatoes are often served as sides with this salad, thus converting it into a one-course meal. You can even pour some of the dressing over the potatoes. This is also excellent as a dressing on endive or on poached shredded cabbage.

Yield: Serves 4 to 6

¾ pound (375g) mixed dandelion, mustard greens, and other greens
5 tablespoons (75ml) apple cider vinegar
3 tablespoons (45ml) white wine vinegar
3 tablespoons (45g) sugar
½ pound (250g) country-style slab bacon cut into tiny dice
2 tablespoons (30ml) bacon drippings
1 tablespoon (15ml) olive oil
2 tablespoons (15g) flour
2 cups (500ml) water
2 eggs
Freshly ground pepper
Chopped hard-boiled eggs (optional)

Wash and drain the greens in a colander or salad spinner. Set aside in a serving bowl. Combine the vinegars in a small work bowl and dissolve the sugar in it. Set aside.

Render the bacon in a skillet over medium heat until brown and crispy. Remove the pan from the heat. Lift out the bacon with a slotted spoon and drain on paper towels. Put two tablespoons of the cooking fat in a deep saucepan with the olive oil. Heat the oil mixture over medium-high heat and add the flour. Cook the flour, stirring constantly with a paddle or wooden spoon until it becomes light yellow. Add the water, mixing as you pour with a wire whisk. Keep whisking until the mixture becomes creamy (about 5 minutes). Then add the reserved vinegar and sugar mixture and continue to whisk until smooth.

Beat the eggs in a medium-size work bowl until thick and lemon colored. Gradually pour half of the hot sauce mixture into the eggs, whisking as you pour so that the dressing becomes warm and slightly thick. Then pour this back into the saucepan with the remaining hot sauce and whisk vigorously over medium heat until the dressing becomes thick and creamy. If it is too thick, thin with hot water to the desired consistency. Add the bacon bits.

Pour over the salad greens, toss together with wooden forks, and serve immediately with freshly ground pepper over the top. Chopped hard-boiled eggs can be added.

Note: The dressing can be made ahead and reheated in the microwave on high for 15 seconds. For a sharper flavor, add an additional tablespoon (15ml) of apple cider vinegar.

Jenny Lind Pie (*Da Jenny Lind ihre Tschintscher-Brod Boi*)

This soft gingerbread pie is still fondly remembered in the Mahantongo Valley of Schuylkill County. Jenny Lind pie was created (or renamed) in the early 1850s in honor of the Swedish singer who at the time had taken the country by storm. A precursor of shoofly pie, it was meant to be handheld and dipped into morning coffee or, as some families preferred, crumbled into the coffee and eaten with a spoon as "coffee soup." The recipe below came from Mrs. Erma Pettich of Valley View, Pennsylvania, an interesting coincidence since another Valley View informant, Grace Starr Shankweiler, mentioned that back in the 1920s and 1930s her mother sold this pie in the family store. Since the pie recipe is not easy to divide in half, I have left it as given.

Yield: two 9-inch (23cm) pies, bottom crust only

2 cups (250g) pastry flour
1 cup (250g) superfine sugar (bar sugar)
1 teaspoon ground cinnamon
1 teaspoon grated nutmeg
¼ teaspoon ground cloves
1 teaspoon baking soda
1 teaspoon baking powder
2 eggs
1 cup (250ml) sour cream or strong coffee

¾ cup (190ml) unsulfured molasses
⅓ cup (85ml) apple cider vinegar

Preheat the oven to 325°F (165°C). Sift together the flour, sugar, cinna-mon, nutmeg, cloves, baking soda, and baking powder into a mixing bowl and make a valley in the center of these dry ingredients. In a separate mix-ing bowl, beat the eggs until frothy and lemon color. Add the sour cream or coffee, molasses, and finally the vinegar. Beat until well blended. Pour the liquid ingredients into the valley in the middle of the dry ingredients and combine gently, taking care not to beat the mixture too hard, as it will begin to foam. Pour this into the pie shells and bake in the preheated oven 1 hour or until fully risen and set in the center. When the pies test dry in the center with a needle, they are ready. Cool on a rack and serve at room temperature.

Lemon-Rice Pie (*Lemmon-Reis Boi*)

This Reformed Mennonite funeral pie was originally treated as a baked pudding and requires a long, slow heat to bake to perfec-tion. It can be sliced and eaten out of hand. The recipe here appeared in the 1851 edition of Gustav Peters's *Die geschickte Hausfrau*, al-though it can be traced to much older mainstream American cook-books.

Yield: one 9-inch (23cm) pie

Pastry for one 9-inch (23cm) pie
1 cup (155g) white long grain rice
2 cups (500ml) water
2 eggs
1 cup (250ml) cream
½ cup (125g) sugar
1½ to 2 teaspoons grated nutmeg
½ teaspoon salt
1 tablespoon grated zest of lemon

Line a 9-inch (23cm) pie pan with short pastry and set aside. Rinse the rice in running water until the water runs clear. Bring the water to a boil and add the rice. Cover and cook over medium heat until all the liquid is absorbed. Fluff with a fork.

Put the rice in a deep work bowl and let it cool to room temperature. Preheat the oven to 325°F (165°C).

Beat the eggs until lemon color, then add the cream, sugar, nutmeg, salt, and lemon zest. Combine this with the rice and pour the mixture into the prepared pie shell. Bake in the preheated oven for 60 to 70 minutes or until fully risen in the center. Cool on a rack and serve at room temperature or slightly chilled.

Lepp Cakes (*Leppkuche*) with Glaze Icing (*Zucker Glessur*)

One of the earliest published recipes for this old-time Pennsylvania Dutch Christmas favorite was featured in *41 bewährte Recepte* (41 Approved Recipes), printed at Millgrove, Pennsylvania, in 1834. As clumsy and poorly written as that recipe was, it still spoke volumes about the popularity of this beloved Christmas honey cake. To be honest, the 1834 recipe is so full of errors that it is obvious the editor was not well versed in cookery. With that in mind, I have taken the recipe and reworked it enough times to make it worth your trouble. The end products are delightful cookies, fat and puffy, just the way most old-timers remember them. You cannot celebrate an authentic Pennsylvania Dutch Christmas without *Leppkuche*. The original recipe has been reduced by half.

FIGURE 47. Honey bucket, Merit Food Company, Bally, Pa., ca. 1915. Photo by Rob Cardillo.

Yield: About 35–40 3-inch (7.5cm) cookies

Cookies

6 cups (750g) spelt flour
2 teaspoons baking soda
2 teaspoons cream of tartar
1 tablespoon ground cinnamon
1 tablespoon ground ginger
1 teaspoon ground cardamom
1 cup (200g) chopped preserved orange peel, minced fine
Finely minced zest of 1 fresh orange
⅔ cup (4 ounces/125g) dark brown sugar
1 cup (250ml) honey
2 large eggs
1 cup (250ml) thick milk (clabbered raw milk) or buttermilk

Into a deep work bowl sift together twice the flour, baking soda, cream of tartar, cinnamon, ginger, and cardamom. Add the minced orange peel. Make a valley in the center of the flour mixture. In a saucepan dissolve the brown sugar in the honey over moderate heat. Once the sugar is dissolved, set aside to cool until lukewarm. Then pour this into the valley in the flour mixture and stir to blend. Beat the eggs until lemon color and frothy, then add the thick milk or buttermilk. Pour this over the honey-flour mixture and stir with a fork or wooden paddle until soft, sticky dough is formed. Dust a clean work surface with additional spelt flour, and work the dough into a soft ball, dusting your hands with flour to prevent sticking. Use only enough extra flour so that the dough does not stick to the fingers. Cover the ball of dough and refrigerate to recover and season for 3 to 4 hours.

Preheat the oven to 350°F (175°C). Roll out the dough while cold to ½ inch (1.25cm) thick. Cut into 3-inch (7.5cm) rounds. Lay them on lightly greased baking sheets and bake for 15 to 20 minutes. Cool on racks. Once cool, the cookies can be decorated with glaze icing (see below).

Glaze Icing

In order to ice all the cookies in one full batch, it is necessary to make 2 batches of icing. Do not double the recipe because it will harden quickly: ice half the cookies with one batch, then the other half with a second batch of icing. Be absolutely certain to remove the granulated sugar mixture from the heat as soon as it achieves the thread stage; otherwise it will recrystallize when the powdered sugar is added. Once it cools and hardens, the icing turns white.

Yield: 1 cup (250ml)

½ cup (125g) granulated sugar
¼ cup (65ml) water
¼ cup (30g) confectioners' sugar
1 teaspoon potato starch
2 tablespoons (30ml) rosewater or lemon juice
Red rose-flavored sugar or white "hail sugar" (Hagelzucker) (optional)

Dissolve the granulated sugar in the water and boil until it reaches the thread stage (230°F/110°C). Remove and beat in the confectioners' sugar and starch. Add the rosewater or lemon juice. Brush the cookies with the glaze icing while it is still hot—work quickly. Scatter optional red sugar over the icing in a cross pattern while the glaze icing is still warm and sticky, or pipe the icing over the cookies in snowflake patterns as shown in Figure 48.

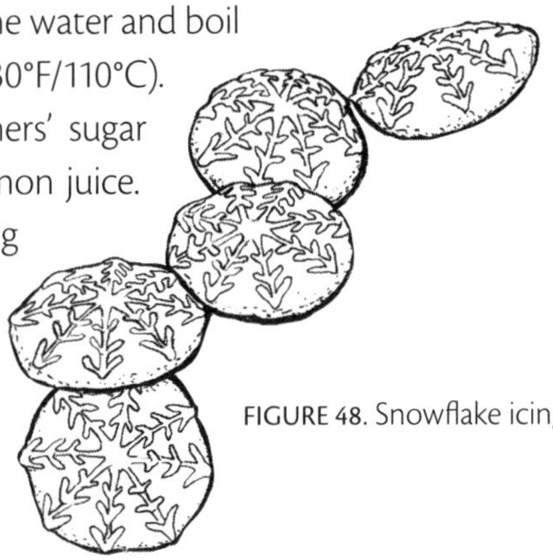

FIGURE 48. Snowflake icing.

◝ Mock Fish (*Blinde Fische*)

The rediscovery of this rare old-time dish was a stroke of pure serendipity. While I was visiting Old Order Mennonite Amos Hoover at his Muddy Creek farm in 1977, another member of his church was visiting the house. We fell into conversation about family recipes that were being forgotten, and the visitor, Mrs. Elizabeth Hahn, brought up *Blinde Fische*. The recipe was recorded in a handwritten cookbook compiled by her grandmother Anna Weaver Martin (1877–1933); this cookbook is still preserved by the family. The dish is made by creating *gleene Gnepplin* (little lumps of dough) in a batter, which is then pan or griddle fried like a fillet of fish. It was intended to use up leftover gravy. To quote Mrs. Hahn: "We like to serve it best with dry beef gravy because that puts the needed accent to it."[9] This is the recipe as recorded in the cookbook and relayed to me by Mrs. Hahn.

Yield: Serves 4

½ cup (125ml) milk
½ cup (125ml) water
½ teaspoon salt or to taste
6 tablespoons (45g) flour, more or less (depending on the flour)

Bring the milk, water, and salt to a gentle boil. Add the flour, stirring constantly with a fork until this forms wet, sticky lumps (*gleene Gnepplin*). Do not stir too briskly or you will break down the lumps, which are important for the texture. Remove from the heat. Using a large tablespoon or serving spoon, drop the batter onto a hot, well-greased griddle or frying pan. Press flat into elongated "fish." Brown on both sides as you would pancakes, then serve hot with the gravy of your choice.

◝ Mock Fish or Rivvel Fish
(*Blinde Fische odder Riwwelfisch*)

After Mrs. Hahn's recipe came to light in 1977, I was presented with yet another type of *Blinde Fische* recipe in 1986 while interviewing people in the Welsh Mountains between Berks and Lancaster Counties. This *Blinde Fische* comes from Magdalena Hildebrandt, who prepared it with goat milk over coals on an open hearth.

Magdalena lived in a 1740s stone cottage that was never electrified; the only source of heat was her hearth. I am glad I lived at the right moment in time to witness this; I walked into the eighteenth century then without quite realizing it. We would consider the lack of electricity an inconvenience, but Magdalena in her infinite simplicity considered it a small price to pay for living closer to nature. In any event she was from the old school: you do not pay a suspicious "foreign" company (outside her county) for the right to use energy that travels unnaturally through wires.

Now that I look back on that magical day, I suspect that Magdalena was totally in tune with the original Earth Mother, whatever that privileged exchange means. At the least it could be said that the Earth Mother was taking good care of her, because at the time Magdalena was eighty-something-plus and as strong as an ox (and just as stubborn). She could claim a full head of hair, though gray, pulled back in a knot under her cap and a complexion totally free of wrinkles. Was it Magdalena's goat milk? I have no idea.

Magdalena was proud of her archaic name. When I fussed too much over the trouble she was exerting to show off her culinary skills in an old pan, she just brushed me away with the flick of her hand and told me that this was an emergency dish prepared quickly to feed a large number of people, calling me *Bu* ("boy"—a term of affection presuming that I was an innocent in these matters). *Blinde Geem* (mock game) is made exactly the same way except that game stock is used instead of milk and buckwheat flour (or a mix of rye and buckwheat) is substituted for wheat flour. Likewise you can use fish stock instead of milk and make *Blinde Fische* that may actually taste like trout.

Yield: About 8 to 10 servings

2 eggs
½ teaspoon salt

1 cup (125g) flour
1 quart (1 liter) goat's milk or cow's milk
1 cup (125g) bread crumbs
Butter or lard for browning
Salt and pepper to taste

Beat 1 egg and the ½ teaspoon of salt until frothy and lemon color. Sift in the flour and stir with a fork to form fine crumbs. The crumbs or *Riwwle* must be small or the "fish" will not hold together. Bring the milk to a boil over medium heat but do not scald. Add the crumbs and stir occasionally to keep the mixture from sticking to the pan. Simmer until thick, then pour onto a greased baking sheet and spread to about ¼ inch (6mm) thick. Allow this to cool and set for about 4 hours. Cut into fillet shapes or small strips.

Beat the remaining egg until frothy and lemon color. Dip the "fish" into this and then cover liberally with bread crumbs. Brown the "fish" on both sides in butter or lard and serve hot with the gravy of your choice and salt and pepper to taste.

Mock Rabbit (*Blinder Haas*)

Pennsylvania Dutch *Blinder Haas* is a general term for a category of meat-based dishes that can vary in texture from coarse meat loaf to an Alsatian-style terrine. The more elaborate recipes often contain liver or tongue, and all of them double as fillings for baked potatoes, dumplings, *Mauldasche,* and meat pies.

Since there are no hares in Pennsylvania, the word *Haas* (*Hase* in standard German) is applied in dialect to rabbits; thus "blind rabbit" is the literal meaning of the Dutch name. Unlike *Blinde Fische* (faux fish), which is truly a poverty dish, *Blinder Haas* recipes are something of an inversion because they are not at all rustic. The recipe below was sent to me by a member of the Holzhauer family from the Myersdale area of Somerset County. In that part of the Dutch Country, mock hare was considered a "parlor dish," a fancy preparation for special company that could be served hot or cold.

It was often baked in earthenware molds (small Bundt pans for example) and served with a topping of onion sauce (recipe page 231) and chopped chives. The cold leftovers make excellent sandwiches seasoned with spicy green tomato catsup.

Yield: Serves 4 to 6

3 large eggs
12 ounces (375g) coarsely ground pork
12 ounces (375g) finely ground veal
8 ounces (250g) ground beef
½ cup (125g) minced onion
¼ cup (65ml) meat stock
1 cup (125g) bread crumbs
1 tablespoon freshly grated nutmeg
Salt and pepper to taste
2 tablespoons (30g) unsalted butter

Preheat the oven to 350°F (180°C). Beat the eggs until lemon color. Put the meat in a deep work bowl and add the eggs. Add the onion, stock, half the bread crumbs, and the nutmeg. Season to taste with salt and pepper. Using your hands, work the meat mixture by kneading and squeezing for about 3 to 4 minutes until it forms a thick, stiff paste. Spread the remaining bread crumbs on a platter or work board. Shape the meat paste into a log or roll about 10 inches (25cm) long. Gently roll this in the bread crumbs several times until the surface is dry and fully coated with crumbs. Set the roll in a baking dish and dot with the butter chopped into little bits. Bake uncovered in the preheated oven for 1 hour. Serve hot or cold.

Comment: Optional additions to this dish are almost infinite, but two that are still popular are 2 ounces (65g) diced slab bacon and 1 teaspoon whole peppercorns. These are added with the meat. If you are baking this in an earthenware mold or terrine pan, grease the pan and dust it generously with bread crumbs before filling it with the meat mixture.

Mock Scrapple (*Blinder Panhas*)

The dilemma of what to do with leftover cooking broth was solved by several of my older informants, who immediately recognized the many ways their mothers had transformed similar by-products into satisfying meals. Cooking stock was never thrown away—any cooking stock can be used. Here it becomes a meatless pot-pudding that in taste and appearance falls somewhere between cornmeal mush and real scrapple. It was commonly eaten with apple butter. If the cooking stock does not measure out to 1 quart (1 liter), top it off with water.

Yield: Serves 4 to 6

1 quart (1 liter) reserved cooking stock from vegetables, peas, or beans
1 cup (200g) parched (dark roasted) cornmeal
½ cup (75g) buckwheat flour
1 tablespoon ground coriander
1 teaspoon ground pepper
1 teaspoon summer savory (dried leaves)
¼ teaspoon ground allspice
1 teaspoon powdered hot pepper (optional)
1½ teaspoons salt or to taste

Put the reserved cooking broth in a large saucepan and bring it to a gentle boil. Sift together the cornmeal and the buckwheat into a bowl and pour 2½ cups (625ml) of the hot broth over this. Whisk smooth to remove all lumps, then pour this into the remaining broth. Bring to a gentle boil, stirring constantly to thicken the mixture. After cooking for 15 minutes, add the ground pepper, savory, allspice, and hot pepper if desired. Season with salt. Continue cooking and stirring until the mixture thickens (20 to 30 minutes). Pour this into a small, greased bread pan or an earthenware terrine. Set aside to cool and set. Chill overnight in the refrigerator.

The next day turn out the mock scrapple, slice, and brown in bacon drippings or lard in a hot iron skillet.

Onion Sauce (*Zwiwwelsass*)

The country Dutch used gravies aplenty, but refined sauces were simply not part of the basic rural diet. On the other hand, when we turn to the large towns and cities, the urban Dutch enjoyed a much more sophisticated cuisine, and this is reflected in the published literature, such as this almanac recipe for onion sauce from *Der alte Germantown Calender* for 1863.[10] It makes an excellent accompaniment for rabbit, liver, veal cutlets, bacon dumplings, or the *Mauldasche* on page 244. If you want the sauce more piquant, add lemon juice to taste; if more mellow, add a spoonful of brown sugar to the onions while cooking them in the butter. The overall flavor should resemble very rich onion soup. This sauce will also work as gravy for cooked giblets or chicken livers over waffles; just replace the half-cup of wine with cream.

Yield: approximately 3 cups (750ml)

1 cup (175g) chopped onion
3 tablespoons (25g) flour
4 tablespoons (60g) unsalted butter
2 cups (500ml) meat stock (preferably beef bouillon)
½ cup (125ml) white wine or water
4 fresh bay leaves
4 thin slices of lemon
1 teaspoon ground coriander
⅛ teaspoon ground cloves (or less)
½ teaspoon freshly grated nutmeg
Salt and pepper to taste
Finely chopped chives

Dust the onion with the flour and heat the butter in a deep saucepan. Once the butter begins to foam, add the onion and cook until soft (about 3 minutes). Add the stock, wine (or water), bay leaves, lemon, and spices but not the chives. Simmer gently until the lemon is soft and has flavored the sauce (about 10 to 15 minutes). Remove the lemon and bay leaves and puree the sauce either in a food processor or by working it through a chinoise. Reheat, check seasoning, and serve liberally garnished with chopped chives. Otherwise freeze for later use.

Onion Tart with Cornmeal Crust (*Zwiwwelkuche mit Welschkarn Gruscht*)

No Pennsylvania Dutch recipe collection would be complete without onion tart, one of the most common snack foods in years gone by. It is not as common as it used to be because the old-style tarts were made with bread dough, and not everyone likes making their own bread. This overlooks the fact that there were easy-to-make cornmeal crusts that could be assembled in about 15 minutes and baked in 20. Thus I have included a recipe using a cornmeal crust because this onion tart is a great snack food that goes with beer as well as wine or hard cider—and the crust is crunchy delicious.

Yield: Serves 6 to 8

Onion Filling

Filling for one 8-inch (20cm) crust

2 ounces (60g) country slab bacon
1½ medium onions
1 large egg
½ cup (125ml) sour cream
¼ teaspoon caraway seeds

Preheat the oven to 425°F (200°C). Cut the bacon into tiny dice and cook in a heavy skillet until the fat is rendered and the bacon is beginning to brown. Lift the bacon out with a slotted spoon and reserve. Cut the onions in half lengthwise, then slice paper thin. Add these to the bacon drippings and cover. Sweat over medium heat until the onion changes color and begins to brown (about 3 to 4 minutes). Remove the onion with a slotted spoon and spread evenly in the prepared cornmeal crust (see below). Scatter the reserved bacon bits over this.

Beat the egg until lemon color and frothy, then add the sour cream. Pour this over the onions so that it spreads evenly. Scatter the caraway over the top and bake in the preheated oven for 20 minutes. Remove and cool on a rack. Slice into 8 pieces of equal size and serve.

Cornmeal Crust

The best way to bake this crust is on a cast-iron griddle, preferably a number 9 Griswold griddle with a handle. These old-time griddles from Erie, Pennsylvania, were the workhorses of the cast-iron cook stoves during the early 1900s, and the walls of many Pennsylvania farmhouses are still lined with rows of them. They are easy to find on eBay and are not expensive. You can also use them for crust pancakes

FIGURE 49. Griswold iron griddle, Erie, Pa., ca. 1910.

(page 195), and many cooks find them ideal for tortillas. The reason the old Griswold griddles are so well suited for this recipe is that once hot, they retain the heat, so you are certain to get the crust nice and crispy toward the center, especially if you let the tart stand on the hot griddle for several minutes after it comes out of the oven. Just be careful to wear the right protection for your hands: that hot griddle handle will burn through thinly woven potholders.

While the crust in this recipe is prepared with yellow cornmeal, you can make a nuttier-tasting version with Pennsylvania Dutch parched cornmeal. This will yield a crust much darker brown in color. Whichever your choice, the crust can be made ahead and frozen for later use—I always keep some on hand. Just defrost it in a microwave for 1 minute on high.

Yield: one 8-inch (20cm) crust

1 cup (125g) all-purpose flour
1 cup (155g) organic yellow cornmeal
1½ teaspoons baking powder
1½ teaspoons salt

¼ cup (65ml) vegetable oil or olive oil
½ cup (125ml) cold water (more or less)

Sift together twice the flour, cornmeal, baking powder, and salt. Put this in a deep work bowl and make a valley in the center. Add the oil and using a fork, stir the oil into the dry ingredients to form a smooth, even crumb. Add the water 2 tablespoons (30ml) at a time, stirring with the fork until soft, pliant dough is formed. Roll this into a ball.

Dust a clean work surface with cornmeal and place the ball of dough on it. Pressing down and pushing outward in all directions, work the dough into an 8-inch (20cm) diameter crust, pinching up the edges so that they are about 1 inch (2.5cm) tall. Transfer the crust to a lightly greased griddle as described above or to a small pizza tin. Fill and bake as directed.

Peach and New Potato Stew
(*Geschmorde Pasching un Neie Grumbiere*)

This recipe surfaced many years ago in the Bald Eagle Valley of Centre County. While the picture of simplicity, it is also unusual and quite refreshing on a hot summer day. It was preserved by the Gingery family of Martha Furnace, which was well known locally for its excellent cooks.[11] The peaches were cut into large bite-size chunks, and the new potatoes (only small ones) were pared and cooked whole or cut into irregular pieces.

Yield: 4 to 6 servings

1 cup (175g) chopped onion or leek
2 tablespoons (30ml) cooking oil
2 quarts (2 liters) chicken stock
2 pounds (1kg) small new potatoes, pared and cut into irregular bite-size pieces
2 pounds (1kg) peaches, pared and cut into irregular bite-size pieces
½ teaspoon grated nutmeg
1 tablespoon chopped parsley
½ cup (125ml) whole milk or cream

1 teaspoon crumbled dry marjoram
Salt and pepper to taste

Put the onion and oil in a deep stewing pan and cover. Sweat over medium heat for about 3 minutes, then add the stock and potatoes. Cook 15 minutes or until the potatoes are al dente and then add the peaches. Once the peaches are tender but not soft, add the nutmeg, parsley, milk (or cream), and marjoram. Add salt and pepper to taste and serve immediately. This is best the day it is cooked but can be reheated in a microwave.

Peach and Yellow Tomato Pie
(Pasching un Geele Tomats Boi)

Peaches and tomatoes, especially yellow tomatoes, are a classic old-time Pennsylvania Dutch combination. They are often canned together or stewed together with the addition of new potatoes. The small, richly flavored heirloom tomato called Golden Juniata was originally developed as a pie tomato during the 1860s at Mt. Wolf in York County.

Yield: one 9-inch (23cm) pie, or 8 servings

1 prepared 9-inch (23cm) pastry crust
4 cups (600g) pared, sliced ripe peaches
2 cups (300g) sliced small yellow tomatoes
3 tablespoons (25g) blanched slivered almonds
2 tablespoons (30ml) lemon juice
¾ cup (185g) sugar, or more depending on sweetness of the peaches
4 tablespoons (30g) potato starch
½ teaspoon grated nutmeg
½ teaspoon salt
¼ teaspoon ground cinnamon

Preheat the oven to 425°F (220°C). Combine the peaches, tomatoes, almonds, and lemon juice in a deep work bowl. In a separate work bowl, sift together the sugar, potato starch, nutmeg, salt, and cinnamon. Then fold this into the peach mixture so that all pieces of fruit are thoroughly coated. Pour the mixture into the prepared pie shell and pat smooth. Bake in the preheated oven for 25 minutes, then reduce the temperature to 375°F (190°C) and continue baking another 25 minutes or until the pie is bubbling in the center. Remove and cool on a rack. Serve at room temperature or chilled.

Peach *Schnitz* Dumplings (*Paschingschnitz Gnepp*)

This excellent dish was preserved by Emma Brownback (1871–1955), who, according to a descendant, obtained the original recipe from a cook at the old Seven Stars Hotel, a 1736 tavern down the road from the church she attended.[12] Back then (the 1920s) the tavern was closed due to Prohibition but continued operation as a farm and cattle auction. These dumplings were part of the menu served to people attending the auctions. The texture of the dumplings should be light and spongy. Weighing the ingredients is critical to achieve this texture. The dumplings can also be cooked separately in boiling water and then served with the hot stock when ready.

Yield: Serves 4, allowing 2 dumplings per person

Dumplings
4 ounces (125g) dried peaches chopped fine (about 2 cups)
10 ounces (310g) boiled, skinned potatoes
10 ounces (310g) flour
4 tablespoons (60g) unsalted butter (soft, at room temperature)
2 large eggs
1 teaspoon salt
6 cups (1.5 liters) of prepared broth (see below)
Chopped dried apricots

Put the chopped dried peaches in a small work bowl and cover with 1 cup (250ml) warm water. Let the peaches stand about 30 minutes to soften. Once the peaches are soft, drain in a colander and press out excess liquid. Rice the boiled potatoes, then sift in the flour and work these together with a wooden spoon. Add the butter and the reconstituted, drained peaches. Beat the eggs until lemon color and frothy, then add them to the dumpling mixture with the salt. Work into a stiff dough. Form out balls of equal size and let them stand at least 1 hour before cooking. While they are maturing, prepare the broth as directed below. Add the dumplings to the simmering broth and cook uncovered for 45 minutes. Adjust seasonings and serve dumplings and stock in soup dishes with chopped dried apricots as a garnish.

Cooking Stock
¼ cup (50g) diced slab bacon
2 tablespoons (30g) unsalted butter
⅔ cup (65g) chopped onion
1 tablespoon (15g) sugar
6 cups (1.5 liters) chicken or ham stock
1 teaspoon thyme leaves coarsely crushed
1 teaspoon salt or to taste

Render the bacon with the butter until clear in a large stewing pan over medium heat, then add the onion and sugar. Cook the onion until it softens, then add the stock. Simmer 1 hour, skimming off foam if necessary. Once the dumplings are ready to cook, add the thyme, salt, and dumplings and proceed as directed above.

Peas and Bacon (*Arrebse-un-Schpeck*)

Not all recipes emanating from Pennsylvania Dutch urban centers were written for the culinary elites. Almanac publishers were well aware of rural clients and their special needs; thus it is possible to find a number of truly frugal poverty dishes in old Pennsylvania Dutch German-language almanacs—in many cases recipes so simple and austere that they may seem quite off-putting today. With the help of field interviews, I was able to gain a better understanding of this particular recipe, which was first published in *Der neue amerikanische Landwirtschafts-Calender* (New American Agricultural Almanac) for 1880, although even then it was extremely old-fashioned when you consider what was being published in cookbooks from the same period.[13] I include it here for its ethnographic value and as a point of comparison highlighting the stark contrast between the food of the Buckwheat Dutch and the cuisine of the well-to-do—in particular mock hare, venison cutlets, and sour marinated rabbit. This was a hearty winter dish for the rural poor, a time of year when eggs were few and butter was short.

Hot from the oven the dish resembles a pudding. Once cool it is similar to cornbread. It was eaten, like *Schlappichdunkes,* from a common bowl in the center of the table, each person dipping in with his or her own spoon or piece of bread. The only "sauce" was apple or pumpkin butter. The bacon, or more likely flitch (unsmoked bacon) or pork side meat, served as both meat and "butter".

Yield: Serves 6 to 8 persons

½ pound (250g) streaky, well-flavored slab bacon (do not slice)
2 cups (500g) split peas or lentils
1½ cups (375ml) clabber (thick milk) or yogurt
1 cup (155g) parched cornmeal (roasted cornmeal)
2 teaspoons baking powder
3 onions
Salt and pepper to taste

Place the slab bacon whole in a deep stewing pan with 1½ quarts (1.5 liters) of cold water. Add the peas. Cover and bring to a gentle boil. Cook until the peas are tender (about 35 minutes). Skim off any foam that might rise to the surface. Remove the bacon and strain out the peas. Cut off 2 slices of bacon and set aside. Reserve the broth for mock scrapple (page 230).

Pulp the peas and bacon in a food processor with 1 cup (250ml) of the cooking stock. Pour this into a deep work bowl and add the clabber or yogurt. Sift together the cornmeal and baking powder and then combine this with the batter. Pour the mixture into a greased *Schales* pan or a 12-inch (30cm) baking dish. Spread the batter so that it is smooth and evenly distributed.

Chop the reserved 2 slices of bacon into small bits. Slice the onions lengthwise down the middle, then slice horizontally into paper-thin pieces. Heat the bacon in a skillet and render the fat. Add the onion, cover, and sweat until soft and turning golden brown (about 5 minutes). Lift the bacon and onion mixture out with a slotted spoon and spread over the top of the pea puree. Bake for 60 to 80 minutes in an oven preheated to 325°F (165°C) or until the puree puffs up a few inches and tests dry in the center. Serve hot with crusty whole wheat or rye bread. Season to taste at the table.

Pickled Okra with Summer Sausage
(*Gepickelte Okra mit Summerwarscht*)

This is one of those creative 1930s country tavern "free lunch" recipes that matches well with cold beer. It is not economical to make this in small quantities because the okra will disappear quickly. The pickling brine can be reused or recycled as starter for sauerkraut. In order for this recipe to develop the best balance of flavors, be certain that the summer sausage (Lebanon bologna) is well smoked—that smokiness is important.

Yield: 1 gallon (4 liters); serves 10 to 20

2 pounds (1kg) tender young okra, trimmed of stems and tough tips
½ pound (250g) sweet Lebanon bologna, cut into cubes or into irregular bite-size pieces
1 medium onion, cut in half lengthwise and then sliced paper thin
12 fresh bay leaves
4 to 5 cloves of garlic sliced in half lengthwise
1 tablespoon fresh thyme leaves or several sprigs to taste
1 teaspoon whole allspice
2 tablespoons whole coriander seeds
1 tablespoon yellow mustard seed

3 cups (750ml) spring water
6½ cups (1.625ml) white wine vinegar
½ cup (125g) sugar
2 tablespoons (30g) pickling salt

Combine the okra, bologna, onion, bay leaves, garlic, and thyme in a deep work bowl. Then add the allspice, coriander, and mustard and mix thoroughly. Pack this mixture into a 1-gallon (4-liter) sterilized jar so that it fills the jar to the shoulders. Heat the water, vinegar, sugar, and pickling salt in a deep pan. Bring to a rolling boil, then pour over the okra mixture. Cover and let stand to mature in a cool place or refrigerate for 3 weeks before serving.

Pit Cabbage (*Grundrezept fer Gruwegraut*)

Gruwegraut was made by the early Pennsylvania Dutch settlers because there was an absence of stoneware in which to ferment the cabbage (sauerkraut cannot be made in redware since it interacts with the glaze; furthermore the clay body is too porous). As local potteries began to turn out large stoneware crocks by the mid-nineteenth century, sauerkraut making was shifted to salt-glaze crocks partially sunken into floors of cellars. Some crocks could hold as much as 20 gallons, which is the ideal size for this type of large-scale production since the crocks should not be filled more than halfway, or at most three-quarters full. The alternative was to make the sauerkraut in barrels either free-standing or sunken into cellar floors; both of these methods are amply documented in Pennsylvania agricultural literature.

Arche Noah, a grassroots seed organization in Austria, recently experimented with this pre-1800s form of making sauerkraut, and not only were the results successful, but also the sauerkraut made this way acquired a unique delicate flavor.[14] The large pieces of preserved cabbage can be shredded with a knife before cooking or simply added to the pot whole with a piece of smoked meat. Among rural Pennsylvania Dutch households this "country-style" sauerkraut was evidently far more common than the finely shredded type of sauerkraut we buy packaged today.

The following recipe is an adaptation for use in stoneware crocks, with the general proportion of 1½ tablespoons (25g) of salt to each 2½ pounds (1.25kg) of cabbage. Slightly more salt is required here since the spring water dilutes the salinity of the resulting brine. Use bottled spring water, not tap water. Tap water contains chemical additives and all sorts of antibiotics processed through the drinking-water system; this will disrupt a healthy enzyme change in the cabbage.

Yield: 12 pounds (6kg)

12 heads of cabbage (approximately 12 pounds/6kg)
8 tablespoons (120g) sea salt or Kosher salt
2 gallons (8 liters) spring water

Remove the outer leaves of the cabbage and wash the heads thoroughly. Cut the heads into quarters or eighths leaving the stems intact. Weigh to be certain you have 12 pounds (6kg)—1 pound (500g) or 2 (1kg) over that will not matter. Clean and sterilize two 6-gallon (24-liter) stoneware crocks. Pack the cabbage cut-side down into the crocks; as you add the cabbage sprinkle it with salt, 3 tablespoons (45g) per crock. Cover the cabbage with spring water, adding 1 gallon (4 liters) per crock. Sprinkle the remaining salt over the top, 1 tablespoon (15g) per crock.

Place a china plate upside down on the cabbage and place a 5-pound (2.5kg) weight on the plate. I use large sterilized glass jugs filled with water for this purpose, but you can use a stone or brick if you desire (first boil the stone or brick to sterilize it). Cover the crocks with clean cloths and set aside in a warm corner of the kitchen for 1 to 2 months, or until fermentation begins. Then move the crocks to a cool storage area such as a pantry to finish the process. Skim off any scum that may form on the top. Patience is required because the cabbage will take some time to soften and sink under the weight on top. Once fermentation commences, be certain to keep the cabbage below the level of the water. Aging should take about 3 months from start to finish. After the pit cabbage is made, it can be frozen in freezer bags for later use.

✑ Pit Cabbage with Pork (*Gruwegraut mit Seifleesch*)

Yield: Serves 6

3 pounds (1.5kg) Gruwegraut (see previous recipe)
3 pounds (1.5kg) pork loin roast cut into long, narrow 3-inch (7.5cm)
  pieces
1 cup (75g) thinly sliced leek or chopped onion
2 cups (75g) apple Schnitz
1 cup (20g) chopped parsley or a mix of parsley and lovage
2 cups (500ml) plain tomato sauce
½ cup (125ml) tarragon vinegar (optional)

Preheat the oven to 375°F (190°C). Slice the pit cabbage into thin pieces, taking care to keep the leaves attached to stems. Line the bottom of a 4-quart (4 liter) baking pan with part of the cabbage. Cover this with the pork. Then scatter the leek or onion, apple *Schnitz*, and parsley over the pork. Cover this with the remaining cabbage and then pour the tomato sauce over the top. Bake in the preheated oven for 60 minutes. If desired, you can add the tarragon vinegar 20 minutes before the cabbage is done. Serve immediately.

✑ Potato Balls (*Grumbiere Balle*)

This recipe originally appeared in the November 1840 issue of a short-lived Lebanon, Pennsylvania, agricultural monthly called *Ceres*.[15] Much of the material in this journal was edited by Dr. Adolf Bauer, who was interested in creating an intellectual forum for Pennsylvania Dutch farmers and their wives. His culinary material may have been overly *bürgerlich* (bourgeois) since most of the dishes, including this one, required specialized equipment (such as the skillet in Figure 50) that was not available in many rural households. While delicate

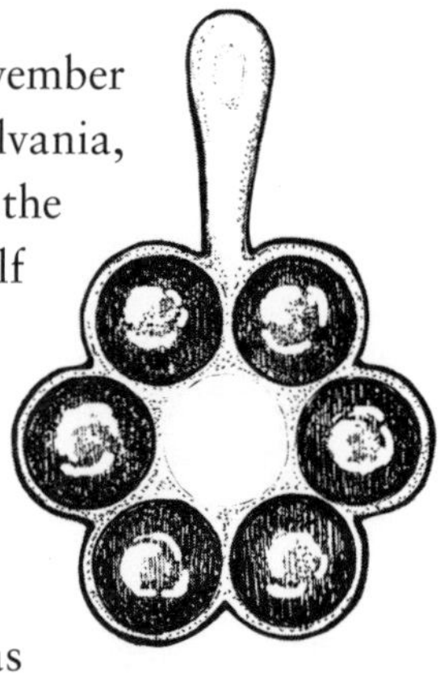

FIGURE 50. Skillet for potato balls.

potato balls may have graced the tables of urban literati such as Dr. Bauer, they were a far cry from the *Hooriche Gnepp* prepared up in the hills. Just the same, country cooks could imitate townish ways by taking day-old *Hooriche Gnepp* and browning them in the same fritter pan used for the dumplings.

Yield: Approximately 24 balls

3 cups (1½ pounds/750g) warm mashed potatoes
1½ tablespoons (10g) spelt flour or organic bread flour
¼ cup (30g) bread crumbs
1 teaspoon baking powder
2 tablespoons minced parsley or chives (optional)
½ teaspoon salt
½ teaspoon freshly ground pepper
2 large eggs, separated
Cracker dust for work surface

Put the warm mashed potatoes in a deep work bowl. In a separate work bowl, combine the flour, bread crumbs, baking powder, parsley, salt, and pepper. Combine this with the warm potatoes, working it well to combine all ingredients. Beat the egg yolks until lemon color and frothy, then fold them into the potatoes. Beat the egg whites until they form peaks, then gently fold them into the potato mixture.

Dust a work surface liberally with cracker dust. Drop scoops of the stiff potato batter onto the work surface and gently roll into balls; they should be dry enough to be handled. Proceed in one of two ways:

Old Way

Put 2 teaspoons of butter or lard in each cup of an old-style iron fritter pan (see Figure 50) and place this over hot coals on a raised hearth or over an open griddle hole in an old plate stove. Fry the balls by turning them from time to time with a spoon until golden brown on all sides. Keep in mind that the center cup will become hotter than the others. Add more cooking fat if necessary. Continue in this manner until all the balls are fried. Serve hot with gravy.

New Way

Deep-fry the balls in oil or fat heated to 375°F (190°C) until crisp and golden brown on the surface. Or grease two 12-cup muffin pans and put a ball in each and then bake in an oven preheated to 375°F (190°C) for 35 minutes or until they begin to turn golden brown.

Potato Pocket Dumplings with Sorrel Gravy (*Grumbiere Mauldasche mit Sauerampel Dunkes*)

Although they were called *Mauldasche* in *Mary at the Farm*, the author Edith Thomas gave their English equivalent as "parsley pies." This latter name was by far the most common among the rural Pennsylvania Dutch, and if you look for them under that designation you will find recipes aplenty. The recipe here is a blend of two separate recipes from Mrs. Leah Culp of Gettysburg; they were circulated among the Dutch community in Adams County and are fairly representative of the dish, although multitudes of other, more-exotic fillings and sauces can be used. I particularly like chervil and morels. The pockets can also be served in broth, in soup, or with rich gravies. Best when hot from the kettle, they are fairly filling, so allow 2 or 3 per person.

Yield: 18 to 20 3-inch (7.5cm) squares

Potatoes

1 pound (500g) mealy potatoes, pared of skins

Boil the potatoes in 2 quarts (2 liters) of water until tender. Drain, re-serve the cooking water, and mash or rice the potatoes. While they are still warm, prepare the filling.

Filling

2 tablespoons (30g) unsalted butter or chicken fat
½ cup (150g) minced leek or onion
½ cup (25g) chopped sorrel
1 pound (500g) warm mashed potatoes as prepared above

1 tablespoon (15g) prepared horseradish (grated in vinegar)
Salt and pepper to taste

Heat the butter or fat in a deep saucepan and add the leek and sorrel. Cover and sweat over medium heat for 3 minutes, then pour this over the warm mashed potatoes. Mix well, then add the horseradish and season to taste. Set aside.

Gravy
3 tablespoons (45g) butter or chicken fat
3 tablespoons (20g) flour
1 cup (125g) chopped leek
2 cups (500ml) cooking liquid from the potatoes
4 ounces (125g) fresh sorrel, coarsely chopped
1 cup (75g) chopped spinach
1 tablespoon (15ml) lemon juice
Salt and pepper to taste

Heat the butter in a large saucepan, then add the flour. Stir until the flour begins to change color. Add the leek. Cover and sweat 3 to 4 minutes or until the leek is tender, then add 1 cup (250ml) of the reserved cooking liquid from the potatoes. Stir thoroughly, then add the sorrel and spinach. Cover and sweat until the greens are soft, then add the remaining cup (250ml) of reserved potato water. Pour the vegetables into a food processor or blender and puree until smooth. Return the sauce to the pan and bring to a gentle boil. Add the lemon juice and season with salt and pepper. Set aside and keep the sauce warm (in a double boiler for example).

Dumpling Dough
2 eggs
½ cup (125ml) lukewarm milk
1 teaspoon melted butter
½ teaspoon salt
1 teaspoon baking powder
2½ cups (315g) flour

To make the dough, beat the eggs until lemon color and frothy, then add the milk and butter. Sift the salt, baking powder, and flour together twice, then put this in a deep work bowl. Make a valley in the center of the flour mixture and add the egg mixture. Work this into stiff dough. Roll out about ¼ inch (6mm) thick on a clean, well-floured surface and cut into 3-inch (7.5cm) squares. Put 1 tablespoon of the filling on each square. To form pockets, fold dough over the filling to form triangles and press the edges shut with your fingers, pinching them together as tightly as possible. Gently slip the dumplings into salted, simmering water and cook until they rise to the surface. Let them cook an additional 8 to 10 minutes, then lift out with a slotted spoon and serve immediately with the sauce (gravy recipe provided above). Garnish liberally with chopped chervil.

Potato Potpie with Saffron (*Grumbiere Botboi mit Safferich*)

Henrietta B. Beam (1843–1931) was an active member of St. Paul's Reformed and Lutheran Church in Bowmansville, Pennsylvania.[16] Her potato potpie was at one time a popular draw at church suppers in the area; if ever there were a truly Pennsylvania Dutch reinvention of common American potpie, this recipe was certainly it. With its layers of pasta and potatoes redolent of local-harvest saffron and spices, it is difficult to imagine this rich, hearty dish served anywhere else but in Pennsylvania. At church suppers it was often served with chicken salad and fried oysters.

Yield: Serves 4 to 6

1 cup (100g) finely diced celery (mix of stems and leaves)
1 cup (100g) chopped leek
1 tablespoon fresh thyme leaves
1 tablespoon coriander seeds
¼ teaspoon powdered saffron (or more to taste)
½ teaspoon ground ginger
⅛ teaspoon ground cinnamon
8 cups (2 liters) rich chicken or veal broth

1 pound (500g) potpie noodles (see note)
1½ pounds (750g) waxy yellow potatoes pared and sliced as thin as
   possible
2 tablespoons (30g) unsalted butter, cut into small pieces
Salt and pepper to taste
Chopped parsley

Preheat the oven to 350°F (175°C). Combine the celery, leek, thyme, and coriander in a small work bowl. In a separate small bowl dissolve the saffron, ginger, and cinnamon in the chicken broth. Take a deep 4- to 6-quart (4- to 6-liter) stewing pan and cover the bottom with potpie noodles. Cover this with a layer of sliced potatoes, then cover this with half the chopped-vegetable mixture. Add another layer of noodles, make another layer with the remaining potatoes, and cover with the rest of the chopped vegetables. Make a top layer with the last of the noodles. Pour the spice-flavored broth over this and dot the top with the chopped butter. Season with salt and pepper, cover, and bake in the pre-heated oven for 1 hour and 20 minutes.

FIGURE 51. Potpie noodles.

Scatter a liberal quantity of chopped parsley over the top and serve hot from the baking pan as a one-pot meal set in the middle of the table.

Note: Freshly made potpie noodles give this dish an entirely different flavor and texture from those of store-bought dry potpies. First of all, traditional cooks made egg pasta with the yolks of "soft eggs," eggs that had not yet been laid. These were removed from chickens when they were butchered and were considered almost as valuable as the chickens. Furthermore home-made potpie swells considerably when cooked and is thus soft and tender. The noodles are also slippery, a texture that many Pennsylvania Dutch like, and the residual flour adhering to them acts as a thickener while they stew. To make your own potpie noodles, follow the recipe below.

Potpie Dough (*Botboi Deeg*)

This recipe will make slightly over the required pound (500g) of noodles for the recipe above. Any additional noodles can be dried for later use or turned into gribble (see page 271). Chicken fat makes noodles more tender than those made with butter. Also refer to the discussion of soft eggs on page 247.

Yield: 4 to 6 servings

2 tablespoons (30g) plus 2 teaspoons (20g) cold unsalted butter or
    chicken fat
3 cups (370g) flour
4 large eggs
4 large egg yolks
¼ teaspoon salt or to taste

Work the butter and flour into fine crumbs in a food processor. Pour them into a work bowl. In a separate work bowl beat the eggs until lemon color and frothy, then make a well in the crumbs and add the eggs. Season with salt and then work this into a soft dough. On a clean, lightly floured surface roll out the dough as thin as possible and cut into 2-inch (5cm) squares or whatever size you prefer. Let the potpie noodles dry 15 to 20 minutes, then use as directed above.

Potato *Schales* (*Grumbiere Schales*)

Yield: Serves 8 to 10

3 tablespoons (45ml) drawn butter, melted lard, or cooking oil of your
    choice
½ cup (75g) finely diced celery
1½ cups (125g) chopped leek
2½ pounds (1.25kg) fingerling potatoes or salad potatoes, shredded on
    the large holes of a vegetable grater
1 tablespoon minced garlic or to taste
¼ cup (65ml) cooking oil

½ *cup (65g) fine bread crumbs*
3 whole eggs
1 tablespoon salt or to taste
1 teaspoon freshly ground pepper
2 tablespoons chopped fresh marjoram or 1 tablespoon dried
1 cup (250ml) milk
Butter
Sour cream and chopped chives

Heat the butter or oil in a sauté pan, add the celery and leek, and cover. Sweat over medium-high heat for 4 minutes, then remove the vegetables from the pan with a slotted spoon and set aside. To the sauté pan add the potato, garlic, and ¼ cup (65ml) oil. Sauté over medium-high heat until the potatoes are hot and cooked tender but not soft (about 6 to 8 minutes). Remove the potato mixture and combine with the reserved celery mixture. Add 3 tablespoons bread crumbs, 3 well-beaten eggs, salt, pepper, marjoram, and milk. Combine to make a thick, stiff batter. Grease a round (11- to 12-inch/28 to 30cm) *Schales* or baking pan and dust with some of the bread crumbs. Add the potato mixture and pat smooth.

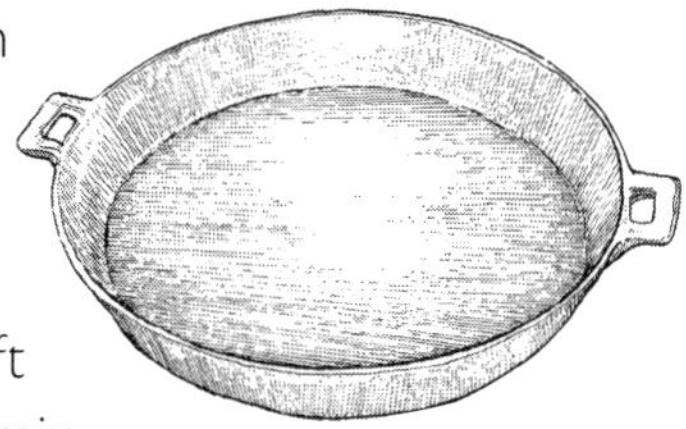

FIGURE 52. *Schales* pan.

FIGURE 53. *Schales* pan.

Dust the top of the potato mixture with the remaining bread crumbs and dot liberally with butter. Bake in an oven preheated to 375°F (190°C) for 40 to 45 minutes or until beginning to brown on top. Serve immediately with a topping of sour cream and chopped chives.

Punxsutawney Spice Cookies
(Punxsutawney Schpeiss-Kichelcher)

During the early 1900s Ida May Fetterman used to make these delightfully brittle melt-in-your-mouth cookies for the Groundhog Club's annual dinners in Punxsutawney.[17] Her popular recipe eventually gained wide circulation among local women's groups and church guilds. These old Dutch–style cookies really are excellent, more so if you use leaf lard, which gives the cookies a special texture. If you do not use lard, you will need 1 full cup (250g) of butter. For added festive flavor, combine the grated zest of one orange with the fruit and nuts.

Yield: Approximately 8 dozen

½ cup (125g) lard
½ cup (125g) unsalted butter
2 cups (315g) brown sugar
3 large eggs (see note)
1 cup (250ml) sour milk (use buttermilk)
3½ cups (440g) pastry flour, sifted before measuring
1 teaspoon salt
1 teaspoon baking soda
1 teaspoon ground cinnamon
1 teaspoon freshly grated nutmeg
1 teaspoon ground allspice
1 teaspoon ground cloves
1 pound (500g) finely chopped raisins
½ pound (125g) coarsely broken walnuts
One large dish of coarsely granulated sugar (at least 2 cups/500g)

Preheat the oven to 350°F (180°C). Cream the lard and butter, then beat this with the brown sugar until it is dissolved and the mixture is light and fluffy. Beat the eggs until lemon color and combine with the sugar and butter. Whisk in the sour milk (buttermilk).

Sift together twice the flour, salt, baking soda, and spices. Then fold these dry ingredients into the batter. Last, fold in the fruit and nuts. Using a teaspoon, dip out scoops of batter and roll gently in the dish of granulated sugar. Set these on greased baking sheets leaving ample room for the cookies to spread (they will spread at least 3 inches/7.5cm). Bake in the middle of the preheated oven for 15 minutes.

Since the cookies are brittle once they cool, lift them as quickly as possible from the hot baking sheets to cool on wire racks.

Note: For half a batch, use 2 eggs.

Sauerkraut *(Grundrezept fer Sauergraut)*

Sauerkraut is a food rich in nutrition and has been a cornerstone of Pennsylvania Dutch cookery since colonial times. It is still made at home by many Pennsylvania Dutch families, but the old method of fermenting it in stoneware crocks has been replaced for the most part by the canning jar. On the one hand, this newer approach is admittedly somewhat easier because of the space constraints in many homes today. On the other hand, crock-style sauerkraut has a flavor and texture that cannot be compared with its jar-made counterparts.

Picking the cabbage after a good fall rain following a hard frost will insure tenderness and high water content in the cabbage, both of which are important for making a proper ferment. Otherwise untreated spring water can be added to create the necessary slurry.

I make my sauerkraut in an heirloom 6-gallon (24-liter) stoneware crock that has been in the family as long as anyone can remember; and I use the recipe of my great-great grandfather—that would be Abraham Weaver (1826–1909)—which I obtained from my Lancaster cousin Betty Weaver Zook. I also have my great-great grandfather's 20-gallon (80-liter) stoneware crock, one of three that was used for making sauerkraut years ago, but it is entirely too bulky to move when full, and frankly I am not feeding the kind of large household with many work hands and servants that he maintained in the 1880s and 1890s. As a weight on the sauerkraut (it must be pressed down during fermentation), I use a well-washed, smaller, 3-gallon (12-liter) crock, which fits neatly inside the larger one. For added weight, the 3-gallon crock can be filled partially with water, although this will depend to some extent on the coarseness of the shredded cabbage (finer, more delicate cabbages do not require as much weight). A gallon glass jug full of water set on an overturned china plate will also work quite as well.

The process begins by washing the cabbage to be certain it is free of caterpillars and aphids (they are notoriously clever at hiding among the leaves). Drain the washed cabbage and then shred it on a vegetable shredder or with a very sharp knife into ⅛-inch (2.5mm) strips.

Take a well-washed stoneware crock and make a layer of shredded cabbage at the bottom. This layer should be about 3 inches (7.5cm) thick, and as a rule of thumb, the weight of each layer should be about 2½ pounds (1.25kg). Scatter 1½ tablespoons coarse sea salt, pickling salt, or Kosher salt over each 2½ pounds (1.25kg) of cabbage and then stamp it vigorously with a kraut stamp or some other wooden device so that the cabbage is bruised and begins to ooze liquid. Add another layer of shredded cabbage, scatter it with the same quantity of salt, and stamp it again. Repeat this until you have filled the crock about ¾ full. If the cabbage does not emit enough liquid during stamping, add untreated spring water 1 cup (250ml) at a time. When pressed down, the cabbage should be covered by about 1 inch (2.5cm) of the liquid. As a further note on procedure, interviewee Rebecca Schwalm of Valley View, Pennsylvania noted that in her family, a few grape leaves were laid over each layer of cabbage; this helped to control the enzyme change and to her mind gave the sauerkraut a better flavor.

Set the smaller crock or some other form of clean, heavy weight on top of the stamped cabbage so that it is pressed down beneath the liquid. Cover the whole with a cloth and tie it down so that gnats and small insects cannot get in (they are attracted by the smell). Let the sauerkraut stand in a warm place 6 days to ferment. You should be able to hear it working by the fifth day. Eventually this gentle fermentation will slow down because the salt will inhibit further breakdown of the cabbage. Skim off any scum that forms on top of the liquid during the early stages of aging, rinse off the weight, then return the weight to the cabbage, cover again, and move the sauerkraut to a cold room to age for 6 to 8 weeks. When the sauerkraut has developed a thick white mold on top similar to what forms on soft cheese, it is ready to eat. This mold is beneficial, and you can dry a piece of it to add to a fresh batch later in the season.

At this point the weight can be removed and the sauerkraut can either be put up in jars or left in the crock as long as it is stored in such a way that it remains beneath the liquid. An old sterilized china plate is often enough to weigh it down for this purpose. Once you have a batch of sauerkraut that has ripened, you can use the juice as starter for another batch and thus continue in this manner every 8 weeks in order to have sauerkraut maturing all winter and into the early spring. You can also freeze the finished sauerkraut in zip-lock freezer bags.

To cook the sauerkraut, put it in a colander and press out all excess liquid, then use the quantity as directed in your recipe.

Sauerkraut Half-Moon Pies
(*Sauergraut Daschekuche odder Halbmund Boi*)

Half-moon pies are the same shape as Latino empanadas or Welsh pasties. Some cooks prefer to use bread dough, others like short crust, and some people even make them with a very flaky butter crust. The choice of dough depends somewhat on the filling and the other items planned for the menu. Eaten by themselves as finger food, they make a very nice light snack, provided you do not eat too many.

This recipe was collected for me by Isaac Clarence Kulp (now deceased) during one of his many excursions among the plain sects in the Big Valley of Mifflin County. The Big Valley is half-moon pie country, and my request was to bring back something

FIGURE 54. Half-moon pies.

representative of the area. While exploring an old mill in the neighborhood of Maitland, which is not in the Big Valley but in a smaller one to the south called Dry Valley, Isaac visited members of his own sect at the Maitland Church of the Brethren. One of the members was a child of Lorena Knepp Fisher, wife of John M. Fisher (1876–1946), who had preserved a collection of recipes that the family had used on their Dry Valley farm. This is the Fisher family recipe for half-moon pies filled with sauerkraut. This same filling was also baked in "English" pies with bottom and top crusts. The mock rabbit recipe on page 228 can also be used as filling in half-moon pies.

Yield: one 9-inch (23cm) "English" pie or about 24 half-moon pies

Pie Filling
3 tablespoons (45ml) cooking oil
2 onions, sliced paper thin
3 cups (525g) sauerkraut
½ cup (100g) diced celery
6 ounces (185g) cooked potatoes, cut into very small dice
½ cup (100g) diced green bell pepper
½ cup (100g) diced red bell pepper
½ teaspoon yellow mustard seed
½ teaspoon celery seed
½ cup (65g) bread crumbs
2 eggs, one of them separated
1 cup (250ml) vegetable stock
1½ tablespoons (35g) dark brown sugar
1 batch half-moon pie dough (see below)
2 tablespoons (30ml) milk or cream

Heat the cooking oil. Cut the onions in half lengthwise, then slice them paper thin. Sweat the onions in the hot oil until they begin to brown. Add the sauerkraut and diced celery, cover, and continue cooking over medium heat for 10 to 15 minutes or until all the liquid has evaporated. Remove from the stove and pour into a deep work bowl. Add the

cooked diced potatoes along with the green and red diced peppers, mustard seed, celery seed, and bread crumbs. Stir well to coat all ingredients
with the crumbs. In a separate bowl beat the egg until light and frothy,
then add the vegetable stock and brown sugar. Pour this over the filling
mixture.

Roll the dough out to about ¼-inch (6mm) thick and then cut into 5-
to 6-inch (13 to 15cm) rounds. Fill each with 1½ tablespoons (50g) of the
sauerkraut mixture, then fold shut, brushing the edges with beaten egg
white and then pressing shut with the tines of a fork. Let the pies recover
and rise in a warm place for about 20 minutes. Beat the reserved egg yolk
with the milk until thoroughly combined, then brush this over the top
surface of each pie. Bake them in an oven preheated to 375°F (190°C) for
20 to 25 minutes. Serve warm from the oven as a handheld snack.

*Note: If the filling is to be baked in a larger pie with or without a top crust,
preheat the oven to 375°F (190°C) and bake 45 to 55 minutes or until the crust
is done and the center tests dry.*

Pie Dough

Yield: Dough for 24 half-moon pies or one 9-inch (23cm) "English" pie

½ ounce (14g) dry active yeast (2 packets)
2 cups (500ml) warm milk
7 cups (880g) sifted all-purpose flour
1 teaspoon salt
8 ounces (250g) unsalted butter

Proof the yeast in the warm milk. Sift together the flour and salt in a
deep work bowl. Make a valley in the center of the flour. Melt the butter
and add it to the valley, then add the yeast. Work this into a soft dough
with a fork. Cover and set aside to double in bulk. Knock down and roll
out as directed above.

Shoofly Pie (*Melassich Riwwelboi*)

I will repeat here what I wrote in *Pennsylvania Dutch Country Cooking,* marketing claims notwithstanding: shoofly pie did not exist before the Civil War. In addition it was a winter dish because molasses was not available during warm weather in the days before refrigeration (otherwise the molasses would ferment). The pie appears to be the end-product of an evolution that began with Jenny Lind pie. Shoofly pie is one of those eggless (thus frugal) by-products of the baking-powder revolution that took hold of Pennsylvania Dutch cookery during the 1870s. The pie entered the scene at the United States Centennial under the name "Centennial Cake." The name "shoofly pie" evolved later, in the 1880s, although historically it was never as common a name as it is today. More often than not the pie was simply called "molasses crumb pie" in Pennsylvania Dutch or "soda rivvel cake." Regardless of its hybrid origins, shoofly pie is a breakfast coffee cake. It is very odd to see it served as dessert after dinner in the tourist spots of Pennsylvania and Ohio unless you are eating it with strong black coffee or, better for the digestion, with a small shot of pear or raspberry schnapps. This recipe is one of the earliest versions of the pie, which does indeed resemble cake. The flavor is similar to chocolate.

Yield: one 9-inch (23cm) pie, or 8 to 10 servings

1½ cups (185g) all-purpose flour
½ cup (125g) white sugar
½ cup (125g) light brown sugar
2 tablespoons (30g) unsalted butter
2 teaspoons ground cinnamon
1 teaspoon grated nutmeg
¼ teaspoon salt
1 teaspoon baking powder
½ cup (125ml) warm strong coffee
½ cup (125ml) dark unsulfured molasses
½ teaspoon baking soda
One 9-inch (23cm) prepared, unbaked pie shell

Preheat the oven to 350°F (175°C). Using a pastry cutter or food processor, work the flour, sugars, butter, cinnamon, nutmeg, salt, and baking powder to form a loose crumb texture. Remove ¼ cup (35g) of crumbs and reserve. In a separate work bowl combine the warm coffee and molasses and stir until the molasses is dissolved. Add the baking soda and stir gently to dissolve it. Pour the liquid into the crumb mixture and fold gently to combine well. Pour this into a prepared pie shell, then scatter the reserved crumbs over the top.

Bake the pie in the middle of the preheated oven for 40 to 45 minutes or until the center of the pie is firm and cakelike. Serve hot from the oven or cool on a rack and serve at room temperature.

Sour Marinated Rabbit (*Hasenpfeffer*)

One dreary March day in 2007 I undertook an excursion to Lancaster County with the specific object of tracking down someone who could tell me much more than I knew about the *Up-to-Date Cook Book* arranged by the Ladies' Aid Society of St. Peter's Lutheran Church in Neffsville. The book was published at Mount Joy in 1924, and unlike many local charitable cookbooks from the Prohibition era, this one contained a rich assortment of distinctively Pennsylvania Dutch recipes—over twenty-nine by my count.

Geraldine Stauffer Weidel (born in 1918) agreed to talk about the cookery of her church; for many years she had helped with the cooking for events held at St. Peter's (her late husband was on the church council), and she still valued her mother's tattered copy of the now-scarce 1924 cookbook. She was only a small girl when it was published, but her mother had been on the cookbook committee, and over time Geraldine had garnered many stories about the original band of women who had gotten it together. Geraldine came from a family of Pennsylvania Dutch tenant farmers (*Lehnsbauere*) who moved from one farmstead to the next raising poultry and livestock for large Lancaster County landowners. While her family was not poor, they did hover close to the edge and were constantly buffeted by shifts in the economy. Her rootless childhood existence was perhaps best expressed by the Grandma Moses–like paintings she had made of all the farms where her parents had lived. They lined the walls of her dining room, and as she narrated their stories it was plain to see that for her, the pictures preserved happy memories. Yet sadly enough, none of those old houses was truly "home."

The social dichotomies of the Pennsylvania Dutch world came together there in Geraldine's diminutive house on the edge of Neffsville. What of the Dutch recipes in the cookbook? Did she ever make them? Her response was revealing: the committee assembled recipes that they thought would sell well; they were raising money but not to promote Pennsylvania Dutch culture or even food that they normally cooked at home. Many recipes came from clippings taken off food packages or from magazines, and yet all of the recipe cullers were pretty much in agreement that even if the dishes were simple, the ingredients had to be fresh. That positive point is especially evident in the section on vegetables.

When I pointed out that there was a recipe for *Hasenpfeffer* in the book, Geraldine was quick to admit that she had never tried it. There were no hunters in the family, and in any case it was viewed as exotic, something outside the immediate cultural sphere of Neffsville. It was a townie thing, and sure enough, the recipe had been donated by Mary Johnson Wacker, wife of Lancaster beer baron Charles V. Wacker of the Wacker Brewing Company.[18] The Wackers were not Lutherans; they were Roman Catholics, members of St. Mary's Church in Lancaster, so their world was indeed far removed from the closed societies of Lancaster Coun-

FIGURE 55. Bottle label for the Wacker Brewing Company's premium beer, 1930s. Roughwood Collection, Devon, Pa.

ty's small towns. There must be an interesting story behind the donation of Mrs. Wacker's *Hasenpfeffer* recipe because she did not give it out to promote her husband's brewery, which had been shut down in 1920 due to Prohibition and would not reopen until 1933. Yet the recipe may suggest something about her status among the women's organizations in the county, and indeed what it meant to be *Hasenpfeffer* Dutch—and quite conscious of it.

This is Mrs. Wacker's recipe with one qualification: she cooked it sauerbraten style as a stove-top stew rather than braising it in vacuo, that is, sealing the lid with bread dough so that no steam escapes. The latter is the technique used in the Pfalz, and as a result the meat there is reduced to goulash consistency. Then again German hares are large and gamey and must be gutted and hung three days before they are skinned, whereas Pennsylvania farm-raised rabbits can be cooked similarly to freshly butchered chickens. If there is leftover rabbit, use it in the hash browns recipe that follows.

Yield: Serves 6

1 rabbit (approximately 4 pounds/2 kg) (see note)
½ lemon, sliced and seeded
8 ounces (250g) onions, sliced
4 fresh bay leaves, bruised
½ teaspoon whole allspice, coarsely crushed
4 cloves, coarsely crushed
½ teaspoon whole peppercorns, coarsely crushed
2 teaspoons salt or to taste
1 cup (250ml) white wine vinegar
3 cups (750ml) spring water
4 tablespoons (65g) butter
4 tablespoons (30g) flour
1 onion minced very fine
Chopped parsley or fresh marjoram for garnish

Joint the rabbit into serving portions and lay them in a sanitized stoneware crock or large glass container. Combine the lemon, onion, and spices in a work bowl, then spread this over the rabbit. Add the salt. Dilute the vinegar with the spring water and pour this over the rabbit. Cover and set aside to marinate overnight in a cold place.

The next day transfer the rabbit and marinade to a heavy stewing pan and bring to a gentle boil. Cover and simmer for about 1 hour or until the rabbit is tender. From time to time remove any scum that rises to the surface of the marinade. When the rabbit is done, lift it out with a slotted spoon and lay it on a hot platter. Cover and place in a warm oven. Strain the cooking liquid to remove the spices and herbs and set it aside.

In a clean stewing pan, melt the butter over high heat and stir in the 4 tablespoons of flour. Cook until a dark nutty brown, then add the onion. Cover and continue to cook only until the onion is soft (about 3 minutes), then add 1 quart (1 liter) of the strained cooking liquid. Boil up vigorously until thick, then pour into a gravy boat and serve immediately with the rabbit. Garnish with chopped parsley or, even better, a liberal quantity of freshly minced marjoram. Fried *Gnepplin* (button dumplings), boiled egg or cabbage dumplings (recipe on page 200), or saffron noodles make agreeable side dishes. You can also make small dumplings with the cooked rabbit liver; just use the recipe for ham-and-cheese dumplings on page 192. Instead of ham and cheese, use 8 ounces (250g) of ground rabbit liver and meat, and drop out the coriander.

Note: If the rabbit is wild, first soak it in salted water for 3 to 5 hours; then drain and place it in the stewing pan as instructed above. A marinade of buttermilk will also take off the strong taste of game.

⚜ Sour Marinated Rabbit in Hash Browns (*Grumbiere Gehacktes mit Haasepeffer odder Haasepeffer Haesch*)

Hash browns are another Pennsylvania Dutch contribution to American cookery; prototypical recipes can be found well into the eighteenth century. The popularity of the dish was probably due to its common appearance in old Pennsylvania Dutch hotels dotting the main roads leading into the Midwest. Dutch settlers also took it into the upper South. It is one of those quick-and-easy preparations that can be expanded and dressed up according to the situation. As the old saying went, all a Pennsylvania Dutch cook needed were a few leftovers, some onions, and a dash of vinegar to make a meal.

The recipe here is one of those old hotel recipes as transmitted to us by the Philadelphia chef and confectioner James Parkinson (1818–1895), a staunch advocate of American regional cookery. He published the recipe in the December 1881 issue of the *Confectioners' Journal* specifically for recycling the remains of precooked meats like *Hasenpfeffer*. If you like, use chopped raw oysters; they must be added about 5 minutes before the potatoes are done.[19]

Yield: Serves 4 to 6 as a side dish

1½ pounds (625g) raw potatoes, pared
4 ounces (125g) cooked sour marinated rabbit (see recipe above) or
    cooked meat of your choice
1 medium onion, minced very fine
3 tablespoons (25g) flour
3 tablespoons (45g) unsalted butter or lard
1 tablespoon (30ml) vinegar (see note)
Salt and pepper to season
1 tablespoon minced fresh sweet marjoram
1 tablespoon chopped chives for garnish

Chop or grate the raw potatoes to a ricelike consistency. Do the same with the meat so that the texture is similar. Combine the potatoes, meat, and onion and dust with the flour. Heat the butter in a broad heavy skillet or sauté pan, and once the butter begins to foam, add the potato mixture. Gently stir-fry over slow, steady heat (about 20 minutes), using a small spatula to scrape and turn the mixture so that it browns evenly. Acidulate with vinegar to taste. Season and add the marjoram. Serve with a garnish of chopped chives.

Note: Since Hasenpfeffer is already sour, only a splash of vinegar is necessary; otherwise use some of the Hasenpfeffer marinade as described in the preceding recipe.

Steamed Yeast Dumplings (*Dampfgnepp*)

MaryAnn Lovell fondly recalled how on special occasions her mother used to cook these dumplings with a sticky molasses sauce. She tore them apart with a fork so that the hot, sweet steam escaped into her mouth. This was one of her fondest childhood memories of growing up in eastern York County. Steamed yeast dumplings are still made by a number of families in areas where traditional cookery is very much alive, especially around Fryburg in Clarion County, as confirmed to me by a member of the Obenrader family from nearby Marble. Cooks in that woodsy section of the state like to serve the dumplings with molasses or locally made maple syrup.

FIGURE 56. *Dampfgnepp.* These same dumplings can also be served with sauerkraut or with *Schnitz-un-Gnepp* (use the steamed dumplings instead of the small dumplings called for in that recipe), or you can stuff the steamed dumplings with various fillings before cooking them—the cooked cabbage dumplings (page 200) make an ideal filling, but a small piece of apple, dried fruit, or even some ground hickory nuts and a little brown sugar will work just as well. Once cooked, they can be frozen for later use or recycled in a variety of ways: in bread puddings; sliced in half, browned in butter, and served with dried beef gravy; or filled with apple butter and eaten as sandwiches.

Yield: 12 dumplings (serves 4 to 6)

¼ oz (7g) dry active yeast
1 cup (250ml) lukewarm milk
3 egg yolks
½ teaspoon salt
2¾ cups (340g) all-purpose flour
2 tablespoons (30g) unsalted butter (optional)

Proof the yeast in the lukewarm milk. Beat the egg yolks until lemon color, then add the proofed yeast mixture. In a large bowl add the salt to the flour, stir well, then make a valley in the center. Add the egg and yeast mixture. Work into a ball of dough, kneading it well for about 4 to 5 minutes, then cover and allow to rise in a warm place until double in bulk. Knock down and form into 2-ounce (60g) balls of dough on a well-floured surface. Set the balls on a greased sheet to rise. Cover and let the dough recover for 15 to 20 minutes.

In the meantime bring 2 cups (500ml) of lightly salted water to a gentle boil in a deep skillet or heavy stewing pan. Add the butter (optional). Set the dumplings in this, spacing them evenly apart. Cover tightly and steam for 1 hour over low simmering heat. The dumplings should puff up like bread. DO NOT LIFT THE LID until the hour is up—better yet, let them steam for 1 hour and 15 minutes. Any draught of air will cause the dumplings to fall and revert into heavy lumps of dough.

Serve immediately by splitting them with an X-cut and then pouring fried bread crumbs or stewed apples over the top. Instead of water, you could boil them in milk and sugar. Another alternative is to add thinly sliced apples to the cooking water and set the dumplings on top of them.

Note: A heavy stewing pan 5 to 6 inches (13 to 15cm) tall and 10 to 11 inches (25 to 28cm) across will work perfectly for this recipe. This is about the same size as a number 28 Le Creuset enamelware pot.

Stewed Squirrel with Steamed Dumplings
(*Geschmorder Eechhaas mit Dampfgnepp*)

Northern Chester County was fairly solid Pennsylvania Dutch until recent suburbanization altered those demographics. The woodsy Brandywine Hills were a longtime favorite with local hunters in search of small game, squirrels in particular. This recipe was circulated among members of St. Peter's Lutheran Church at Knauertown, where it has been traced to Amanda Keim (1884–1961), whose husband was well known in local hunting circles. The steamed dumplings can be cooked in one of two ways: with the squirrel or separately. Many people prefer to cook them separately because you make gravy from the pan liquids and the dumplings get in the way. If you are dubious about squirrel, substitute two rabbits. If you are adventurous, use two young groundhogs instead of rabbits. The Keims cooked all three types of game with this same basic recipe. However, squirrel is by far the most delicate, especially when it is stewed with a little dandelion wine.

Aside from steamed dumplings, *Gnepplin* (button dumplings), raisin dumplings, peach *Schnitz* dumplings (recipe page 236), and bacon dumplings also go extremely well with this dish.

Yield: Serves 4 to 6

4 squirrels, dressed and cleaned
½ cup (65g) flour
6 tablespoons (90g) bacon drippings or lard
2 onions chopped very fine
½ lemon sliced paper thin (seeds removed)
1 teaspoon salt or to taste
½ cup (125ml) "rainwater" sherry or well-aged dandelion wine
3 tablespoons (45g) butter
3 tablespoons (25g) flour
Salt and pepper to season
Freshly minced rosemary or marjoram
One batch steamed dumplings (page 262)

Cut up the squirrels into pieces, dividing them into legs, thighs, and backs similarly to carving rabbit or chicken. Dust these with the half cup of flour. Heat the bacon drippings (or cooking oil of your choice) in a large heavy stew pan. Once this begins to crackle and smoke, add the meat and brown on both sides over brisk heat (about 8 to 10 minutes total cooking time). Reduce the heat and add the onions. Stir to mingle the onions with the meat. Cover and sweat for 3 minutes or until the onions are clear. Uncover and add 2 quarts (2 liters) of boiling water, the lemon, and salt. Simmer gently for about 1½ hours or until the meat is almost falling from the bones. Add the sherry or dandelion wine.

Remove the meat with a slotted spoon and set aside on a hot serving platter in a warm oven. Melt the 3 tablespoons of butter in a skillet and stir in the flour. Stir constantly and brown over medium-high heat for about 3 minutes, then add 2 cups of the stock from the squirrel. Stir to thicken and then pour into the stewing pot and bring to a gentle boil so that the gravy thickens. Season with salt and pepper. Serve the squirrel piled high in the center of the hot platter with the dumplings (see note below) around the edge. The gravy is either poured over this or served separately. Minced rosemary can be added to the gravy or scattered over the meat when it is served.

Note: Rather than use Amanda Keim's steamed dumpling recipe (which was a common type of baking-powder biscuit), use the recipe for steamed dumplings on page 262. That recipe will supply enough dumplings for the squirrels.

Stuffed Pig Stomach (*Seimawe*)

Before You Start

Always buy a pig stomach that has been previously cleaned by a butcher who knows how to trim stomachs for stuffing. Each stomach has three holes that must be closed tightly in order to make the recipe work effectively. Good Pennsylvania Dutch butchers know how to clean the stomachs without leaving large holes, in which case it is easier to simply tie them shut with string or heavy thread. Otherwise sew them shut by turning the stomach inside out, leaving one hole for the stuffing. Then turn the stomach right-side out and fill it through the remaining hole. All pig stomachs should be sterilized by soaking in salted water for 6 hours or overnight. This should result in the water turning light pink, a sign that the salt is doing its job. Discard the water and rinse the stomach. Tie or sew up and proceed with the recipes below.

Stuffed Pig Stomach with Mashed Potato Filling (*Seimawe mit Grumbiere Fillsel*)

This recipe comes from the late Pearl B. Bortz of Macungie and is one of the least complicated and most fail-safe pig stomach recipes I have encountered. While I have restructured it to follow better procedure, the result is faithful to Mrs. Bortz's original, which is unusual because it contains no meat.[20]

Yield: Serves 6 to 8

1 cleaned pig stomach (about 12 to 14 ounces/375g to 440g)
2 tablespoons (30g) unsalted butter
2 tablespoons (30g) lard (or butter if you prefer)
1½ cups (375g) minced onion
1 cup (125g) bread crumbs
2 pounds (1kg) warm mashed potatoes
½ cup (10g) minced parsley
3 eggs well beaten
½ cup (125ml) hot milk
1½ teaspoons salt or to taste
1 tablespoon coarsely ground peppercorns

Place the pig stomach in a bowl with salted water and let this stand overnight in the refrigerator. In the morning rinse in fresh water two or three times and then pat dry with a towel.

To prepare the stuffing, melt the butter and lard in a large skillet, then add the onion and bread crumbs and brown until they turn golden. Combine this with the mashed potatoes and then add the parsley. Beat the eggs until lemon color and then fold them into the potato mixture, adding the hot milk as you stir. Season with salt and pepper.

Take a spoon or scoop and fill the pig stomach with the potato mixture. Tie up the opening with string as tight as possible so that it does not leak. Do not fill the stomach so that it is packed tight; you must allow for the expansion of the filling while it cooks.

Bring 1 gallon (4 liters) of water to a rolling boil and season it with 1 tablespoon of salt. Once the water is boiling, reduce the heat to a gentle simmer and add the pig stomach, gently lowering it into the water; dropping it too quickly may cause the skin to split. Cover the pot and poach about 3 hours or until done (it should feel plump and firm like a sausage). Roll it over from time to time so that it cooks evenly on all sides. Remove from the water and drain. Serve hot or cold. Cut into slices and brown them lightly on both sides in a skillet. Serve plain or with gravy.

Note: The flavorful water in which the stomach is cooking can be used for boiling sausages and potatoes (or turnips and carrots), which can be added about 30 minutes before the stomach is done. This broth can then be reused as the basis for scrapple by adding meaty pork bones, a pork liver, a pig foot, or whatever else you prefer. Thicken with cornmeal and buckwheat, using the spices for the Blinder Panhas recipe on page 230. By itself the cooking broth can also be used as the basis for soup, as a broth for serving Mauldasche, or as liquid for cooking pork and sauerkraut. You can also freeze it for later use.

Stuffed Pig Stomach with Meat Filling (*Seimawe mit Fleesch Fillsel*)

Fresh sausage in the skins has much better flavor than the sausage sold loose (the recipes are different), so always choose it for stuffing. Also the smokier the smoked sausage the better, because this will help enhance the flavors of the other ingredients. Otherwise pork stuffing such as this will hold its own provided it is well seasoned with fresh herbs.

Yield: Serves 6 to 8

1 cleaned pig stomach
12 ounces (350g) fresh ground pork sausage in the skins
1 cup (200g) diced ham or cooked smoked pork tongue
1 cup (150g) smoked pork sausage, cut in half lengthwise, then sliced into half-moon pieces
2 tablespoons (30g) unsalted butter
2 cups (250g) minced onion
½ cup (50g) chopped celery

1 cup (155g) cooked diced potatoes
1 cup (125g) bread crumbs
½ cup (10g) minced parsley
2 tablespoons ground coriander
1½ teaspoons salt
1 teaspoon coarsely ground peppercorns
1 teaspoon freshly grated nutmeg
3 eggs

Set aside the pig stomach in a deep bowl of well-salted water. Soak 6 hours or overnight (the water should turn pink). While the stomach is soaking, prepare the stuffing as follows. Remove the uncooked sausage from the skins and put it in a deep work bowl, discarding the skins. Add the diced ham and the smoked sausage cut into half-moon pieces.

Heat the butter in a broad sauté pan and add the onion and celery. Sweat over medium-high heat for three minutes or until tender, then pour the contents of the pan over the meats. Add the diced potatoes, bread crumbs, parsley, coriander, salt, peppercorn, and nutmeg. Beat the eggs until lemon color, then add them to the filling mixture.

Using a wooden spoon, combine all the ingredients until thick. Stuff the stomach, tie or sew up the remaining hole, then poach for 3 hours in simmering water as described in the preceding recipe. After 3 hours remove from the water, reserve the cooking water for soup, and put the stomach in a small shallow pan.

Preheat the oven to 375°F (190°C) and bake the stomach for about 25 minutes, basting it frequently with butter or bacon drippings until the skin achieves a golden brown color. Serve immediately in slices or serve later after browning each slice in a sauté pan until golden on each side. This can also be sliced and eaten cold like pâté.

Sweet-and-Sour Marinated Shad
(*Siess-un-Sauere Schaed*)

Shad is oily like its close relative the herring, thus it takes well to vinegar marinades. The roe shad is recommended, since the females are oilier than the bucks. The addition of several sprigs of fresh thyme will improve the flavor. Fresh bay leaves are critical, and there should be enough hot pepper that you can detect the heat.

Yield: Serves 6 to 8

1½ pounds (750g) boned fillet of shad
1 or 2 small seeded pods of cayenne or to taste
1 teaspoon whole cloves
1 teaspoon whole allspice
½ medium onion (75g) sliced paper thin
6 fresh bay leaves
½ teaspoon coarsely ground black pepper
2 cups (500ml) white wine vinegar
2 teaspoons sea salt
⅓ cup (90g) sugar
1 cup (250ml) dry white wine

Cut the fish into small, bite-size pieces. Put the fish, cayenne, cloves, allspice, onion, bay leaves, and pepper in a deep glass bowl. Stir to mix the ingredients thoroughly. Heat the vinegar in a nonreactive saucepan and dissolve the salt and sugar in it. Boil hard 3 minutes, then remove from the heat and set aside to cool. Once the vinegar cools to room temperature, add the wine. Pour this over the fish and cover. Marinate in the refrigerator 1 to 2 days before serving. This will keep under refrigeration for at least 2 weeks.

Sweet Buckwheat Bread (*Siess Buchweetzebrod*)

This tasty half-bread, half-cake comes from Perry County courtesy of a member of the Longenecker family of New Bloomfield. There are several Perry County variants: some more like cake; others more like dense loaf bread. I think the results are best when the bread is baked in a traditional, shallow 11½- to 12-inch (27.5 to 30cm) diameter earthenware *Schales* pan. The Pennsylvania potter Dorothy Long (1933–2009) used to make these heavy dishes in limited editions during the early 1980s. If you are lucky enough to find one at a flea market or antique shop, snap it up. Ceramic plates like Dotty's are wonderful for baking because they retain radiant heat. Incidentally, I once ran out of buckwheat flour, so as an experiment I substituted wild-rice flour. It worked, and the bread tasted as though it had chocolate in it. It was a great hit! If you do not like anise, try something different: 1 teaspoon of ground Chinese five spices instead.

Yield: 8 to 10 servings

3 cups (375g) organic buckwheat flour
½ cup (65g) organic spelt flour (or bread flour)
1 teaspoon baking soda
1 teaspoon ground anise
4 tablespoons (60g) unsalted butter
6 tablespoons (90g) brown sugar
4 tablespoons (40g) poppy seeds
1 tablespoon (5g) minced fresh rosemary
4 large eggs
2 cups (500ml) buttermilk or natural yogurt
White bread crumbs

Preheat the oven to 375°F (190°C). Sift together the buckwheat and spelt flours, soda, and anise three times. Using a sieve or colander, rub the butter and sugar with the flour mixture to form crumbs. Or crumb the mixture in a food processor. Then add 3 tablespoons (30g) of the poppy seeds and the rosemary.

Beat the eggs until lemon color and combine with the buttermilk. Stir this into the crumb mixture.

Grease the baking dish and dust it liberally with bread crumbs. Pour the batter into it and spread evenly. Scatter the remaining poppy seeds over the top. Bake in the preheated oven for 40 minutes or until done in the center. Cool on a rack and serve at room temperature with sour cream or cream cheese.

Sweet Gribble Pie (*Siesse Grippelboi*)

This recipe was created for the menu of the Black Horse Hotel in Reinholds, Pennsylvania, by the cook and owner Clara Bowman. Her creative cooking was legendary during the 1920s, and she was one of the first local cooks in Pennsylvania to elevate the cuisine to a new level of culinary expression, albeit in small steps. Her customers came to the Black Horse for her popular chicken-and-waffle dinners; she then tempted them with novelties such as this dish. Aside

FIGURE 57. The Black Horse Hotel, Reinholds, Pa., ca. 1910. Built in 1751 and once famous for its Pennsylvania Dutch cookery, the hotel was demolished in 1978 to make way for a fast-food store. Old photograph courtesy of the Cocalico Valley Historical Society, Ephrata, Pa.

from the almond-and-sour-cherry version, which is best when eaten hot or at room temperature, Clara also made a saffron version and the one most commented upon by restaurant critics: chocolate gribble pie (next cookbook!). Clara Bowman's gribble pies were actually culinary revivals because traditional gribble began to disappear from mainstream Pennsylvania Dutch cookery after the Civil War. Like several other cooks in her generation, she was interested in taking old dishes and reinventing them.

Yield: Serves 6 to 8

½ batch potpie dough (page 248)
2 large eggs
½ cup (125ml) fresh sour cream
½ cup (125g) sugar
Salt to taste
½ teaspoon ground cinnamon
½ teaspoon grated zest of lemon
½ cup (100g) dried sour cherries
½ cup (50g) sliced almonds
9-inch (23cm) pie shell
Topping:
¼ cup (25g) sliced almonds
1 teaspoon sugar
¼ teaspoon ground cinnamon

Roll out the dough ¼ inch (6.6mm) thick on a well-floured surface. Using a sharp knife cut the dough into pencil-thin slices. Let them dry for about half an hour, then chop into tiny bits the size of pinhead oatmeal or split peas. This should yield 2 cups (300g) of gribble. Spread the gribble on a cookie sheet to dry overnight or at least 4 to 6 hours.

To cook the gribble, bring 2 quarts (2 liters) of lightly salted water to a rolling boil, then reduce the temperature to a gentle simmer. Add the gribble and let it cook about 10 to 11 minutes or until tender. Strain and set aside in a deep work bowl. Add a little melted butter or chicken fat so that the gribble does not stick together.

Beat the eggs until lemon color, then add the sour cream and sugar. Pour this over the gribble and stir well. Season with salt, then add the cinnamon and lemon zest. Add the chopped dried sour cherries and the sliced almonds. Mix thoroughly, then pour the mixture into a prepared 9-inch (23cm) pie shell. Bake in an oven preheated to 375°F (190°C) for 45 to 50 minutes. As soon as the pie leaves the oven scatter over it a mixture of sugar, sliced almonds, and cinnamon. Serve with stewed pears and dark coffee.

Thick Milk Pie (Clabber Pie) or Slop Tart (*Dickemillich Boi odder Schlappkuche*)

This type of pie was popular with visitors to the Kutztown Folk Festival, and in the past several of the food concessions offered them for sale. They are still available on the Zion Church menu, although this recipe comes from the Quakertown area of Bucks County.

Yield: one 9-inch (23cm) pie

2 tablespoons rice flour or pastry flour
1 teaspoon ground cinnamon
½ teaspoon ground cloves
½ teaspoon baking soda
1 tablespoon cream of tartar
2 large eggs, room temperature
2 cups (500ml) thick milk (clabbered milk) or very thick buttermilk
1 cup (250g) sugar
1 9-inch (23cm) prepared pie shell

Preheat the oven to 350°F (175°C). Sift together the rice flour, cinnamon, cloves, baking soda, and cream of tartar. In a separate bowl, beat the eggs until lemon color, then add the milk and sugar. Beat until the sugar is fully dissolved, then sift in the flour and spice mixture. Whisk until combined and beginning to foam, then pour into the prepared pie shell. Bake in the preheated oven for 45 minutes or until set in the center. Cool on a rack and serve at room temperature or slightly chilled.

Trinkle's Lehigh County Corn Pie
('em Joseph Trinkel sei Lechaw Kaundi Welschkarn Boi)

When I interviewed Dr. Don Yoder about his early work in Pennsylvania Dutch folk studies, among his most vivid memories of his year teaching at Muhlenberg College in 1948 were weekly lunches at Joseph Trinkle's Cetronia Hotel on the edge of Allentown. Trinkle's hotel was a magnet for local farmers coming into the city for market, and one of the culinary highlights of the hotel bar was Trinkle's locally famous handheld corn pie. A glass of Horlacher's beer, a bowl of hearty potato soup, and one of these corn pies were all you needed to satisfy an appetite on a cold winter day. The bar scene was a center of lively Dutch conversation, and as the farmers left the barroom, they often belched to signify their appreciation of a meal well cooked. With a little help from several rare 1940s Trinkle's menus and a few newspaper clippings about the food served there, the recipe that follows comes so close to the original that when Dr. Yoder tried one, he declared it a true "living memory."

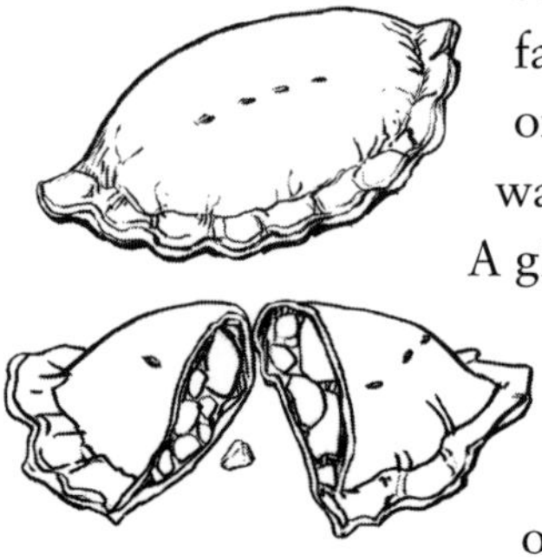

FIGURE 58. Corn pies.

Yield: 24 half-moon pies

3 cups (450g) cooked sweet corn
½ cup (75g) diced cooked potato
1 cup (150g) chopped fried chicken
1 cup (175g) chopped onion
½ cup (65g) bread crumbs
½ cup (10g) chopped parsley
1 tablespoon sugar
1 tablespoon dry summer savory
3 tablespoons (45g) melted butter
2 large eggs
Salt and pepper to taste
1 batch half-moon pie dough (page 255)

1 egg, separated
2 tablespoons (30ml) milk or cream

Prepare 1 batch of half-moon pie dough (page 255) and set aside in a warm place to double in bulk. Preheat the oven to 350°F (175°C). Combine the corn, potato, chicken, onion, bread crumbs, parsley, sugar, and summer savory in a deep work bowl. Add the melted butter and combine thoroughly. Beat the eggs until lemon color and frothy, then fold into the filling mixture. Season to taste.

Once the dough has doubled in bulk, knock down and knead for about 4 minutes. Roll out ¼ inch (6mm) thick and cut into 5- to 6-inch (13 to 15cm) rounds. Place about 1½ tablespoons (50g) of filling in the center of each round of dough. Fold over, brush the edges with beaten egg white, and press with a fork to seal the edges. Poke 4 holes with a fork in the top of each pie, then set aside to recover for 20 minutes. Once the pies have recovered and the dough has started to puff nicely, set them on lightly greased baking sheets. Beat the egg yolk and milk until fully combined and brush this over the surface of each pie. Bake in the preheated oven for 20 to 25 minutes. Serve hot or at room temperature. These pies can be frozen for later use and reheated in a microwave oven.

Recipes by Category

Glossary of Pennsylvania Dutch Food Terms

Amische Roascht: Amish roast, a type of pudding or casserole made of potatoes, bread, and shredded or chopped chicken. The name is borrowed from English, while the recipe evolved out of chicken dumplings.

Bach Adel: "Creek Gentry," a euphemism for rich millers, especially those who acted as local bankers for traditional farm transactions.

Backet/Baecket: Boiled potatoes that are cut in half lengthwise and cooked golden brown on a griddle. An inexpensive snack food.

Blind: A term for faux dishes, as in *Blinde Fische* (mock fish), *Blinde Geem* (mock game), and *Blinder Haas* (mock rabbit or hare).

Boddegeschmack: taste of place, the special flavor food derives from the soil, as in French *terroir*.

Brate: To roast, specifically to spit roast but also used in the sense of frying.

Brieh: Juice or stock. This is either the juice pressed out of something or leftover cooking stock that is flavored by the food cooked in it. Thus *Zwiwwelbrieh* is either the raw juice pressed out of onions or a broth created by boiling onions in water.

Brodsupp: Bread soup, a type of casserole made with large pieces of stale bread. A common name for any type of *Schlupper* (bread casserole).

Buhnesuppeleit: The "Bean Soupers," an annual Civil War picnic in Snyder County that features bean soup.

Buweschenkel: "Boys thighs," a type of boiled, stuffed dumpling. In the Allentown area these were oversized *Mauldasche*.

Buweschpitzle: "Boys bits" or "boys pricks," a type of quenelle made of potatoes and pan-fried or deep-fried.

Dampfgnepp: Steamed dumplings, steam-baked in a skillet or deep stewing pan. *Dampfgnopp*: a large dumpling about the size of a pie prepared in the same manner as the smaller dumplings.

Drechtergnepp: Boiled dumplings made with a funnel.

Drechterkuche: Funnel cakes.

Dunkes: Gravy thickened with flour or milk or both. The word comes from *dunke,* a verb for dipping or dunking bread into food.

Dunkesbrod: Sops, bread used to wipe up plates during a meal.

Endepeffer: Sour marinated duck, duck marinated in vinegar or wine before it is stewed.

Faektribrod: Factory bread, bread produced in large-scale commercial bakeries.

Fillsel: Filling, both a stuffing in poultry or meat dishes and a baked casserole. Normally a mixture of potatoes and bread.

Fisch-Boi: Fish pie, a dessert pie made in the Mahantongo area and consisting of a crust similar to cookie dough and a sweet filling made with molasses or syrup.

Fleesch: Meat, also used for specific dishes such as *Fleeschpeffer:* sour marinated pork and beef tenderloin or eye of the round cooked together in the same pot.

Gehacktes: Hash, any food minced very fine.

Gehacktesupp: Chopped soup, Pennsylvania Dutch egg drop soup.

Gereeschte Mehlsupp: Browned flour soup or roux soup. Normally flour and butter or lard browned in a pan, then thinned with stock. The browned flour gives the soup both a creamy texture and flavor.

Geschwelde Grumbiere: Potatoes boiled whole usually in their skins. Also called simply *Geschwelde* (plural).

Gnepp: Any type of dumpling. *Gnepplin* are small dumplings about the size of small buttons or currants, hence the Pennsylvania term "button dumplings." They are often incorrectly equated with

Swabian *Spätzle*, which are more stringlike in shape; otherwise the dough is the same.

Gnepplinbrett: A dumpling board, a small handheld board designed to hold dough so that it can be chopped and then dropped into boiling water.

Gneppschpatz: A small spatula designed specifically for slicing dough to make small string dumplings called *Spätzle* in German. The German word for the dumplings derives from this ancient tool—*spatullus* in Celto-Roman. The Pennsylvania Dutch use the same small spatulas to make their own types of dumpling.

Grautgnepp: Cabbage dumplings, usually about the size of walnuts.

Grippel: Gribble. Crumbs of dough about the size of pinhead oatmeal created by chopping dough into tiny bits. A poverty version of this dish is made with buckwheat flour and water, which is chopped while heated in a skillet. Sweet gribble is created by chopping egg pasta into small bits, which were called "pop-robins" by Pennsylvania Quakers and often added to soup. Gribble made with the yolks of turtle eggs is added to pepper pot soup.

Grimmele: Crumbs, especially dry bread crumbs.

Grossbauer: The owner of a very large farm or of several farms. The Pennsylvania Dutch equivalent of landed gentry. They often rent land to tenant farmers.

Grumbiere Balle: Potato balls, a type of fried dumpling.

Grumbier Gehacktes: Hash brown potatoes.

Grumme: The crumb or white part of a loaf of bread. Also written *Brodgrumme*.

Gruscht Pannkuche: Bread crust pancakes, pancakes made with bread crust batter.

Gumbis: Also written *Gumbisch* or *Kumbisch*. The term derives from Latin *compositum* and refers to a deep-dish casserole made of layers of shredded cabbage and other ingredients. *Gumbistopp* is both the name of the earthen pot or pan in which the recipe is baked and a synonym for the food inside.

Haasepeffer Haesch: A type of hash brown potatoes mixed with minced rabbit.

Harzepeffer: Sour marinated beef hearts, marinated in wine or vinegar before cooking. Usually cut into strips when cooked.

Harsch Schnidde: Venison cutlets, a luxury dish.

Hasenpfeffer: Written in dialect as *Haasepeffer*. Rabbit stewed in a sour marinade.

Hooriche Gnepp: "Hairy" dumplings. Dumplings made from shredded potatoes; the shreds give the dumplings a fuzzy appearance, hence the name.

Kaffeesupp: Coffee soup, a soup made by breaking bread into a cup of hot coffee.

Koche: To boil but also more generally to cook.

Lehnsbauer: Tenant farmer, normally involved in truck farming or with products for local farm markets. An important component in the Pennsylvania Dutch food system.

Leppkuche: Lepp cakes or honey cakes. A popular Christmas cookie with a dry, porous texture intended for dipping in hard cider, wine, or coffee.

Lulu Bapp: LuLu paste. A cracker spread sold in Pennsylvania Dutch farm markets north of Harrisburg. The name refers to a beer-cheese dip for hot soft pretzels that was developed at the LuLu Country Club established by the Shriners in 1912 near Philadelphia. The original recipe was only one of several imitation Liptauer cheese spreads served in Philadelphia's German hotels and cafés and in Pennsylvania Dutch taverns and eating saloons. LuLu paste was popularized locally because it was served at Shriner picnics and in the dining cars of the Pennsylvania Railroad during Shriner excursions. The original 1920s recipe was based on true Philadelphia cream cheese; the rural adaptations use other types of cheese, especially "hung cheese," a type of dense, small-curd cottage cheese. Sometimes used as a filling in *Mauldasche*.

Mauldasche: Boiled pocket dumplings euphemistically called "mouth slappers." Normally triangular in shape. Similar to Italian ravioli.

Metzelsupp: Butchering day stew, or a gift of butchering day meats distributed to friends or the needy.

Millichbrod: Milk bread, the best sort of sourdough bread made with milk rather than water.

Millichflitsch: Another name for *Schlappkuche* (slop pie).

Neideitsche Kiche: New Dutch cuisine. A movement that began in the late 1920s to reinvent the traditional cookery along more contemporary lines. Not influenced by French nouvelle cuisine.

Nesselkuche: Nettle tart, a pizzalike pie covered with sautéed onions, pan-wilted nettle greens, and an egg-and-sour-cream topping. A nettle quiche.

Nudelsupp: Noodle soup.

Oiersupp: Egg drop soup, a synonym for chopped soup.

Panhas: Pennsylvania Dutch dialect synonym for scrapple. Scrapple, originally spelled *schrappel*, is a Lower Rhineland term also found in Holland Dutch. *Panhas* is a Westphalian term of Celtic origin written as *pannas*, literally "food made in a pan." The common explanation that *Panhas* means "pan rabbit" is a false etymology.

Riwwelfisch: Another name for *Blinde Fische* in reference to the pasta crumbs from which the mock fish were made.

Riwwelsupp: Any soup thickened with pasta crumbs made by rubbing the dough between the fingers. The crumb texture is smaller than gribble.

Rollitsch: Stuffed pickled beef tripe made mostly in York and Adams counties. The presumed origin of the term is Holland Dutch, from *rolletje*.

Rutscher: An earthenware or cast-iron pan with a handle on one end and a spout on the other. Used for braising meats, for roasting poultry, or for deep-dish casseroles. The name derives from the verb *rutsche*, "to slide, push, or jiggle" something in and out of the oven. Children who cannot sit still are said to *rutsch* too much.

Schales: A shallow-dish casserole taking its name from Schale, a "shell," in reference to the medieval shape of the baking dish. Synonymous with a small Spanish paella pan.

Schaumkuche: Literally "foam omelet," a type of omelet in which the egg whites are separated, beaten, and folded in last.

Schlagt nei: "Dig in." Used in the plural form when addressing people at the dinner table. The Pennsylvania Dutch equivalent of *bon appétit*.

Schlappichdunkes: Slop pot gravy, a euphemism for dishes eaten out of a common bowl into which people at the table dip bread or spoons.

Schlappkuche: Slop pie, normally a pie crust filled with milk sweetened with sugar. A common snack for children.

Schmierkeeskuche: Cottage cheese pie, normally a flat, pizzalike pie covered with small-curd cottage cheese, onions, and perhaps also apple butter.

Schnitz-un-Gnepp: A stew of dried sliced apples and dumplings; meat is sometimes added.

Schtammtisch: A table in a bar or saloon reserved for regulars who meet there often. An elaborately carved *Schtammtisch* from Kuechler's Roost is now in the collection of the Berks County Historical Society.

Schtreivlin: A Swabian term for funnel cakes. The term is sometimes used in Pennsylvania Dutch.

Schtupp: Stove room or *Stube* (in standard German). A room apart from the kitchen that was heated with a cast-iron plate stove. This is where Pennsylvania Dutch families normally ate their meals. With the advent of the cast-iron cook stove during the 1840s, the stove room shifted to the kitchen as the focal point for family meals.

Schuppe: To sauté by means of jostling a skillet or frying pan to make the contents rise into the air. Hence *Schuppgnepplin*, sautéed dumplings, another name for *Buweschpitzle*.

Schwatze Brei: Black mush, a porridge of cornmeal mixed with buckwheat flour.

Schwowegnepp: Swabian dumplings, a term for either large boiled dumplings or large steamed dumplings.

Seimawe: Stuffed pig stomach, normally filled with a mixture of potatoes, sausage, meat, and perhaps bread crumbs.

Summerwarscht: Summer sausage. This smoked beef sausage is often sold under the misnomer Lebanon bologna, as though it were invented in Lebanon County (it was not). There are commonly two kinds, one sweet and one sour, but styles of preparation vary from county to county.

Wasserschtreivlin: Boiled dumplings made in the shape of funnel cakes.

Welschkarn Gruscht: Cornmeal crust, any type of pie crust made with cornmeal.

Zwiwwelkuche: Onion tart or onion pie, a traditional farm dish akin to the French quiche. The French word *quiche* derives from Alsatian German *Kuche*.

Notes

CHAPTER 1

1 Christian Germershausen, *Die Hausmutter in allen ihren Geschäfften*, volume 2 (Leipzig: Johann Friedrich Junius, 1778), pages 450–451.

2 Interview, Isaac Clarence Kulp, Pennsburg, Pa., June 13, 2005.

3 Ibid.

CHAPTER 2

1 Julius Friedrich Sachse, *The German Sectarians of Pennsylvania*, 2 volumes (Philadelphia: Privately printed, 1899) , volume 1, page 115.

2 Paul Peirce, *Suppers* (New York: Barse & Hopkins, 1907), pages 23–24.

3 Peirce, *Suppers*, pages 25–26.

CHAPTER 3

1 William Vollmer, *United States Cook Book* (Philadelphia: John Weik, 1859), page 51.

2 Johann Georg Hohman, *Das Evangelium Nicodemus* (Reading, Pa.: C. A. Bruckman, 1819), page 226.

3 *Vollständiges Nürnbergisches Koch-Buch* (Nuremberg: Wolfgang Moritz Endters, 1691), page 542.

4 Interview, Ivan Glick, Lancaster, Pa., April 23, 2010. Annie Glick was Ivan's mother.

5 Vollmer, *United States Cook Book*, pages 37–38.

6 Friedrike Löffler, *Oekonomisches Handbuch für Frauenzimmer* (Stuttgart: Johann Friedrich Steinkopf, 1795), pages 31–32.

CHAPTER 5

1 Helen R. Martin, The *Crossways* (New York: Century Company, 1910), page 4.

2 William Woys Weaver, *Country Scrapple: An American Tradition* (Mechanicsburg, Pa.: Stackpole Books, 2003), pages 1–76.

3 Eszter Kisbán, *Népi Kultúra, Közkultúra, Jelkép: A Gulyás, Pörkölt, Paprikás* (Budapest: MTA Néprajzi Kutatócsoport, 1989).

4 Refer to William Woys Weaver, *Pennsylvania Dutch Country Cooking* (New York: Abbeville, 1993), pages 47–48, 52, and the illustration on page 67.

5 *Kooche,* also written *Kooch,* was an old local Nuremberg dialect term for *Brei,* meaning "porridge" or "gruel." See *Vollständiges Nürnbergisches Koch-Buch* (Nuremberg: Wolfgang Moritz Endters, 1691), page 87.

6 Eliza Leslie, *New Receipts for Cookery* (Philadelphia: T. B. Peterson, 1854), page 416.

7 Edith M. Thomas, *Mary at the Farm* (Norristown, Pa.: John Hartenstine, 1915), page 221.

8 Leslie, *New Receipts*, page 412.

CHAPTER 6

1 *The Gettysburg Centennial Cook Book* (Lancaster, Pa.: Inquirer Printing, 1876), page 51.

2 Helen R. Martin, *Sabina: A Tale of the Amish* (New York: Century Company, 1905), page 6.

3 William Woys Weaver, *Sauerkraut Yankees* (Philadelphia: University of Pennsylvania Press, 1983), page 129.

4 Abraham Brubaker (died 1935) was the last of the German preachers at Longenecker's, although English had been in common use even in the 1860s.

5 Meixner's philosophies are outlined by Klaus Freckmann in "Hausforschung im Dritten Reich," *Zeitschrift für Volkskunde* 78:2 (1983): 169–186. Her works are now illegal in Germany and cannot be accessed online.

6 David Weaver-Zercher, *The Amish in the American Imagination* (Baltimore: Johns Hopkins University Press, 2001), page 87.

7 Letter of Mary Jane Hershey to Dr. Don Yoder, Lederach, Pa., November 14, 1972.

8 Elsie Singmaster, *The Magic Mirror* (Boston: Houghton, Mifflin, 1934), page 202.

9 Bland Johaneson, "Victualary among the Pennsylvania Germans," *American Mercury* 15 (October 1926): 196–198.

CHAPTER 7

1 The technique for storing pit cabbage in the ground was also recommended for whole heads of cabbage intended for overwinter fodder or for market; straw or corn stalks were used as insulation around the heads of cabbage. Many articles appeared in the *American Agriculturist* treating this as an economical and safe way to keep cabbage fresh during cold weather. This is confirmed in specialist literature such as James J. H. Gregory's *Cabbages: How to Grow Them* (Salem, Mass.: James J. H. Gregory, 1870). The preferred varieties for fermented pit cabbage were Early Schweinfurth, Quintal (also called Gros chou d'Alsace), Flat Dutch, Drumhead, and Sugar Loaf.

2 *Neue Gemeinnütziger Pennsylvanischen Calender auf das Jahr 1872* (Lancaster: Johann Bär, [1871]), unpag.

3 Berenice Steinfeldt, *The Amish of Lancaster County* (Lancaster, Pa.: Arthur G. Steinfeldt, 1937), page 30.

4 This herbal is translated and analyzed in William Woys Weaver, *Sauer's Herbal Cures: America's First Book of Botanic Healing* (New York/London: Routledge, 2001).

5 Theodore Zwinger, *Theatrum Botanicum; das ist, Vollkommenes Kräuter-Buch* (Basel: Hans Jacob Bischoff, 1744), page 456. The first edition appeared in 1696.

CHAPTER 8

1 Peter Seibert Davis, *The Young Parson* (1861; repr., Philadelphia: Smith, English & Co., 1863), page 224.

2 Elsie Singmaster, "The Vacillation of Benjamin Gaumer," *Century Magazine* 71:5 (March 1906): 708.

CHAPTER 10

1 Ralph Wood, *The Pennsylvania Germans* (Princeton, N.J.: Princeton University Press, 1942), page viii.

2 Ann Hark, *Hex Marks the Spot* (Philadelphia: J. B. Lippincott, 1938), page 282.

3 Hark, *Hex Marks the Spot*, page 283.

4 Interview, John B. Fisher, Morgantown, Pa., April 25, 2006.

5 Frederick Klees, *The Pennsylvania Dutch* (New York: Macmillan, 1950), page 414.

6   Guy McConnell, "The Peace People of Pennsylvania," *Family Circle* 17 (June 14, 1940): 13.

CHAPTER 11

1   Olive G. Zehner, "It's Fashionable to Be Pennsylvania Dutch Today," *Pennsylvania Dutchman* 4:14 (April 1953): 16.
2   Maynard Owen Williams, "The Pennsylvania Dutch Folk Festival," *National Geographic* 102:4 (October 1952): 505–516.
3   Because of the sensitivity of working with the festival organizers, this interviewee asked that her name not be printed. Criticism of the festival's food came from a sincere desire to see an improvement in the culinary offerings, especially good food more representative of the culture.

CHAPTER 12

1   Whoopee Pies entered Amish popular culture via several points of contact with the outside world during the 1960s. One of the early disseminators of the cake was *Family Life*, an Amish magazine that is no longer published. A recipe adapted to home cooking appeared in the November 1968 issue under the title "What Shall We Put in School Buckets?" It came from Anna Mae Burkholder, a contributor from Indiana. Although baked and packaged in Roxbury, Massachusetts, by the Berwick Cake Company, the original commercial pies were evidently distributed or subcontracted in the Chicago area from the 1950s into the early 1970s before the bakery went out of business in 1977. From there they entered into local Amish cooking in Illinois and Indiana, where they were known for quite a few years before they became common among the Amish in Pennsylvania. The Big Valley Amish in Mifflin County were the first Pennsylvania Amish to adopt the pies, probably because they served the same practical function as half-moon pies. From a nutritional standpoint, half-moon pies are a lot more healthful.

Food writers outside Pennsylvania generally refer to the Amish Whoopee Pies as Pennsylvania Dutch, but that claim is certainly tenuous because it is mostly the Amish who make them, not the Pennsylvania Dutch majority. Furthermore several bakeries in western Pennsylvania, among them the Washington Bakery in Bedford, tried to copy Whoopee Pies and sell them under that name during the early 1930s. They ran afoul of copyright infringement, so other local names evolved: for example, Gobs, which is an off-color term borrowed from mining slang.

2 *Old Family Recipes from St. Martin's Parish* (Radnor, Pa.: Women's Auxiliary of St. Martin's Church, 1934), advertisement page at the end of the book.

RECIPES

1 J. Levan, *Berks County Cook Book of Pennsylvania Dutch Recipes* (Reading, Pa.: J. Levan, 1934), page 42. This was one of the first cookbooks in the 1930s to use the term "Pennsylvania Dutch" in its title—a clear response to political upheavals in Germany. Levan was an acquaintance of J. George Frederick and was affiliated with the Society of Pennsylvania German Gastronomes. This book was renamed the *Pennsylvania Dutch Cook Book of Fine Old Recipes* in late 1934 when rights were purchased by the Culinary Arts Press of Reading, Pennsylvania. See Dorman and Davidow in the bibliography.

2 For traditional techniques for making *Schnitz*, see Henry Showalter, "Snitz Pie," *Pennsylvania Dutchman* 5:9 (January 1, 1954), page 16.

3 George Girardey, *Höchst nützliches Handbuch über Kochkunst* (Cincinnati: F. U. James, 1841), pages 17–18.

4 Mark W. Hoffman, *Sixty Wholesome Potato Dishes* (New Tripoli, Pa.: Privately printed, ca. 1935), page 12.

5 "Brod-Kuchen," *Der amerikanische Bauer* 4 (1854): 60.

6 *Pennsylvania State Grange Cook Book* (Harrisburg, Pa.: Evangelical Press, 1932), page 128.

7 Irene B. Arthur's numerous recipes originally appeared in the *Allentown Morning Call*. Her filling recipe was published in a slightly different form in the December 11, 1948, edition. She later corresponded with Ora Yoder (mother of Dr. Don Yoder), whom she met at the Kutztown Folk Festival. Mrs. Arthur was born in 1921 and became the wife of Stanley D. Arthur (1909–1959). Several of her letters and recipes are preserved in the collection of the author.

8 Missionary Society of St. Paul's Reformed Church (Bowmansville, Pa.), *Household Guide and Cook Book* (Denver, Pa.: Steffy & Co., 1916), page 35.

9 Correspondence with Amos B. Hoover, Ephrata, Pa., October 20, 2011.

10 *Der alte Germantown Calender für das Jahr 1863* (Philadelphia: Sauer & Barnes, [1862]), page 23.

11 Interview with Don Yoder, September 27, 2008. This family recipe was recorded by his mother, Ora Cronister Yoder.

12 This recipe was transmitted to me by Sarah Freely (now deceased), who was acquainted with the pastor of Brownback's United Church of Christ (Spring City, Pa.), where Emma Brownback and her husband were members. Both Emma and George Brownback are buried in the graveyard nearby.

13 *Der amerikanische Landwirtschafts-Calender auf das Jahr 1880* (Reading, Pa.: Ritter & Company, 1879), unpag.

14 "Arche Noah Projekt: Das Grubenkraut," *Arche Noah* (November 2009): 11.

15 "Kartoffel Ballen," *Ceres* 2:4 (November 1840): 56.

16 Henrietta Beam was the wife of John K. Beam (1840–1918). She is buried beside her husband in the Bowmansville Union Cemetery. Her recipe was published in several Lancaster County fund-raising cookbooks, but for the most part the printed versions are not only skeletal; they are also sometimes deviously misleading—such as quadrupling the potatoes and leaving out the spices. It was thus necessary to speak with cooks who remembered preparing the dish in the church kitchen well into the 1950s.

17 Ida May Fetterman (1875–1948) was the wife of William H. Fetterman (1865–1946). They are buried in the Circle Hill Cemetery at Punxsutawney. Her husband was affiliated with the groundhog .club in Punxsutawney.

18 Mary A. Johnson Wacker (1852–1936). The Wacker Brewing Company began in 1859 as the Eagle Brewery, which was sold by Elizabeth Sprenger in 1863 to the Württemberg immigrant Joseph Wacker (father-in-law of Mary). The Wacker Brewing Company went out of business in 1956.

19 "Potatoes (Parkinson Style)," *Confectioners' Journal* 7:83 (December 1881): 42.

20 "'S Pennsylfawnisch Deitsch Eck," *Allentown Morning Call,* December 11, 1948.

Bibliography

Amish Cooking. Aylmar, Ontario/LaGrange, Ind.: Pathway Publishing, 1979.

Apfel, Mrs. T. Roberts, and Mrs. Calvin N. Wenrich. *Old Pennsylvania Recipes.* Lancaster, Pa.: Privately printed, 1933.

"Arche Noah Projekt: Das Grubenkraut." *Arche Noah* (November 2009): 11.

Backenstose, D. Lee. *Stuffing the Pig Stomach.* Schaefferstown, Pa.: Franklin House, ca. 1990.

The Berks-Lehigh Farmer. *Recipes and Their Cooks.* Kutztown, Pa.: D. H. Conover, 1967. This is volume 2 of a collection of recipes submitted by members of the local granges in Berks and Lehigh Counties.

Best, Martha S. "Food Varieties at the Festival." *Pennsylvania Folklife* 22 (Folk Festival Supplement 1973): 14–18.

———. "Leaving the Festival with Thoughts of Food." *Pennsylvania Folklife* 20:4 (Summer 1971): 37–39.

Brauns, Ernst Ludwig. *Practische Belehrungen und Ratschläge für Reisende und Auswanderer nach Amerika* [Practical Advice and Useful Hints for Travelers and Emigrants to America]. Braunschweig: Herzogliches Waisenhaus Buchdruckerei, 1829.

Burkholder, Anna Mae. "What Shall We Put in School Buckets?" *Family Life* 1:11 (November 1968): 26–27.

Ceres, eine Zeitschrift für den Landwirth [Ceres, a Journal for Farmers]. 3 volumes. Lebanon, Pa.: Samuel Miller, 1839–1841.

Chandler, Julia Davis. "Moravian Domestic Life." *Boston Cooking-School* 10:7 (February 1906): 311–317.

Davis, Peter Seibert. *The Young Parson.* 1861. Repr., Philadelphia: Smith, English & Co., 1863.

DeChant, Alliene Saeger. "Sixteen Years of the Folk Festival." *Pennsylvania Folklife* 14:4 (Summer 1965): 10–13.

Der alte Germantown Calender für das Jahr 1863. Philadelphia: Sauer & Barnes, [1862].

Devlin, Ron. "For Almost 30 Years, Maidencreek Woman Wears Unofficial Title of Funnel Cake Queen." *Reading Eagle*, May 16, 2010.

Dorman, William K., and Leonard Davidow. *Pennsylvania Dutch Cook Book of Fine Old Recipes*. Reading, Pa.: Privately printed, 1934. This is J. Levan's *Berks County Cook Book* reissued under a new title.

Ecenbarger, William. "The Amish under Siege." *Philadelphia Inquirer Magazine,* January 26, 1986, pages 16–21, 26.

Edwords, Clarence E. *Bohemian San Francisco*. San Francisco: Paul Elder, 1914.

Fasolt, Nancy. *Clear Toy Candy*. Mechanicsburg, Pa.: Stackpole Books, 2010.

41 Bewährte Recepte für Handwerker und Hausväter [Forty-One Approved Recipes for Craftsmen and Home Use]. Millgrove, Pa: Samuel and Solomon Siegfried, 1834.

Freckmann, Klaus. "Hausforschung im Dritten Reich" [Research on Folk Architecture during the Third Reich], *Zeitschrift für Volkskunde* 78:2 (1983): 169–186.

Frederick, J. George. *The Pennsylvania Dutch and Their Cookery*. New York: Business Bourse, 1935.

"Frische Brodwärscht, gebrodne Grumbiere un Peffergraut." *Pfälzer Feierowend* 3:34 (August 25, 1951): 6.

Fritsch, Peter V. *Der Haahne Greht: Pennsylvania Dutch Poems and Scherenschnitte*. Morgantown, Pa.: Masthof Press, 2006.

Fryer, Benjamin. "Kuechler's Roost." *Historical Review of Berks County* (October 1935): 15–18.

Germershausen, Christian Friedrich. *Die Hausmutter in allen ihren Geschäfften* [The Housewife in All Her Duties]. Volume 2. Leipzig: Johann Friedrich Junius, 1778. This is part of a multivolume series, although each volume stands alone.

The Gettysburg Centennial Cook Book. Lancaster, Pa.: Inquirer Printing, 1876.

Gibbons, Phebe Earle. *"Pennsylvania Dutch" and Other Essays*. Philadelphia: J. B. Lippincott, 1872.

Giger, Emma Alder. *Colonial Receipt Book*. Philadelphia: John C. Winston Co., 1907.

Gilcher, Klaudia. "Grumbeerwaffeln: Die Specialität, die einst Arme-Leute-Essen war" [Potato Waffles: The Specialty That Was Once Poor People's Food]. *Die Rheinpfalz* 64:74 (March 29, 2008).

Girardey, George. *Höchst nützliches Handbuch über Kochkunst* [A Highly Useful Manual of Cookery]. Cincinnati: F. U. James, 1841.

Globe-Times. *The Globe-Times Cook Book of Old-Fashioned Recipes*. Bethlehem, Pa.: Globe-Times, 1934. This contains recipes gathered from food columns in the newspaper.

Good, Phyllis Pellman, and Rachel Thomas Pellman. *From Amish and Mennonite Kitchens*. Intercourse, Pa.: Good Books, 1984.

Gregory, James J. H. *Cabbages: How to Grow Them*. Salem, Mass.: James J. H. Gregory, 1870.

Groff, Betty, and José Wilson. *Good Earth & Country Cooking*. Harrisburg, Pa.: Stackpole Books, 1974.

Groff, Douglas Withers. *The Slumbering Groundhog Lodge of Quarryville, Pennsylvania*. Lancaster, Pa.: Whitmore Printing, 2000.

Haldeman, S. S. *Pennsylvania Dutch: A Dialect of South German with an Infusion of English*. London: Trübner & Co., 1872.

Harbaugh, Henry. *Harbaugh's Harfe*. Philadelphia: Reformed Church Publication Board, 1870.

Hark, Ann. *Hex Marks the Spot*. Philadelphia: J. B. Lippincott, 1938.

———. *The Story of the Pennsylvania Dutch*. New York: Harper & Brothers, 1943.

———. "Who Are the Pennsylvania Dutch?" *House & Garden* 79:6 (June 1941): 21 and 64.

Hark, Ann, and Preston A. Barba. *Pennsylvania German Cookery*. Allentown, Pa.: Schlechter's, 1950.

Heilman, U. Henry. "Descriptive and Historical Memorials of Heilman Dale." *Proceedings of the Lebanon County Historical Society* 4:13 (1909): 407–459.

Heinmann, Berthold. *Von Äpfelkraut bis Zimtschnecke: Das Lexikon der rheinischen Küche* [From Apple-Kraut to Cinnamon Snails: A Lexicon of Rhineland Cuisine]. Cologne: Greven, 2011.

Heller, Edna Eby. *The Art of Pennsylvania Dutch Cooking*. Garden City, N.Y.: Doubleday & Company, 1968.

———. *A Pinch of This and a Handful of That*. Lancaster: Pennsylvania Dutch Folklore Center, 1951. Volume 2 was issued under the same title in 1952.

———. "Restaurants, Too, Go Dutch." *The Dutchman* 6:1 (June 1954): 9 and 23.

———. "Saffron Cookery." *Pennsylvania Folklife: Folk Festival Issue* (July 1964), pages 40–41.

———. *Shoo-Fly Cookery*. Lancaster: Pennsylvania Dutch Folklore Center, 1953. The revised 1960 edition was given a new title: *Edna Eby Heller's Dutch Cookbook*.

"Henry G. Croll, 70, Dies at Skippack." *Norristown Times Herald*, October 10, 1930.

Hergesheimer, Joseph. *From an Old House*. New York: Alfred A. Knopf, 1926.

Hershey, Adele H., and Ruth H. Irion. *Pennsylvania Dutch Recipe Frakturs*. Allentown, Pa.: Schlechter's, 1947. This is a lavishly produced series of framable graphics with recipes.

Hill, Susan Colestock. *Heart Language: Elsie Singmaster and Her Pennsylvania German Writings*. University Park, Pa.: Penn State University Press, 2009.

Hines, Duncan. *Adventures in Good Eating*. Bowling Green, Ky.: Adventures in Good Eating, Inc., 1941.

Hoffman, Mark W. *Sixty Wholesome Potato Dishes*. New Tripoli, Pa.: Privately printed, ca. 1935.

Hohman, Johann Georg. *Das Evangelium Nicodemus*. Reading, Pa.: C. A. Bruckman, 1819.

"In Era of Kuechler's Roost, People Had Time to Enjoy Life." *Reading Times*, October 11, 1962.

Johaneson, Bland. "Victualary among the Pennsylvania Germans." *American Mercury, 15* (October 1926): 196–198.

———. *Victualary among the Pennsylvania Germans*. Cedar Rapids, Iowa: Society of Pennsylvania German Gastronomes, 1928. Reprint of the 1926 essay bound in pamphlet format.

Kauffmann, Judith. *Der Saumagen: Entdeckungsreise ins Innes eines Pfälzer Küchenklassikers* [Stuffed Pig Stomach: A Trail of Discovery into the Inner Story of a Palatine Culinary Classic]. Annweiler: Plöger Medien, 2003. 2nd printing, 2010.

Keller, Mrs. J. A. *The Pennsylvania German Cook Book*. Alliance, Ohio: Privately printed, 1904.

Kisbán, Eszter. *Népi Kultúra, Közkultúra, Jelkép: A Gulyás, Pörkölt,*

Paprikás. Budapest: MTA Néprajzi Kutatócsoport, 1989. This is a full volume of material in the series Életmód és Tradíció.

Klees, Frederick. *The Pennsylvania Dutch*. New York: Macmillan, 1950.

Kohl, Johann Georg. *Travels in Canada, and through the States of New York and Pennsylvania*. London: George Manwaring, 1861.

Krauss, Irene. *Gelungen, Geschlungen: Das Grosse Buch der Brezel* [The Perfect Bow: The Big Pretzel Book]. Tübingen: Silberburg-Verlag, 2003.

Ladies' Aid Society of St. Peter's Lutheran Church [Neffsville, Pa.]. *Up-to-Date Cook Book*. Mount Joy, Pa.: Bulletin Press, 1924.

Lea, Elizabeth Ellicott. *Domestic Cookery*. Baltimore: Cushings & Bailey, 1853. Edited by William Woys Weaver under the title *A Quaker Woman's Cookbook* (Philadelphia: University of Pennsylvania Press, 1982; new ed., Mechanicsburg, Pa.: Stackpole Books, 2004).

Leslie, Eliza. *New Receipts for Cooking*. Philadelphia: T. B. Peterson, 1854.

Levan, J. *Berks County Cook Book of Pennsylvania Dutch Recipes*. Reading, Pa.: J. Levan, 1934. Reissued as William K. Dorman and Leonard Davidow, *Pennsylvania Dutch Cook Book of Fine Old Recipes* (Reading, Pa.: Privately printed, 1934).

Lloyd, Nelson. "Among the Dunkards." *Scribner's Magazine* 30:5 (November 1901): 513–528.

Löffler, Friedricke. *Oekonomisches Handbuch für Frauenzimmer* [The Gentlewoman's Handbook of Domestic Economy]. Stuttgart: Johann Friedrich Steinkopf, 1795.

Martin, Helen R. *The Crossways*. New York: Century Company, 1910.

———. *Sabina: A Tale of the Amish*. New York: Century Company, 1905.

———. *Tillie: A Mennonite Maid*. New York: Grosset & Dunlap, 1904.

McConnell, Guy. "The Peace People of Pennsylvania." *Family Circle* (June 14, 1940): 12–13, 16–17, 20.

Miller, Mark Eric, ed. *Amish Cooking*. New York: Crescent Books, 1991.

Missionary Society of St. Paul's Reformed Church [Bowmansville, Pa.]. *Household Guide and Cook Book*. Denver, Pa.: Steffy & Co., 1916.

Troxell, William S. *Aus Pennsylfawnia.* Philadelphia: University of Pennsylvania Press, 1938.

Tyndall, Ruth R. *Eat Yourself Full: Pennsylvania Dutch Cookery for Feinschmeckers.* New York: David McKay, 1967.

Vollmer, William. *The United States Cook Book.* Philadelphia: John Weik, 1859.

Vollständiges Kochbuch für die deutsch-amerikanische Küche [Complete Cookbook for the German-American Kitchen]. Philadelphia: Loes & Sebald, ca. 1856.

Vollständiges Nürnbergisches Koch-Buch [Complete Nuremberg Cookbook]. Nuremberg: Wolfgang Moritz Endters, 1691.

Walbert, David. *Garden Spot: Lancaster County, the Old Order Amish, and the Selling of Rural America.* Oxford: Oxford University Press, 2002.

Weaver, William Woys. *Country Scrapple: An American Tradition.* Mechanicsburg, Pa.: Stackpole Books, 2003.

———. *Culinary Ephemera: An Illustrated History.* Berkeley: University of California Press, 2010.

———. "The Kutztown Folk Festival and Its Stereotyping of Pennsylvania Dutch Cookery." *Repast* 24:1 (Winter 2008): 16–19.

———. *Pennsylvania Dutch Country Cooking.* New York: Abbeville, 1993.

———. "Pennsylvania Dutch Identity and the Sauerkraut *Grenze.*" In *Pfälzer in Amerika,* ed. Werner Kremp, Roland Paul, and Helmut Schmahl, 117–126. Trier: Wissenschaftlicher Verlag, 2010.

———. *Sauerkraut Yankees.* Philadelphia: University of Pennsylvania Press, 1983.

———. *Sauer's Herbal Cures: America's First Book of Botanic Healing.* New York/London: Routledge, 2001.

———. "The Water Gate Inn: Pennsylvania Dutch Cuisine Goes Mainstream." *Gastronomica* 9:3 (Summer 2009): 25–31.

Weaver-Zercher, David. *The Amish in the American Imagination.* Baltimore: Johns Hopkins University Press, 2001.

Weygandt, Cornelius. *The Dutch Country.* New York: D. Appleton-Century, 1939.

———. "Our Pennsylvania Dutch." *Travel* (October 1940): 25–29.

———. *Philadelphia Folks.* New York: D. Appleton-Century, 1938.

———. *The Red Hills.* Philadelphia: University of Pennsylvania Press, 1929.

Wheeler, Mary Alice. "Ann Hark: Writer and Lecturer on the Pennsylvania Dutch." *Der Reggeboge* 40:1 (2006): 3–20.

White, Allene. "They Made Whoopie!" *Maine Sunday Telegram,* October 16, 1988, pages 1–2.

Williams, Maynard Owen. "The Pennsylvania Dutch Folk Festival." *National Geographic* 102:4 (October 1952): 505–516.

Wood, Ralph. *The Pennsylvania Germans.* Princeton, N.J.: Princeton University Press, 1942.

Yoder, Don. "Pennsylvania German Folklore Research: An Historical Analysis." In *The German Language in America: A Symposium,* ed. Glenn G. Gilbert, 70–105. Austin: University of Texas Press, 1971.

———. "Sauerkraut in the Pennsylvania Folk-Culture." *Pennsylvania Folklife* 12:2 (Summer 1961, Special Festival Issue): 56–69.

———. "Twenty-Five Years of the Folk Festival." *Pennsylvania Folklife* 23 (1974, Folk Festival Supplement): 2–7.

Zehner, Olive G. "It's Fashionable to Be Pennsylvania Dutch Today." *Pennsylvania Dutchman* 4:14 (April 1953): 16.

Ziegler, Charles C. *Drauss un Deheem.* Leipzig: Hesse & Becker, 1891.

Zwinger, Theodore. *Theatrum Botanicum; das ist, Vollkommenes Kräuter-Buch* [The Botanical Theater; or, Complete Herbal]. Basel: Hans Jacob Bischoff, 1744.

PRINTED MENUS SPECIFICALLY REFERENCED IN THE TEXT

Allentown, Pa., 1933–1934. *Keystone Trail Inn, 19th and Roth Avenue.* Menu. Joseph Trinkle, Proprietor. Roughwood Collection, Devon, Pa.

Allentown, Pa., July 6, 1949. *Walp's Pennsylvania Dutch Style Cooking. U.S. Route 22, Allentown, Pa.* Menu. Roughwood Collection, Devon, Pa.

Lancaster, Pa., 1937. *Amish of Lancaster County. Air Conditioned. German Village. Lancaster, Pa.* Menu. Paul Heine Jr., President. Menu design dated and signed Hede Kurtz. Roughwood Collection, Devon, Pa.

Lenhartsville, Pa., 1941. *Lenhartsville Hotel and Seafood Restaurant.* Menu design dated and signed Johnny Ott. This is the old name of Ott's Deitsch Eck and includes a retail price list for beer cheese, one of his specialties. Roughwood Collection, Devon, Pa.

Newlonsburg (now Murrysville), Pa., 1938. *House by the Side of the Road*. Menu. Roughwood Collection, Devon, Pa.

Norristown, Pa., October 3, 1902. *Twelfth Annual Banquet, Pennsylvania German Society, Y.M.C.A. Building, 406 Dekalb Street*. Lewis G. Stritzinger, Caterer. Roughwood Collection, Devon, Pa.

Ronks, Pa., 1954. *Miller's Ess Blatz*. Menu. Text in Pennsylvania Dutch. Roughwood Collection, Devon, Pa.

Sarasota, Fl., 2002. *Troyer's Dutch Heritage Restaurant*. Menu. Roughwood Collection, Devon, Pa.

Washington, D.C.., June 2, 1958. *Marjory Hendrick's Water Gate Inn*. Menu. Text in Pennsylvania Dutch and English. Roughwood Collection, Devon, Pa.

INTERVIEWS

Adam, Theo, and Gertrude Adam. Obermohr, Rheinland-Pfalz (Germany), June 15, 2009. Poverty foods; Frau Adam is a well-known traditional cook in the region around Kaiserslautern.

Beidelman, Robert, and Lucille Beidelman Schwartz. Macungie, Pa., September 4, 2009. Both siblings grew up in Beidelman's Hotel (now demolished) at Macungie.

Beiler, Salome. Narvon, Pa., November 12, 2009. Old Order Amish, wife of building contractor.

Blank, Steven, and Lavinia. Parkesburg, Pa., December 14, 2011. Old Order Amish; interview centered on Amish roast and traditional customs associated with it.

Breininger, Lester. Robesonia, Pa., January 20, 2008. Retired schoolteacher, traditional redware potter. Now deceased.

Brendle, Glenn. Gap, Pa., May 23, 2010. Farmer and produce broker. Grew up in Strasburg, Lancaster County, Pa.

Brendle, Miriam Smoker. Strasburg, Pa., December 10, 2010. Grew up Amish in the Atglen area of Chester County, Pa.; widow of poultry farmer Martin Brendle.

Bumbaugh, Lamar W. Lyons Station, Pa., March 6, 1993. Herbalist, folk healer, and dealer in furs. Now deceased.

Care, Faye Delp. Fleetwood, Pa., March 9, 2007. Father owned Delp's Meats; trained in traditional butchering practices.

Denlinger, Dr. Everett E. Ronks, Pa., December 14, 2011. Veterinarian for the Lancaster County Amish community and author of a self-published autobiography about his work among the Amish.

Dietrich, Verna. Krumsville, Pa., February 22, 2007. Traditional butcher, proprietor of Dietrich's Country Meats.

Dotterer, Luella George. Kempton, Pa., November 21, 2011. Traditional cook, grew up in a tenant farming family in Weisenberg Township, Lehigh County, Pa.

Eckert, Charles Franklin. Aspers, Pa., August 1947. Retired Adams County butcher. Interviewed by Dr. Don Yoder, whose field notes are now in the possession of the author. Eckert was the subject of a full chapter in Yoder's *Discovering American Folklife* (1990). Now deceased.

Enck, Miriam. Lebanon, Pa., February 28, 2008. Grew up Mennonite, now president of the East Indies Tea Company.

Faust, Mima Yoder. Hegins, Pa. August 27, 1953. School teacher and wife of E. Franklin Faust, Reformed clergyman. Now deceased. Interviewed by Dr. Don Yoder (her nephew).

Fegley, Charles. Royersford, Pa., November 5, 2007. Retired college professor.

Fisher, John B. Morgantown, Pa., April 25, 2006. Ex–Old Order Amish building contractor and teacher, author of an autobiography, *Outside of Paradise* (2011).

Fritsch, Peter. Alburtis, Pa., January 17, 2008. Dialect poet and folk artist.

German, Deborah Snyder. Allentown, Pa., October 8, 2011. Interviewed at the German Family Reunion, New Tripoli, Pa.; grew up on a farm in Lynn Township, Lehigh Co., Pa.

Gilcher, Volker. Freinsheim, Rheinland-Pfalz (Germany), June 13, 2009. Chef and owner of the Restaurant-Weinkeller von Busch-Hof in Freinsheim; noted regional cook.

Glick, Ivan. Lancaster, Pa., April 23, 2010. Former Beachy Amish and farmer. Now deceased.

Groff, Betty. Mount Joy, Pa., March 12, 2008. Former restaurateur and cookbook author.

Haas, Lee W., and Evelyn Bachman Haas. Slatington, Pa., December 4, 2010. Head of the Grundsau Lodge movement, dialect speaker, great-grandson of famous powwow doctor Dennis Rex.

Hahn, Elizabeth Hoover. East Earl, Pa., June 5, 1977. Old Order Mennonite, Weaverland Conference. *Blinde Fische* recipes. Follow-up correspondence, October 2011.

Hamm, Kerry, and Sandra Hamm. New Tripoli, Pa., October 8, 2011. Kerry Hamm grew up on a farm in Lynn Township, Lehigh

County; his wife grew up in Northampton County. Both are enthusiasts of Pennsylvania Dutch cookery.

Hartman, Roy. Little Oley, Pa., November 18, 2010. Retired farmer.

Henninger, Grace Merkel. Lenhartsville, Pa., November 14, 2010. Farm wife and former restaurant cook. Now deceased.

Hermann, Gisela. St. Julian, Rheinland-Pfalz (Germany), November 5, 1983. Poverty foods. Traditional cook specializing in potato dishes from the Kusel area. Now deceased.

Hess, Catherine. Boyertown, Pa., December 29, 2008. Former restaurateur and caterer.

Hildebrandt, Magdalena. Green Bank, Pa., August 4, 1986. Grew up in a remote part of the Welsh Mountains and lived most of her life in an unmodernized 1740s stone cottage. Cooked on an open hearth and raised goats. Now deceased.

Hoover, Amos B., and wife Nora Martin Hoover. Ephrata, Pa., July 26, 2011. Hog farmer, collector of rare books on Mennonite culture, founder of the Muddy Creek Farm Library. Old Order Mennonites (Weaverland Conference).

Kern, Lucy. East Greenville, Pa., June 21, 2011. Home cook and organizer of the first women's Grundsau Lodge.

Kline, Robert. Newmanstown, Pa., February 28, 2008. Dialect speaker, physician, and grower of saffron; expert on native species of morels; board member, Pennsylvania German Society.

Klint, Doris Snyder. Auburn, Pa., October 8, 2011. Interviewed at the German Family Reunion, New Tripoli, Pa. Grew up on a farm in Lynn Township, Lehigh Co., Pa.

Koch, Crystal. East Texas, Pa., May 2, 2007. Chef and former proprietor of The Willows restaurant.

Krauss, Betty. Palm, Pa., February 4, 2008. Schwenkfelder farm wife.

Kulp, Isaac Clarence. Pennsburg, Pa., June 13, 2005. Dunkard (Church of the Brethren) folklorist and local historian. Now deceased.

Laubenstein, Samuel. Friedensburg, Pa., November 29, 2011. Traditional cook and butcher; butchers privately for individuals, hunt clubs, and some restaurants; specializes in game and venison.

Lorish, Linda. Huff's Church, Pa., March 12, 2007. Works with women's committee in the local church to produce food events and chow chow sales.

Lovell, MaryAnn Elstrodt. Hegins, Pa., November 30, 2011. Grew up in the Stoney Brook area of York County, Pa.; granddaughter of well-known powwow doctor Emanuel Landis, who lived in the historic 1734 Schultz House.

Lute, Mary Jane Schrope. Wayne, Pa., October 17, 2009. Folk artist from Hegins, Pa.

McNally, Lydia Brown. Phoenixville, Pa., October 25, 2010. Reformed Mennonite and hooked rug artist; born on a farm near West Point, Va.

Morgan, Sarah. Pine Grove, Pa., October 26, 1992. Heirloom gardener and traditional cook. Now deceased.

Neff, Alda. Orrstown, Pa., July 1949. Interviewed by Dr. Don Yoder in connection with a manuscript cookbook compiled by Alda Leedy. Field notes in possession of the author. Now deceased.

Paul, Liselotte Weber. Steinwenden, Rheinland-Pfalz (Germany), November 2, 1983. Discussed techniques for making *Dippehaas* (Pennsylvania Dutch *Hasenpfeffer*). Frau Paul prepared the recipe in an 1805 *Dippe,* an earthenware pan made especially for this festive dish. Now deceased.

Pletsch, Eugen. Ramstein, Rheinland-Pfalz (Germany), November 6, 1983. Traditional butcher. Discussed differences between Palatine and Pennsylvania Dutch butchering practices.

Reinoehl, Sally. Valley View, Pa., November 29, 2011. Grew up on a farm near Lykens, Pa.; well-known traditional cook who participates in county and state cooking competitions.

Roan, Nancy. Bechtelsville, Pa., November 2, 2006. Traditional cook and organizer of the Goshenhoppen Historians and Goshenhoppen fair.

Ryland, Ida. Pine Grove, Pa., November 29, 2011. Grew up on a farm in the Beaver Valley not far from Sarah Morgan, who is pictured in *Pennsylvania Dutch Country Cooking*; traditional cook.

Schwalm, Rebecca. Valley View, Pa., November 29, 2011. Grew up in the village of Valley View; traditional cook.

Shaner, Richard, and Eleanor Shaner. Kutztown, Pa., August 16, 2009. Local historians.

Shankweiler, Grace Starr. Valley View, Pa., October 18, 2011. Grew up in a country store in Valley View, Pa.

Snyder, Carl. New Tripoli, Pa., April 11, 2007. Board member, Pennsylvania German Society and collector of Grundsau lodge materials. Now deceased.

Snyder, Nelma. Pitman, Pa., November 30, 2011. Grew up on a farm in the Mahantongo Valley; traditional cook.

Stetzler, Steven. Lenhartsville, Pa., May 22, 2007. Chef and proprietor of the Deitsch Eck restaurant. Grandson of interviewee Luella George Dotterer.

Strawser, Barbara. Schaefferstown, Pa., March 11, 2008. Folk artist and traditional cook.

Troutman, Steven. Klingerstown, Pa., October 27, 1992. Traditional butcher, partner in Troutman Brothers Meat.

Weaver, Grace Hickman. West Chester, Pa., October 10, 1987. Grew up on a farm in Pocopson Township, Chester County, Pa.; father was a pork butcher. Discussed citron melons and citron melon recipes. Now deceased.

Weaver, James. Bowers, Pa., July 29, 2007. Old Order Mennonite (Groffdale Conference) and vegetable farmer. Interview included several members of his extended family.

Weidel, Geraldine Stauffer. Neffsville, Pa., March 1, 2007. Cook at Neffsville Lutheran Church, specialist in traditional Pennsylvania Dutch cookery.

Yoder, Don. Devon, Pa., December 10, 2005, and September 27, 2008. Pennsylvania Dutch scholar and one of the cofounders of the Kutztown Folk Festival.

Zion's Windsor Castle Church Food Committee. Hamburg, Pa., May 9, 2007. Operates a food tent at the Kutztown Folk Festival.

MISCELLANEOUS CORRESPONDENCE

Hershey, Mary Jane Lederach. Four-page letter to Dr. Don Yoder, Lederach, Pa., November 14, 1972, regarding the funeral of her grandfather Jacob B. Mensch (1835–1912). Unpublished typescript, author's collection.

Hoover, Amos B. One-page letter with attached genealogical material to William Woys Weaver, Ephrata, Pa., October 20, 2011, regarding Blinde Fische and Mrs. Elizabeth Hahn. Handwritten, author's collection.

Witmer, Christopher. Two-page letter to William Woys Weaver, Palmyra, Pa., January 13, 1982, concerning foods and foodways in Perry County, Pa. Handwritten, author's collection.

Index

Page references in italics refer to illustrations.

Acknowledgments

Since the core material in this book was assembled over the course of forty years of fieldwork, the list of people to whom I owe special gratitude is exceptionally long, and several of them have passed away. Permit me to begin with the interviewees, who were willing to share their thoughts on Pennsylvania Dutch culture and especially their "food memories."

The late Isaac Clarence Kulp deserves similar recognition. He was a colorful individual who lived his plain life by his own rules. From his many forays into sections of the Dutch Country I have never seen, he brought back recipes, stories, contacts—all the tools I needed in order to take my food research to another level.

The late Ivan Glick did the same. He lived on part of my old ancestral property in Lancaster County in an architectural gem built by Weavers in the 1780s. Our weekend trips into the Dutch countryside will always remain with me; Ivan could walk up to a strange house and within the space of five minutes convince the owners that they had been waiting for our visit with open arms. I always thought that someone would shoot at us to get us off the property, but "Ivan's Way" inevitably prevailed. There and then I learned as much about the good side of human nature as I did about food and Pennsylvania Dutch culture.

Among the living yet (as we say in Dutch), who is more deserving of thanks than the Reverend Carl Shankweiler? He put me up and carted me around in order to visit all the wonderful people I was able to interview (and then some; this is never finished work) in the spectacularly beautiful, worlds-away landscapes of the Lykens and Mahantongo valleys.

Kimberly Richards Brown of the Historical Society of Berks County must be thanked for taking a personal interest in my Kuechler's Roost research problems, solving all of them, and retrieving from a dusty archive the perfectly charming 1893 photo of the old hermit himself. Likewise Jeff McGranahan at the Historical Society of Montgomery County spent the good part of a day untangling the Croll family genealogy and the succession of buildings the family once owned in Skippack so that we could determine once and for all exactly where it was that the seven sweets and seven sours were invented. J. M. Duffin, archivist at the University of Pennsylvania, was also helpful, especially in sleuthing through obituaries that clarified background information on J. George Fredericks, Edith M. Thomas, and several other Pennsylvania Dutch authors about whom very little was known.

Of course the éminence grise behind it all was Dr. Don Yoder, one of my interview subjects but also a comrade in arms during fieldwork. I invited him to come along during many of my interviews, which was no small undertaking for someone who is now ninety years old. The results were spectacular, mainly because he knew people from past generations, and this opened the flow of food memories down channels of time I could never have anticipated.

I also want to mention my doctoral mentor, Dr. Patricia Lysaght, at University College, Dublin. One of the conditions of my course of study in Ireland was that I publish several books based on my research. This is the first. Patricia knew that I needed to do this work, and she knew that the narrative was worth telling, although my Irish colleagues were absolutely dumbfounded by the complexity of Pennsylvania Dutch culture.

The artist Signe Sundberg-Hall, who has contributed the beautiful line art in this book, as she has done in others, brings to her art the special understanding of one who is herself part Pennsylvania Dutch. Our culture has produced a huge family of extraordinary talent, and I am blessed with the likes of Signe, who understands our food culture without detailed explanation. I think her drawings convey exactly how delicious our traditional dishes are.

And finally I dedicate this book to my long-time friend Don Davis of Zions Grove, Pennsylvania, not only because he and his wife Wendy make the best sauerkraut in the state, but also because Don has been in the business of antiques since I first met him. His keen instinct for the rarest kind of culinary equipment, not to mention some of the odd-ball materials illustrated in this book, have filled my house and library with treasures of great scholarly value. Don is a consummate connoisseur of all things Pennsylvania Dutch, so I know he will delight in the stories recounted in these pages.